The Image and the Region –
Making Mega-City Regions Visible!

The Image and the Region – Making Mega-City Regions Visible!

edited by Alain Thierstein, Agnes Förster

Lars Müller Publishers

Contents

- 7   **Preface**
- 9   **Calling for Pictures**
  Agnes Förster, Alain Thierstein
- 37   **Mapping Hybrid Value-Added Landscapes**
  Christian Kruse
- 59   **Governing Polycentric Urban Regions**
  Simin Davoudi
- 69   **Accessing Global City Regions**
  Maurits Schaafsma
- 81   **Cooperating and Competing**
  Wilhelm Natrup
- 97   **Managing Reputation**
  Reinhard Frei
- 107   **Visioning and Visualizing**
  Wil Zonneveld
- 127   **Revealing the Social Topography of Mega-City Regions**
  Heiri Leuthold
- 141   **Experiencing Urban Regions**
  Ursula Stein, Henrik Schultz
- 155   **Stimulating the Second Space**
  Julian Petrin
- 169   **Visualizing Desires, not Cities**
  Remo Burkhard
- 181   **Perceiving and Visualizing Changing Environments**
  Eckart Lange
- 189   **Going Beyond Identity**
  Urs Primas
- 207   **Setting up a Perception Instrument**
  Meret Wandeler
- 227   **Creating Identity**
  Beatrix Bencseky
- 253   **Adding Value to Spatial Development**
  Agnes Förster, Alain Thierstein
- 275   **Appendix**

Alain Thierstein
Agnes Förster

Preface

Mega-city regions are an emerging new large-scale urban phenomenon that is currently being discussed from both an analytical-functional and a political-normative perspective. In research the constituent elements and driving forces of mega-city regions are increasingly coming to light. They are feeding the comprehension of the mega-city regions' decisive role in economic, social and cultural development on the national and European level. Hence spatial development faces new challenges and tasks at the novel spatial scale of mega-city regions. The relevant and responsible stakeholders and players are being challenged – large-scale metropolitan governance is called for. On this point a problem of transmission arises. All over Europe there seems to be little awareness still among the relevant players of the prominence of mega-city regions. To politicians, citizens and administrators, mega-city regions remain invisible in many respects: They are rarely mapped, lack a name, image and attendant concept, and hardly offer any direct sensual perception in everyday life.

This work is based on the hypothesis that getting a picture of mega-city regions is crucial for comprehension, identification, motivation and commitment, and is thus a prerequisite to establishing large-scale metropolitan governance. Mega-city regions as an analytical or normative concept have to be transformed into a space of perception in order to finally become a space of collective action. The task of "Making Mega-City Regions Visible!" as presented in this book is an ample and complex one and demands a multifaceted process. The book brings together contributions from scholars and practitioners from different disciplines. The approach is explorative. Starting from the experience of familiar spatial scales, the book approximates the new and still unfamiliar spatial scale of mega-city regions. The selection of the articles and disciplines presented does not claim to be comprehensive in any respect. It has to be regarded as a starting point to further research and practice.

The book draws on contributions to the international conference "The Image and the Region – Making Mega-City Regions Visible!" which took place in Munich in February 2006 at the Chair of Spatial and Territorial Development, the Faculty of Architecture, Munich University of Technology.

ca

Agnes Förster
Alain Thierstein

Calling for Pictures

The Need for Getting a Picture of Mega-City Regions

The title of this book consists of two components. The main title, "The Image and the Region," picks up on a question that has been around for quite some time. What is the reciprocal interrelationship between a region (a spatial entity as administrative, economic, social or cultural construct) and its image (the way this construct is experienced, represented and conceived)? This book is about mega-city regions, or more accurately about the "polycentric metropolis." Regions – this includes mega-city regions – are not of a fixed nature but are part of the perpetual transformation of the spatial system in which regions emerge, exist for some time and may then disappear (Paasi 2000). When talking about the relationship between the "image" and the "region," this dynamic nature is of special interest. What is the image's role and importance in the changes that affect a region's emergence? What qualities of images go along with the different steps of the region's process of institutionalization?

The subtitle of the book, "Making Mega-City Regions Visible!" aims to employ this interaction in the process of emergence of Mega-City Regions. First of all, it was an invitation to the authors gathered at a symposium in Munich in early 2006. Their lectures (the corresponding articles are presented in this book) explore preconditions, starting points, techniques, modes and possible contexts for getting a picture of mega-city regions. If we bring together and superpose these different approaches in one book, "Making Mega-City Regions Visible!" turns out to be a program or work plan rather than a ready product. The fruitful interaction of the "image" and the "region" has to be tested and exercised in practice; it demands an active character and openness for individual experience. The work plan addresses all kinds of responsible players within mega-city regions, whether coming from the political domain, administrations, the planning domain or private enterprise.

The fourteen contributions in this book are complemented by the editors' introduction to the general topic of "The Image and the Region" and the concluding main lessons learnt for a program of "Making Mega-City Regions Visible!" Besides introducing the general topic, this first article aims to provide the reader with guidance. It illustrates the motivation for the choice of disciplinary perspectives reflected in the collected articles as well as the task assigned to the authors. The introduction has three sections. First, the nature and current state of mega-city regions as an object of analytical research and strategy of spatial planning policies is looked at. Second, the question of perception is presented as an essential building block towards the achievement of large-scale metropolitan governance. Third, a tentative framework of the perceptional work on mega-city regions is sketched out, providing a starting point for the articles collected in this book.

I   Emerging Mega-City Regions – A New Challenge to Spatial Development

The hypothesis of the polycentric mega-city region combines two distinct concepts, viz., Friedmann's world cities approach and Sassen's global cities approach. Both concepts state the rise of a transnational urban network of so-called world or global cities. Friedmann refers to a major geographical transformation of the capitalist world-economy when production is internationalized. This restructuring results in a new international division of labor, whose main agents are multinational enterprises and their corresponding complex organizational structures. World cities can be understood as control points or geographical places of economic power within these organizations. The territorial basis of a world city is more than the central city; it refers to the economic space of a region. World cities very often are polycentric urban regions that consist of a number of historically distinct cities that are located in more or less close proximity. Prominent examples such as the Kansai Region in Japan, Randstad Holland or the Ruhr also lack a clear leading city which dominates in political, economic or cultural aspects (Friedmann 1986). The concept of the global city, however, focuses on the location strategies of advanced producer service firms as a spearhead of the rising global knowledge economy. Sassen discovers a new geography of centrality in which the city centers or central business districts form the heart of a global urban network. The functional centrality of global cities brings about the increasing disconnection from their broader hinterlands or adjacent metropolitan regions (Sassen 2001). "Sassen's focus on centrality leads her to conceptualizing 'global cities' as focal points that operate separately from their hinterlands. Friedmann's focus on the relative concentration of power, in contrast, implies that a 'world city' may consist of multiple cities and their hinterlands that may themselves be subject to urbanization processes" (Derudder 2006: 2034).

The concept of polycentric mega-city regions, on the one hand, comprises the geographical dimension of world cities as large-scale polycentric city-regions. On the other hand, the knowledge-intensive business services (KIBS) that the global city concept refers to are likewise recognized as a major driving force in the formation process of these regions. Consequently, a mainly static description of mega-city regions can only be a first approximation of the new urban phenomenon. In this regard mega-city regions require a critical mass and a concentration of main functions such as control and regulation functions, gateway functions, innovation and competition functions (Blotevogel 2002). A second approach, however, emphasizes that mega-city regions are not a static and completed state of urbanization. Mega-city regions are in the process of emerging; they are a multi-scalar urban process that is currently unfolding on two spatial scales. First, at an international and European level, there are increasing functional linkages between the core cities of each mega-city region. Second, at a metropolitan regional level, there are evident and increasing interdependencies between highly global cores and their surrounding areas. The main driving forces of the emergence of mega-city regions are knowledge-intensive business sectors, leading to a dense network of interaction such as virtual communications and business travel within and between advanced producer service firms (Halbert, Convery and Thierstein 2006). "Mega-city regions are a series of anything between ten and 50 cities and towns, physically separate but functionally networked, clustered around one or more larger central cities, and drawing enormous economic strength from a new functional division of labor. These places exist both as separate entities, in which residents work locally and most workers are local residents, and as parts of a wider functional urban region connected by dense flows of people and information carried along motorways, high-speed rail lines and telecommunication cables" (Hall and Pain 2006: 3).

Mega-city regions turn out to be the functional spaces of the knowledge economy. They are the hubs within the globally organized net of this leading economic sector. Consequently, mega-city regions are of key importance for the economic and social development at both the European and national spatial scale. Their strategic role in spatial development is increasingly recognized; their emergence is being driven in different respects. Mega-city regions are the object of analytical research, normative political concepts as well as strategies of communication and marketing within the global competition of location. Depending on these different purposes, the nomenclature of emerging new large-scale urban spaces varies. Distinct terms basically denote the same phenomenon. From an analytical background "polycentric urban region," "polynucleated metropolitan region," or "metropolitan agglomeration area" can be regarded as synonyms. Normative concepts use terms such as "metropolitan region" or "metropolitan area" and communication applications often favor names such as "Greater Zurich Area," "Greater Munich Area," or "Greater Boston Area." The notion of "mega-city region" has been primarily shaped by Peter Hall and Kathy Pain and the corresponding transnational project team in the POLYNET study. This term reflects the large-scale nature and the developing polycentric structure of the new urban phenomenon that has to be distinguished from the more current term of "city-region."

The Polycentric Metropolis
What is the current state of mega-city regions? The Interreg III B Study Project POLYNET – Sustainable Management of European Polycentric Mega-City Regions – is one of the most recent research activities addressing this emerging new large-scale urban phenomenon (Hall and Pain 2006). The project drew on the following hypothesis: Mega-city regions arise from a process of very extended decentralization from big central cities to adjacent smaller ones, old and new. "A key feature of these regions is that in different degrees they are polycentric. POLYNET adopts a basic hypothesis that they are becoming more so over time, as an increasing share of popu-

lation and employment locates outside the largest central city or cities, and as other smaller cities and towns become increasingly networked with each other, exchanging information which bypasses the large central city altogether" (Hall and Pain 2006:3).

Within mega-city regions multiple cities and towns are bound together. Their critical mass makes it possible to provide the infrastructure that is needed for superior high-quality knowledge production and global-knowledge exchange. The different locations and areas within mega-city regions are characterized by increasing functional specializations and corresponding spatial differentiation; a new functional hierarchy within the mega-city region is emerging. The POLYNET project aimed at investigating this ongoing process with the resulting degree of polycentricity and current state of functional division of labor within the mega-city region.

Therefore, the methodology of the Globalization and World Cities Study Group led by Peter Taylor was adapted to the new phenomenon of mega-city regions. When analyzing the world city network, the focus is on intercity relations in terms of the organizational structure of the global economy (Taylor 2001, 2004). Starting from a fundamental criticism of previous urban research that focused on attributes mostly in a national context, the relationships between the cities should be measured on the basis of flows taking a global perspective (Hall and Pain 2006). Relationships between cities are not measured directly, in terms of actual flows of information. Instead, Peter Taylor and his study group use a proxy: the internal structures of large advanced producer service firms are analyzed, revealing the relationship between head office and other office locations. World or global cities are defined in terms of their external information exchange. When applying this approach to polycentric global mega-city regions, they should be defined in terms of corresponding internal linkages (Hall and Pain 2006).

Within the POLYNET project eight mega-city regions in Northwestern Europe were examined in three steps. First, the analysis of commuting helped provide the working definition for functional urban regions. Second, quantitative as well as qualitative analyses of advanced producer services delivered maps of intrafirm as well as of interfirm connectivities. Third, policy analysis and policy focus group workshops complemented the research project. Using the POLYNET approach, we shall illustrate some newly elaborated findings for the Mega-City Region of Munich.

Example: The Mega-City Region of Munich[1]
The research project "Interconnectedness and Locations of Knowledge-Intensive Firms. The Case of the Mega-City Region of Munich" started in 2006 and investigates spatial patterns of the knowledge economy in a study area of about 150 x 180 km that includes the city of Munich. In addition to the POLYNET approach, the quantitative analysis of intrafirm networks not only looks at multilocations of advanced producer service firms but also includes knowledge-intensive high-tech sectors.

Urban morphology and commuter patterns strongly suggest that the mega-city region is a highly monocentric region with Munich being by far the primary center. Apart from this first assessment, subtle differentiations appear when looking at the knowledge economy's driving forces in spatial development. Starting from this nonphysical functional approach, the major questions are: Beyond the obvious monocentricity, can an emerging fine-grained polycentricity of the mega-city region be recognized? Does an increasing division of labor – accompanied by a process of specialization and differentiation – between the different areas of the mega-city region become apparent?

The results of quantitative analysis are deepened in the further steps of the project by applying qualitative research on the interfirm connectivities.

1. The Definition of the Mega-City Region of Munich

Commuter patterns of the workforce between municipalities are suitable for defining the single functional urban areas of the Mega-City Region of Munich; they are meaningful on a regional scale (Figure 1). Commuting is based upon the physical movements of players and therefore bound to build infrastructure. Consequently, these findings are not sufficient to identify nonphysical functional interrelationships at the spatial scale of a mega-city region.

As a starting point to further analysis of the nonphysical interrelations, a preliminary delimitation of the Mega-City Region of Munich has to be defined. All functional urban areas within the potential reach of Munich defined by a radius of about 60 minutes travel time plus the functional urban area of Regensburg are constituent portions of the Mega-City Region of Munich (Figure 2). Commuter patterns between the functional urban areas reveal the physical interconnectedness within the Mega-City Region of Munich. In addition to the strong monocentric patterns directed towards the functional urban area of Munich, lateral physical connectivities appear (Figure 3).

Figure 1:
Commuting patterns in the Mega-City Region of Munich: commuting between municipalities.

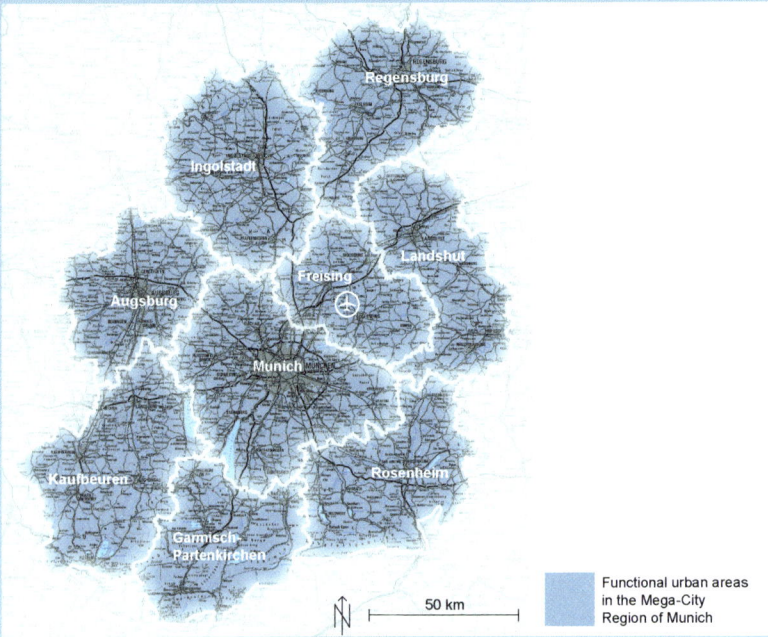

Figure 2:
Study Area: the preliminary perimeter of the Mega-City Region of Munich.

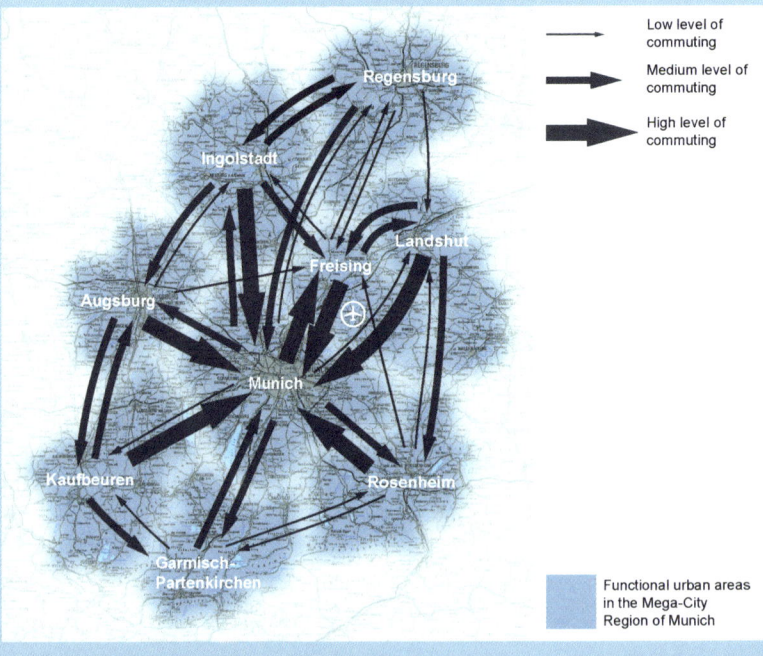

Figure 3:
Commuting patterns in the Mega-City Region of Munich: commuting between functional urban areas.

2. Analysis of Intrafirm Connectivities in Three Steps

The networks of multibranch firms of the advanced producer services as well as the high-tech sector are analyzed at different spatial scales, viz., regional, national and international. These networks are an approximation for the underlying flows of information and communication.

2.1 Patterns of Connectivity

Advanced producer service firms often form a systematic network with a location in different portions of the mega-city region; they look for proximity to customers. Munich is the core within this dense network, but lateral connectivities that bypass the dominating center are emerging.

Within the mega-city region, Munich and Regensburg have the strongest intrafirm connectivities. Putting Munich at center stage, relatively strong connectivities with Ingolstadt and Augsburg become evident (Figure 4).

When looking at the functional urban area of Regensburg, patterns of connectivity with national as well as international locations reveal their major interlinkage with Munich, which in turn is a strong indication that Regensburg is an important secondary city within the Mega-City Region of Munich (Figure 5).

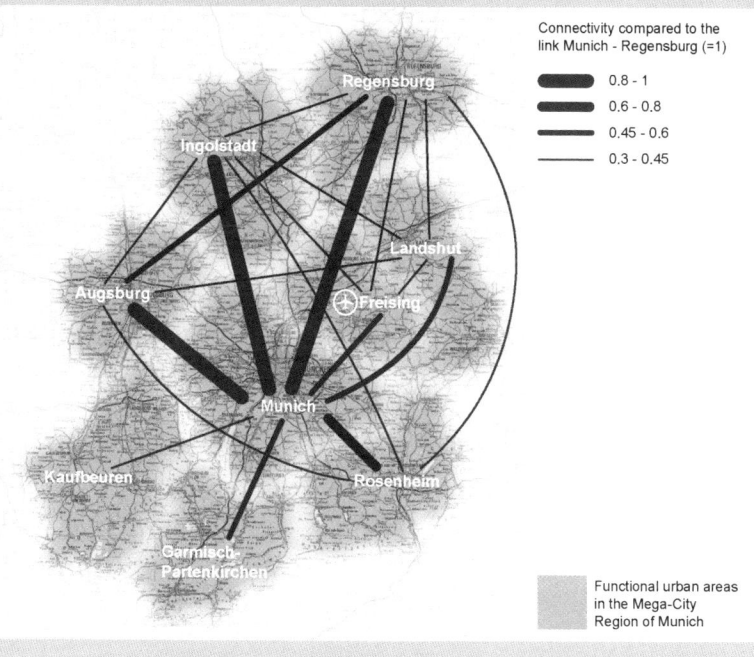

Figure 4:
Intraregional linkages of intrafirm networks of advanced producer services within the Mega-City Region of Munich.

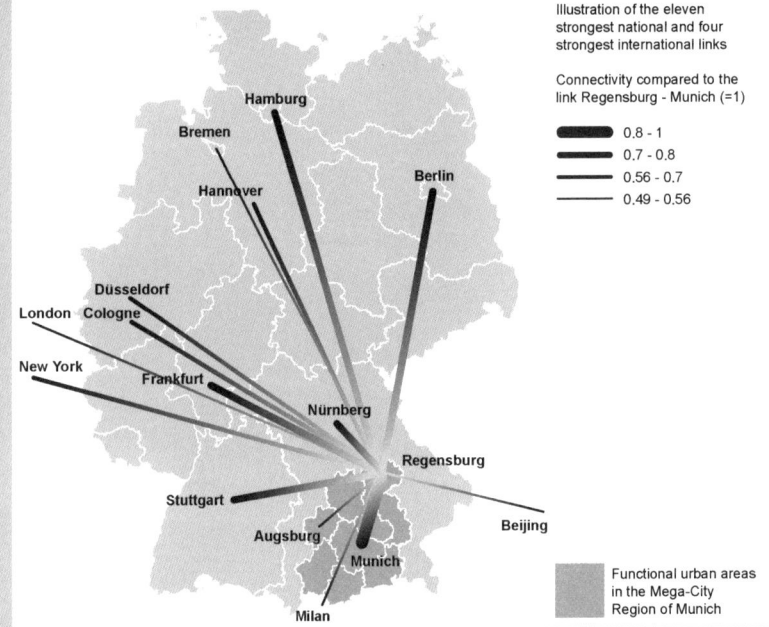

Figure 5:
Connectivities of Regensburg: intensity of intrafirm connectivity of advanced producer service firms to national and international locations.

2.2 Intensity and Hierarchy of Connectivity

Within the knowledge economy spatial patterns differ; there are significant differences between the connectivities of advanced producer service and high-tech firms.

Regarding the advanced producer services sector, Munich is the strongest linked with four big national cities, followed by Paris and London as global cities. To all other functional urban areas of the mega-city region, Munich is mostly the dominating center (Figure 6).

The high-tech sector is characterized by a major role of international locations. Munich is the most intensely connected internationally. The other functional urban areas, however, are also dominated by international and national connections rather than primary connections to Munich. Each functional urban region has an individual profile of connectivities depending on the residing firms (Figure 7).

Figure 6:
Intensity of intrafirm connectivity of advanced producer services to international and national locations.

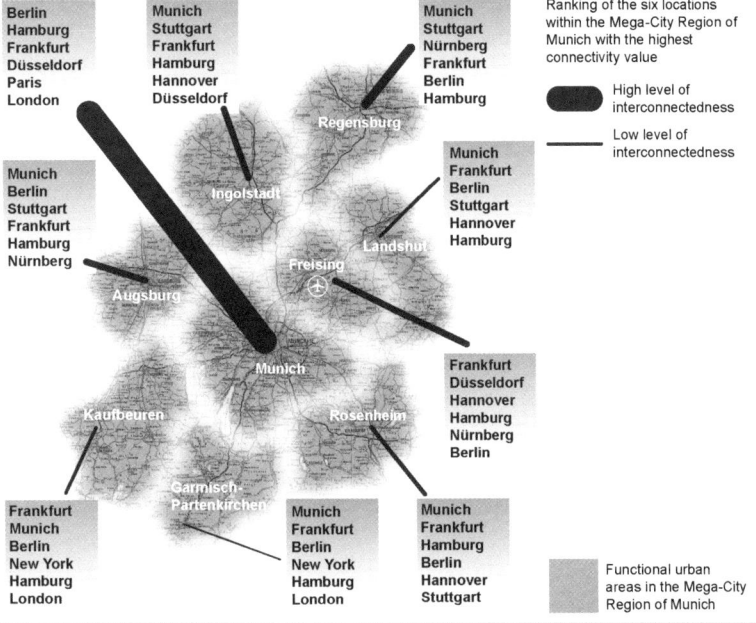

Figure 7:
Intensity of intrafirm connectivity of high-tech firms to international and national locations.

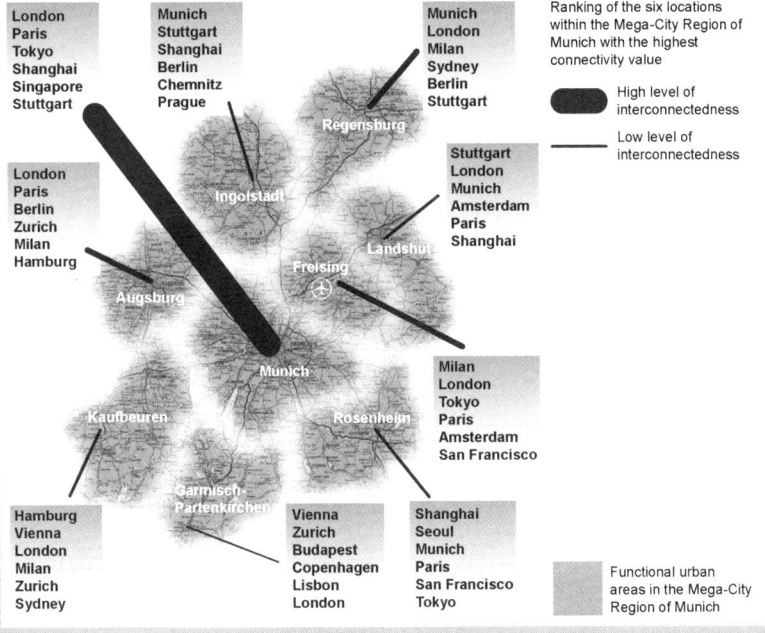

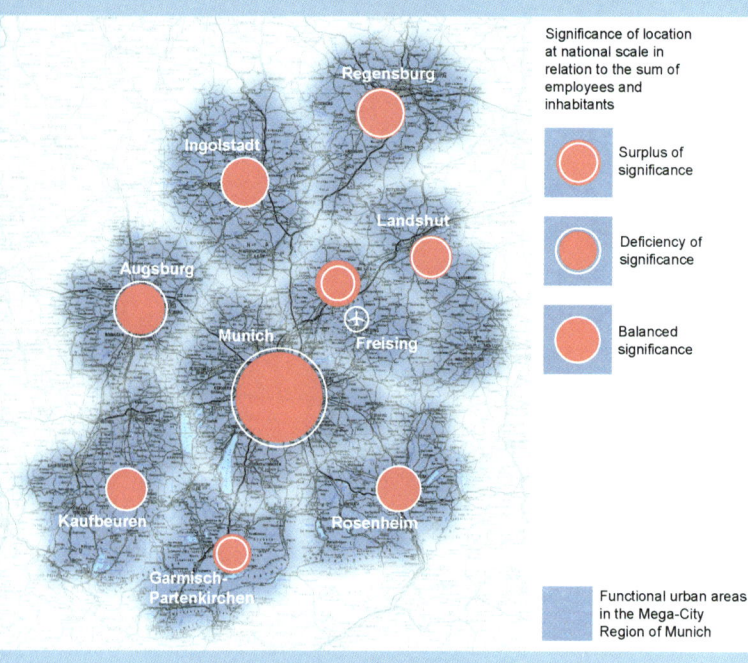

Figure 8:
National importance of the functional urban areas within the mega-city region: advanced producer service firms.

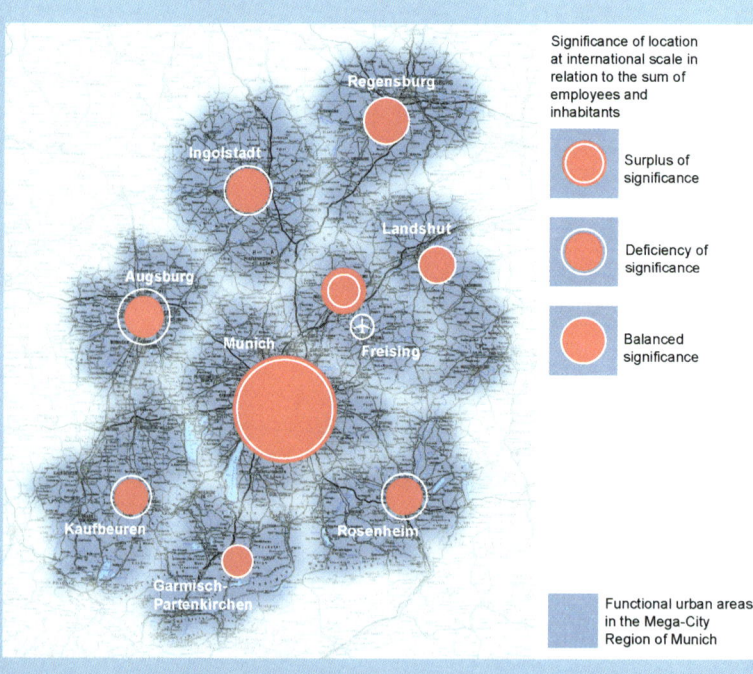

Figure 9:
International importance of the functional urban areas within the mega-city region: advanced producer service firms.

3. Relative Importance of the Different Functional Urban Areas

When putting the national and international importance of the different areas within the mega-city region in relation to the sum of their inhabitants and jobs, both the surplus and deficit of meaning of the different locations can be identified (Figures 8 and 9).

Between the different functional urban areas a division of labor appears concerning the connectivity with different spatial scales. While Munich acts as a global and European "knowledge hub," the surrounding functional urban areas are of predominantly national importance.

Freising as a smaller functional urban area is an exception; its strong surplus of international importance is mainly due to its proximity to Munich's international airport. In this respect Freising and Munich are not substitutes but complementary locations within the same functional urban space.

The Awareness Issue

The mega-city region hypothesis describes an emerging new large-scale urban phenomenon. The process of its emergence, however, does not proceed at an equal pace; the ongoing "spatial development on the quiet" as revealed by analysis does not conform to the current state of the corresponding policy strategies and structures. The POLYNET study examined the policy implications that arise from the analytical findings about the emerging mega-city regions. In this way the crucial importance of awareness of the spatial scale of mega-city regions became apparent (Halbert, Convery and Thierstein 2006).

"It came as a surprise to the whole POLYNET project team to learn how crucial is an awareness of the spatial scale of mega-city regions. With regard to policy-making – especially on a regional, national and supra-national level – a gap in perception still seems to exist between the documented and normative policy approaches on polycentric development of mega-city regions – as in the ESDP – and the knowledge and recognition about the factual degrees of functional polycentricity and the spatial scale of mega-city regions" (Halbert, Convery and Thierstein 2006: 113).

The results of POLYNET stress the essential and pressing awareness issue in all of the eight mega-city regions. The lack of attention and awareness leads to a gap between the growing knowledge about mega-city regions provided by research, on the one hand, and spatial policy in mega-city regions, on the other. Governance processes on a metropolitan scale have hardly started yet, and awareness of the importance and the particular functionality of mega-city regions is not apparent in EU policy in the years 1999 – 2000, nor in policy at the regional and national levels in the year 2005. As there is little concern for the crucial connection between the changing requirements of knowledge-intensive firms and urban change, the ability to use this knowledge for local and regional development and spatial planning purposes is still weak (Halbert, Pain and Thierstein 2006).

The lack of awareness of the new spatial scale of MCRs results in the inability to establish stable and successful multilevel governance. Consequently, contemporary spatial planning policies are characterized by a gap between the functional logic of the economic driving forces of spatial development and the territorial normative approaches public bodies are bound to. This mismatch becomes apparent on different spatial scales as in the example of the mega-city region of Paris. The lack of functional polycentricity in the Paris region, with its still relatively concentrated functional patterns and locations of knowledge-intensive firms, can partly be explained by an inappropriate normative polycentric planning policy at two other competing spatial scales, viz., the national scale and the agglomeration scale, two territorial approaches that fail the mega-city region's functional logic (Halbert 2006).

This mismatch affects the ability to pursue sustainable spatial development in mega-city regions. The political bodies and institutions that have an impact on mega-city regions indeed have planning objectives of sustainability, but their strong territorial logic does not consider the driving functional forces of spatial development. As a consequence, the concept of sustainability is not reflected in the context of the complex system of interaction of mega-city regions on a global/European as well as regional/local spatial scale. Mega-city regions are more or less open economic and ecological systems, which means that policy measures taken in one mega-city region may have effects in other regions (Halbert, Pain and Thierstein 2006).

The main questions still to be asked, which are crucial for future policy in mega-city regions aimed at sustainable spatial development, touch on four distinct themes, i.e., economic development, social inequities, environmental sustainability and territorial cohesion (Halbert, Pain and Thierstein 2006). The interrelationship of these themes with the new spatial scale of mega-city regions is far from simple and obvious, and much more attention must be given to this question, in policy-making as well as in research.

II Perception – an Essential Building Block

Before discussing models for large-scale metropolitan governance or possible answers to the implications of the concept of sustainability in the context of mega-city regions, one has to address the essential prerequisite to all these efforts. Who is fully aware of the mega-city region's spatial scale? The question of perception precedes every attempt to develop strategies for or adapt governance structures to the new challenges.

One can either condemn the ignorance and lack of understanding of major stakeholders and players or simply get on with that task. We want to comprehend the question of perception as a substantial challenge in the context of mega-city regions; instead of a sideline it is a priority issue. This exactly is what happened during the POLYNET project. After having revealed analytically the new scale of the mega-city region of Northern Switzerland, the project team wanted to tackle policy questions. When doing so, the major issue of perception took center stage. In stakeholder workshops the whole problem of the latent invisibility gradually became evident. In the concluding workshop in June 2005, participants were asked to individually map – as an "educated guess" – the spatial reach of each of six main policy fields, all of which have a major territorial impact. Participants, furthermore, had to indicate whether these policy fields undergo any dynamics with regard to their strategies or instruments. This exercise had no analytical purpose of its own but led quickly to a lively debate about adequate territorial organization. The aggregate map of the six policy fields discussed displayed some distinct patterns that represented common as well as diverging perceptions of the participants about spatial reach and the dynamics of the respective policies.

How then to specify the challenge of "Making Mega-City Regions Visible!"? The perception and recognition of the new spatial scale of mega-city regions from a local, regional and metropolitan perspective underlies a double complexity. The first difficulty can be attached to the object itself; the spatial characteristics of mega-city regions hinder their immediate sensory perception. The second one is tied to the observer's perspective; the fragmentation of political responsibilities results in a concurrence of views, backgrounds and interests of different actors that have to be integrated in a metropolitan governance process. In the following sections these two perspectives will be elaborated on.

Complexity of Perceiving Mega-City Regions I:
Invisible Qualities and Characteristics

What are the spatial characteristics of the mega-city regions found in POLYNET that make perception so difficult and demanding for the different actors involved?

A New Spatial Scale

The mere size of mega-city regions – they are bigger than a city and its agglomeration – challenges our perception in two respects. First it breaks down our common notions of spatial categories and consequently counters our mental dispositions as the basis for our perception. As shown in the example of the Zurich-Basel metropolitan region in Switzerland, the new scale of this emerging mega-city region has an impact upon the traditional perception of the country as rural or semi-rural with little urban character (Gabi et al. 2006). Additionally, when extending beyond administrative borders and other familiar boundaries, Mega-city regions also disturb every historically founded understanding of the territory. Secondly the new scale brings about the sheer impossibility of an intuitive sensual perception in everyday life. The identification of regional contexts already imposes considerable difficulties on many players. In the context of mega-city regions these questions are raised in a new context of scale and size.

Flexible, Ever-Changing Boundaries

The nonphysical functional approach to mega-city regions implies the loss of fixed, static boundaries. One cannot exactly say where mega-city regions start and where they end; borderlines are blurred.

"...Everywhere it proved impossible to identify precise mega-city region boundaries. The dynamic nature of emergence of mega-city regions prevents their fixed delimitation..." (Halbert, Pain and Thierstein 2006: 207).

Mega-city regions are of a variable geometry. They extend over the area where the economic players interact in a dynamic way. Mega-city regions as a concept of spatial development does not even aim at generating fixed borders but rather endorses thinking in flexible, functional defined spaces. So leaving behind the still-present territorial logic does not only imply bridging borders and scaling up cooperation but giving up the predominance of static borders. This seems to be especially difficult because identification and self-conception of a region's inhabitants and decision-makers significantly rely on the constituent power of boundaries.

Invisibility of the Constituent Elements

The definition of mega-city regions mainly by means of their nonphysical functions and networks means that its constituent elements are not directly perceptible. "Spatial development on the quiet" refers to the (at first glance invisible) influence of physical and virtual connections and relationships between enterprises as part of the current economic and social processes on spatial development (Thierstein et al. 2006).

"Visible changes by no means tell the whole story of the underlying development tendencies. Beneath the surface of expansion of the built environment there exists an intensive network of virtual exchange of knowledge, data and information. Recent research has shown that the activities of the knowledge-intensive business firms and their location strategies are major driving forces of spatial development" (Gabi et al. 2006: 157).

Shifting Perspectives and Coexistence of Opposite Dynamics

This functional analysis of mega-city regions reveals simultaneities of different and overlapping spatial scales. In order to really understand the ongoing mega-city region formation processes, it is necessary to permanently change the perspectives – again an unusual and ambitious procedure – between different spatial scales such as global, national, metropolitan, regional and local. And by doing so, there appear simultaneities of opposing processes in mega-city regions, such as concentration and dispersion, centralization and decentralization. The ESPON project on "Potentials for polycentric development in Europe" illustrates how, at the European scale (macrolevel), "regional polycentric integration will tend to increase the contrast between core and periphery if implemented across the board... At the national and transnational scales (mesolevel), a policy for increased polycentricity and spatial balance at the European level will strengthen the strongest urban regions." At the subnational level likewise "the strengthening of secondary cities with the aim of balancing the capital region may increase the difference between them and smaller cities" (ESPON 2004: 239).

Lacking Congruence of Functional, Morphological and Administrative Shape

Different analytical approaches with the associated differing notions of space bring about different versions and spatial shapes of mega-city regions. Once the nonphysical functional correlations within mega-city regions are revealed, one observes that the invisible functional shape thus far discovered does, in the majority of cases, differ from the initially visible morphological shape of the territory. The interrelations between the functional and morphological spaces are not evident and are difficult to understand. This divergence adds to the more obvious gap between small-scale administrative borders, on the one hand, and the organization of everyday life in large-scale city-regions, on the other.

Discontinuity and Diversity

Finally, the nonphysical functional spatial approach to mega-city regions brings about a perimeter that includes manifold and morphologically heterogeneous parts that partly invalidate common spatial categories such as the distinction between urban and rural spaces (Thierstein et al. 2006). Mega-city regions include a very diverse range of different categories of space, including highly urban centers, hybrid urban landscapes and semirural areas. The often functionally as well as morphologically polycentric mega-city regions lack homogeneity. On the contrary, it is complementarity, the functional division of labor, that glues the parts together. This also implies a discontinuity of space; in mega-city regions highly concentrated urban nodes of functional and physical density alternate with big empty spaces or in-between spaces.

To conclude, as nonphysical, dynamic functional forces form their internal cohesion, emerging mega-city regions seem to be rather counterintuitive with regard to catchy notions and thus challenge perception and comprehension.

Complexity of Perceiving Mega-City Regions II:
Multiple Recipients and Worlds

When shifting from the description of the object to the perspective of the observer, a second complexity in the recognition of the emerging new urban phenomenon of mega-city regions arises. It is induced by the institutional fragmentation of mega-city regions that also brings about a fragmentation of perception.

In most cases there exists no political institution at the scale of mega-city regions. Instead a multitude of political bodies from different spatial scales, regional as well as municipal, have to be integrated in a process of multilevel governance. As functional forces are crucial driving forces in spatial development in mega-city regions, other important actors for spatial development that have to be considered come from outside the administration (see Davoudi's article in the present book). According to their economic, social, civil or cultural function, position and affiliation, these different players perceive mega-city regions in different ways. They focus different contents, topics and challenges; they have different interests and scopes of action.

In the case of the Rhine-Main mega-city region, the POLYNET project has found a concurrence of various regionalizations, a multiplicity of regional views compiled by different coalitions of actors (Freytag, Hoyler and Mager 2006). According to the authors, the region remains internally fragmented despite the high international visibility of Frankfurt. In the RhineRuhr case the research team even speaks of an "unborn" giant because of fragmented institutional landscape, fuzzy strategic concepts and uncoordinated policies (Danielzyk, Knapp and Schmitt 2006).

Considering the multiplicity of players and stakeholders is only a first step towards understanding the complexity of perception from the recipient's point of view. There is a second and probably more important aspect. The hub function of mega-city regions brings about another kind of inconsistency of perception. Mega-city regions are described as interfaces and gateways between economic activities on different spatial scales, from local to global (Thierstein et al. 2006). One expression of this function is the crucial importance of international gateway infrastructures, such as air- or seaports. As a consequence, mega-city regions are also an intersection point of people and actors with different ranges to their spatial activities. The different areas of reference also implicate a different kind of logic and motivation for their action. Differing logic behind actions and different interests imply a variation in spatial reach of respective actions. Manufacturing firms mostly locate their individual activities along their value chain following their industrial logic of global functionality. Whereas administrative bodies follow an institutional logic, which is determined by the territorial boundaries of their (localized) jurisdiction. These different worlds mix and confront one another in mega-city regions more than on any other spatial scale. This is where they interact directly or indirectly by sharing the same space.

The sociological concept of *économies de la grandeur* is instrumental in interpreting the simultaneous and overlapping worlds of various interests and actors (Boltanski and Thévenot 1991). It helps to understand the articulation between traditional institutional boundaries and new spaces of areas such as mega-city regions. Therefore, we are interested in the way the numerous actors within the mega-city regions justify and rationalize the different dimensions of the emergent new spatial scale, the mega-city region. The concept of the *économies de la grandeur* distinguishes six different "worlds," or justifications, that actors use to legitimize their activities. Although originally developed in a corporate context, the sociological concept seems apt to be applied in regional contexts as well. The six "worlds" each have a distinct spatial realm of activity, an individual logic of action, and a few overarching guiding principles. They are:
- Competitiveness (representing the merchant world)
- Territorial cohesion (the domestic world)
- Efficiency (the industrial world)
- Image (the world of opinions)
- Solidarity (civil society)
- Creativity (the world of inspiration)

In a large-scale space containing different flows, such as mega-city regions, these six worlds are naturally closely interrelated. The superposition or even confrontation of such different "worlds" in one place can be understood by analogy to the description of the simultaneity and superposition of different "scapes," different concepts of space belonging to different social groups (Hauser 2003). In one and the same place it is possible for different claims of interpretation, conventions and land use that compete and come into conflict to coexist. At first glance these different concepts of space are quite invisible and even the different actors are not always aware of them.

So far the major challenges of the perceptional work have been looked at from the object's as well as from the observer's perspective. Before specifying the program of "Making Mega-City Regions Visible!" the potential role of perception to governance processes shall be briefly considered. What might the productive interplay of "image" and "region" consist in? How can it be conceptualized and verified?

Reflecting Perception's Role in Governance Processes
The OEDC describes governance as the organization and administration of regional authorities and institutions on different levels as well as processes of decision-making, cooperation, and exertion of influence (OECD 2001). Governance aims at the horizontal self-organization among mutually interdependent actors. Therefore new spatial alliances and partnerships between the central government, territorial public authorities, the private sector and civil society are debated (Thierstein, Held and Gabi 2003). Achieving large-scale metropolitan governance as it is required in mega-city regions depends on a collective learning process that has to be initiated. The change favored by government institutions can only be accomplished by an evolutive understanding of spatial development. Within this change process the cycle of "awareness, products and processes" as a "key to insight" plays a crucial role (Thierstein,

Held and Gabi 2003). A successful long-term development of mega-city regions needs the interaction of these three components. Creating awareness of problems and involvement enables the development of adequate actions and solutions in single sectoral fields. Their implementation depends on governing processes being initiated, stimulating regional societal learning processes at the same time. As a result actors deepen their awareness and strengthen the endeavor to better action. It is by this spiral course that the three interrelated levels of action, which governance is based upon, are gradually established: strategy, structures and culture. Within this process of spatial development, building up and deepening awareness and hence working on the perceptibility of mega-city regions can be understood as a permanent task.

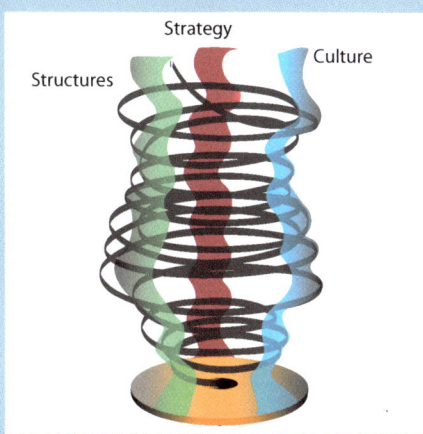

Figure 10:
Evolutive understanding of spatial development: governance strategies, structures and culture are constantly and mutually reviewed and adapted.

Awareness is an active attitude that is closely related to attention. Attention is a significant and scarce resource; it forms the first step towards action in the sense of AIDA-attention, interest, desire, and action. It is a cognitive process of the human mind that is very much tied to perception. As such it is a gateway to the rest of cognition, such as decision-making, memory, or emotion (Brockhaus Enzyklopädie online 2005a). Attention implies withdrawal from some things in order to deal effectively with others. Thus, trying to establish attention for mega-city regions has to take into account the situation of concurrence that might exist with regards to other spatial scales that the endeavor of political bodies is bound to.

Awareness can be understood in a double sense; it consists of two components that are closely linked up, first, to recognize a problem and second, to recognize one's involvement. When discussing concepts of spatial or regional identity it becomes apparent that questions of perception are a prerequisite to the identity formation processes of players, stakeholders and citizens. Weichart distinguishes three steps within such processes: first, "identification of" relates to the perceived identity of places; second, "being identified" means to identify oneself as being part of the place or region and hence to realize one's role, interests and responsibilities; third, "identification with" points to the symbolic function of places that permits them to become objects of identification (Weichart 1990). Establishing identification of mega-city regions is the very first step towards the identification of the players with this new spatial scale that the governance issue demands. It is in this realm that Paasi (2003) conceives the question of regional identity: "'Regional identity' is, in a way, an interpretation of the process through which a region becomes institutionalized, a process consisting of the production of territorial boundaries, symbolism and institutions" (Paasi 2003: 478). The OECD makes a similar argument when stating that improved metropolitan governance would not result solely from the reform of institutions and finances. It was rather a question of changing behavior and governance culture as well (OECD 2001; Thierstein, Held and Gabi 2003). The required governance culture implies behavior patterns, in particular cultural attitudes, values, principles and norms, the recurring routines and trusted forms. Common culture and behavior help create identity and a sense of belonging (Thierstein et al. 2005). Healey's "concepts of place" in a similar way stress the importance of a "common language" of place that is more than quantitative analytical data. Questions of meaning and identity of place thereby play a crucial role (Healey 2002).

The perceptibility of mega-city regions is a precondition for the identification of the citizens, players and stakeholders with this new spatial scale. So far mega-city regions can be regarded as an analytical and normative concept. But when mega-city regions really do become an effective reference area for spatial planning and development, they also have to become perceptional regions with day-to-day relevance that can also be identified with. There seems to be a cumulative causation; political enforceability (a), or the establishment of large-scale metropolitan governance, largely depends on the perceptibility (b), in the sense of identification of, that subsequently enables feelings of belonging (c) to be established, which afterwards give rise to public acceptance (Weichart 1999).

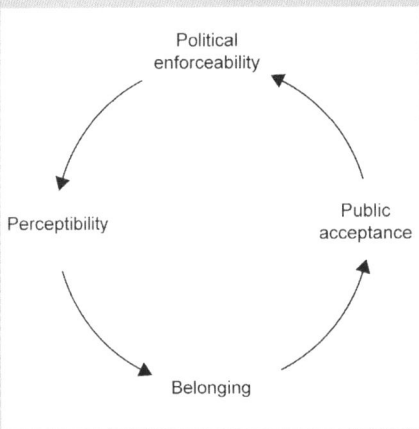

Figure 11:
Planning regions as objects of perception and identification: the potential role of a region's perceptibility to spatial development.

III "Making Mega-City Regions Visible!" – Conceptualizing the Perceptional Work

This book aims to explore the question of visualizing mega-city regions in a general and systematic way. An integral part of the book is to examine the necessary width and depth of the program of "Making Mega-City Regions Visible!" The authors' investigations do not refer to a predefined framework of the perceptional work to be done. As the field of research in the program is wide and open, the contributions have different starting points. Nevertheless, in the following section we want to distinguish three basic dimensions of images that are involved in the process of spatial perception. Their application and function to the emerging phenomenon of mega-city regions will be outlined. Following that, these different dimensions with their multiple facets are the focus of the different articles presented in this book. The confrontation and superposition of these contributions demands conceptualizing their interaction and application within evolutive planning processes; the concluding article will address these questions.

The image of the region will be conceived as an answer to the immanent invisibility of mega-city regions. The term image has ample meanings that have to be specified for our large-scale spatial context. When trying to improve perception of mega-city regions it might be useful to briefly consider how perception works.

How do we perceive space and what are therefore the relevant layers of intervention? Understanding the perceptional process is the focus of many scientific as well as practical disciplines. In this book Petrin's article explores a couple of these different approaches in relation to large-scale spatial contexts. Following his hypothesis, space is basically produced in the human brain. Consequently, when thinking about modes of intervention in order to improve or change perception he introduces a dualism of spatial production: In addition to material space (first space), there is a second, immaterial space that can be understood as a synthesized model of perception or imagination. It is these two layers that can be the object of spatial production (see Petrin's article in the present book). Perception is driven by immediate sensations as well as our mental projections. The concept of the mental model is one of many possible illustrations for the process of spatial perception. It tries to explain the transfer from the sensory stimulus to a context. Mental models are images of reality in human perception. As cultural views, convictions, prejudices, mental patterns, fixed ideas and other intuitive explanations, mental models help individuals to interpret their environment. Thus memory and experience play a crucial role. Mental models are necessary to integrate new information into a context in order to properly understand, comprehend and judge it. When absorbing the new information and impressions in this way, the possibilities of representing reality in the mental model are constantly being enlarged for future perception. This is when a learning process takes place. Learning influences our mental models because in the experience of learning our views, experience and expectations are changed (Hasebrook 1995).

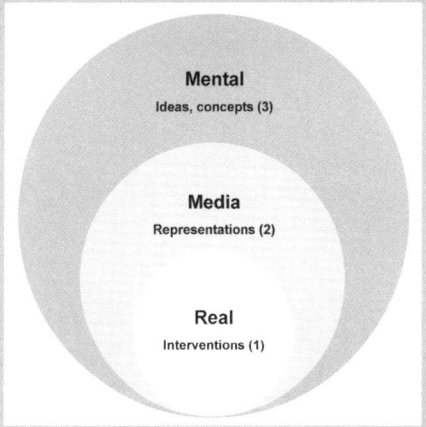

Figure 12:
Three dimensions of "Making Mega-City Regions Visible!"

Three Dimensions of "Image" Steering Perception

When understanding perception as a learning process, the program of "Making Mega-City Regions Visible!" can be started from a double perspective. It implies that work on the object (the emerging phenomenon of mega-city regions) as well as work on the observer (the players, stakeholders and citizens) is involved in processes of metropolitan governance. In the observer's mind the image, idea and concept of mega-city regions has to be established and reinforced. In real space the perceptibility of these large-scale polycentric urban regions has to be strengthened. Referring to the idea of a learning process, a third, intermediary layer of intervention plays a crucial role: images in the sense of visualizations help to communicate between these two poles.

The selection of perspectives, approaches and disciplines in this book draws on the hypothesis that the program of "Making Mega-City Regions Visible!" needs to be based upon a tripartite notion of the term image, reflecting the successive steps of the perception of space. The German Brockhaus gives three meanings to the term *Bild*, or image in English. First, image can mean outlook, view, and perspective – the perception of an object with the human eye. Second, image can be understood as illustration, picture – a two- or three-dimensional representation of an object. Third, image may refer to idea or concept – it can only be experienced and seen in people's mind. It is a mental representation of real or fictional objects (Brockhaus-Enzyklopädie 1987). When applying these three categories of images to spatial phenomena and contexts one can assess their meaning and substance in the context of mega-city regions.

Real Images

Real images refer to spatial qualities of mega-city regions that can be directly perceived and experienced in everyday life. These spatial characteristics may be foremost locations and places within the region: city centers, living areas, commercial areas, airports or protected landscapes. Second, the real images can relate to physical, spatial objects like buildings, infrastructures or parks. Third, the ways of using space are involved: highly synchronized timetables, space information system, media and culture or sports activities or festivities (Schönwandt 2006). When reflecting about a region's potential real images, the question of significance, sense and importance of these real elements and aspects arises. What spatial elements will the mega-city region's map be made up of? What is significant and important at the new spatial scale of mega-city regions in what respects – in functional, physical, emotional, symbolic, historical and other?

One main function of real images may consist of visualizing a region in day-to-day life. Those characteristics of space that can be experienced in everyday life are potential focal points of processes of identification (Ipsen 1997). Additionally real images are points of reference for media and mental images and thus become part of the way space is communicated inside or outside the mega-city region. By interventions in space these real images can be deliberately created, manipulated and strengthened.

Media Images

Media images include, on the one hand, representations of real spatial images that can be perceived and experienced directly. Thus these real images are reproduced and can be communicated. On the other hand, and this aspect seems to be even more important, not directly perceptible spatial qualities of mega-city regions can be visualized as well. This might relate to the illustration or mapping of physical and nonphysical functional relations such as commuting or communication patterns. Media images are generated by different techniques of visualization, including maps, photographs, models, diagrams or interactive visualizations.

When dealing with media images the program of "Making Mega-City Regions Visible!" can be better understood if we take into consideration four interrelated layers: content, technique, recipient and function (see Burkhart's article in the present book). Reflecting the complexity of perceiving mega-city regions as described in the preceding section, the main challenges appear to concern content and recipient. The nonphysical functional analytical approach implies the endeavor of developing adequate techniques of visualization corresponding to the relational understanding of space. In this respect major difficulties arise. When taking into consideration the recipient's and the function's perspective on these images (whom will the images get through to? what will they provoke?), the issue gets even more complex. While mega-city regions are closely related to a relational understanding of space, essentialist concepts of space and the corresponding self-evident importance of morphological space are still very familiar and dominant (Healey 2004). This also raises questions concerning form, style and design. Will media images purposely break up with or look for ways to tie into these present ideas of space?

The special importance of media images consists in their role as a starting point for the process of creating awareness. It is by this category of images that the spatial construct of mega-city regions is "discovered" analytically. In time media images may change mental ones and may form a basis for real images to be recognized and purposefully developed.

Mental Images

This category of images includes at least three different aspects. First, mental images refer to the notion of conception or idea. It is thus closely related to the process of classification and arrangement. This is of relevance in two fields. According to Paasi (2003), naming a region in the day-to-day life of the citizens is important and part of the spatial symbolism "…naming is showing, creating, bringing into existence. This emerges from the fact that human knowledge bears on classification, and identification is basic to classification" (Paasi 2003: 480). The name stands for a mental construct that has found its way into everyday life. When applied to spatial development and planning, ideas such as theoretical constructs of space are powerful in forming categories of thinking, empirical research and normative action. This is very much the case with Christaller's theory of Central Places in the German planning tradition that dominated spatial thinking and action for a long time. This is subliminally expressed by the use of Christaller's hexagon symbol (originally used for central places) for German mega-city regions in the official maps by the Ministerial Conference on Spatial Planning up to the year 2000 (Bundesamt für Bauwesen und Raumordnung 2000).

Secondly mental images may point to the "mindware" – reputation is a synonym – of a region. It is about the cognitive attraction factors of a place, the image a locality evokes in the outside world. This image is not objective but bound to the subjective and fragmentary knowledge people have of space. Hospers argues that the image of a place, the "mindware," becomes more and more important for location decisions as "hardware" (physical and human capital) and "software" (social capital) of different places are increasingly assimilated (Hospers 2006). This concept of image is comparable to that of a corporate or product image. It exceeds the visual sphere and features a wholeness of emotions and feelings, factual information, and intended action. It consolidates in the course of time through internal and external perception and experience (Brockhaus Enzyklopädie online 2005b).

When turning to the way mega-city regions are perceived from inside, a third meaning of mental image becomes relevant. Mental images as subjective mental projections of the region determine the identity formation processes of players, stakeholders and citizens. These kind of mental maps are based upon the cognitive and emotional relations that the inhabitants bind to their region.

The importance of mental images is due to their function as a filter in the process of perception; they precede and result from the processing of sensations. They give orientation, steer attention and help to interpret the environment.

Mental images of mega-city regions are rare, almost nonexistent. On the other hand, they are in great demand. In the global competition of locations, place marketing and branding have to promote increasingly spacious objects such as Greater Boston, Greater Lyon, Greater Zurich, Greater Milan or Greater Munich. They therefore strongly look for potentials of forming and communicating these kinds of images.

Daring the Interplay

When approaching the program of "Making Mega-City Regions Visible!" (such is our hypothesis), all three notions of images have to be considered together. There is a mutual correspondence between real, media and mental images; they comprise and influence one another. Real images can act upon media and mental images; media images affect mental images. Coming back to the spiral course of awareness, products and processes that helps large-scale metropolitan governance to gradually take root, fostering perception turns out to be a multi-faceted task. The single components of this perceptional work draw on the three dimensions of images and have to be conceived in succession related to the evolutive understanding of spatial development. Thus the task is not only to reveal and enrich the different modes of "making visible," but to think about their integration and sequence within planning processes alike.

"Conceptualizing the perceptional work" in the preceding section offers a first tentative framework as a starting point for the program of "Making Mega-City Regions Visible!" As the collection of approaches in this book aims to explore the potentials, varying importance and possible interferences of all three layers of images in the large-scale context of mega-city regions, we soon had to recognize the need for the integration and interaction of different disciplines. We decided to invite scholars and practitioners from different disciplinary backgrounds to participate in a symposium early in the year 2006, and eventually in the present book in order to address the task collectively.

In two respects the book is based on an approach that is more speculative than systematic. The book aims to gather sometimes quite scattered disciplinary perspectives. At the same time the selection of disciplines is neither thought to be representative nor complete. It is an integral part of this book to reflect on the different disciplinary approaches that the program of "Making Mega-City Regions Visible!" demands. The second aspect relates to the task we assigned the authors. Until now "making visible" the new spatial scale of mega-city regions left little room for original experience and research. Trusted knowledge and experience from familiar spatial scales had to be projected onto the new dimension of mega-city regions. This exercise in scaling up existing knowledge implies a highly explorative procedure.

The following fourteen articles reflect and test the spectrum of the perspectives needed for the program of "Making Mega-City Regions Visible!" The sequence presented here does not stand for any hierarchy of the contents. The book concludes with an attempt by the editors to embrace the collected disciplinary perspectives and a quick sketch of the main lessons learnt.

Notes

[1] This chapter is based upon the research project *Interconnectedness and Locations of Knowledge-Intensive Firms. The Case of the Mega-City Region of Munich* of the Chair of Spatial and Territorial Development, Munich University of Technology, 2006 – 2007 (Thierstein, Goebel and Lüthi 2007).

References

Blotevogel, H.H. 2002. "Deutsche Metropolregionen in der Vernetzung." *Informationen zur Raumentwicklung* (6/7): 345-351.

Boltanski, L. and L. Thévenot. 1991. *De la justification. Les économies de la grandeur*. Paris: Gallimard.

Brockhaus-Enzyklopädie. 1987. "Bild." 19th ed. 24 vols. Vol. 3: 301. Mannheim: F.A. Brockhaus.

Brockhaus Enzyklopädie online. 2005a. "Aufmerksamkeit." 21st ed. Bibliographisches Institut & F. A. Brockhaus AG.

Brockhaus Enzyklopädie online. 2005b. "Image." 21st ed. Bibliographisches Institut & F. A. Brockhaus AG.

Bundesamt für Bauwesen und Raumordnung. 2000. "Raumordnungsbericht 2000." *Berichte*, Vol. 7. Bonn: Selbstverlag des BBR.

Danielzyk, R., W. Knapp and P. Schmitt. 2006. "RhineRuhr: Towards Compatibility? Strategic Spatial Policies for a Specific Configuration of Polycentricity." *Built Environment* 32 (2): 137-147.

Derudder, B. 2006. "On Conceptual Confusion in Empirical Analyses of a Transnational Urban Network." *Urban Studies* 43 (11): 2027-2046.

ESPON. 2004. *ESPON 1.1.1. Potentials for polycentric development in Europe. Project Report*. Final Report. Luxembourg: Co-financed by the European Community through the Interreg III ESPON.

Freytag, T., M. Hoyler and C. Mager. 2006. "Advantageous Fragmentation? Reimagining Metropolitan Governance and Spatial Planning in Rhine-Main." *Built Environment* 32 (2): 124-136.

Friedmann, J. 1986. "The World City Hypothesis. Development and Change". In *The Global Cities Reader*, edited by N. Brenner and R. Kell. Oxon: Routledge: 67-71.

Gabi, S., A. Thierstein, C. Kruse and L. Glanzmann. 2006. "Governance Strategies for the Zürich-Basel Metropolitan Region in Switzerland." *Built Environment* 32 (2): 157-171.

Halbert, L. 2006. "The Polycentric City Region That Never Was: The Paris Agglomeration, Bassin Parisien and Spatial Planning Strategies in France." *Built Environment* 32 (2): 184-193.

Halbert, L., F.J. Convery and A. Thierstein. 2006. "Reflections on the Polycentric Metropolis." *Built Environment* 32 (2): 110-113.

Halbert, L., K. Pain and A. Thierstein. 2006. "European Polycentricity and Emerging Mega-City Regions: 'One Size Fits All' Policy?" *Built Environment* 32 (2): 205-218.

Hall, P. and K. Pain. 2006. "From Metropolis to Polypolis." In *The Polycentric Metropolis. Learning from Mega-City Regions in Europe*, edited by P. Hall and K. Pain. London: Earthscan: 3-16.

Hasebrook, J. 1995. *Multimedia-Psychologie. Eine neue Perspektive menschlicher Kommunikation*. Heidelberg, Berlin, Oxford: Spektrum Akademischer Verlag.

Hauser, S. 2003. "Stadt ohne Bild. Zur Wahrnehmung der Agglomeration." In *100 % Stadt – Der Abschied vom Nicht-Städtischen*, edited by E. Hubeli, H. Saiko and K. Vöckler. Graz: Haus der Architektur Graz: 105-121.

Healey, P. 2002. "Spatial Planning as Mediator for Regional Governance. Conceptions of Place in the Formation of Regional Governance Capacity." In *Regional Governance – New Models of Self-Government in the European Community*, edited by D. Fürst and J. Knieling. Hannover: Verlag der ARL: 13-25.

Healey, P. 2004. "The Treatment of Space and Place in the New Strategic Spatial Planning in Europe." *International Journal of Urban and Regional Research* 28 (1): 45-67.

Hospers, G.-J. 2006. "Borders, Bridges and Branding: The Transformation of the Øresund Region into an Imagined Space." *European Planning Studies* 14 (8): 1015-1033.

Ipsen, D. 1997. *Raumbilder. Kultur und Ökonomie räumlicher Entwicklung*. Pfaffenweiler: Centaurus-Verlagsgesellschaft.

OECD. 2001. *Cities for Citizens. Improving Metropolitan Governance*. Paris: OECD Publishing.

Paasi, A. 2000. "Re-constructing Regions and Regional Identity." Paper read at Alexander von Humboldt Lectures in Human Geography, 7.11, at Nijmegen, The Netherlands.

Paasi, A. 2003. "Region and Place: Regional Identity in Question." *Progress in Human Geography* 27 (4): 475-485.

Sassen, S. 2001. *The Global City: New York, London, Tokyo*. 2nd ed. Princeton, New Jersey: Princeton University Press.

Schönwandt, W.L. 2006. "Analysieren – Visualisieren – Kommunizieren: Mit welchen "Werkzeugen" arbeiten wir?" Paper read at Öffentlicher Abendvortrag am Lehrstuhl für Raumentwicklung TU München, 3.7., at München.

Taylor, P.J. 2001. "Specification on the World City Network." *Geographical Analysis* (33): 181-194.

Taylor, P.J. 2004. *World City Network: A Global Urban Analysis*. London: Routledge.

Thierstein, A., S. Gabi, C. Kruse and L. Glanzmann. 2005. "Sustainable Management of the Polycentric European Metropolitan Region of Northern Switzerland." Paper read at AESOP 05, at Wien.

Thierstein, A., V. Goebel and S. Lüthi. 2007. *Standortverflechtungen der Metropolregion München. Über Konnektivität in der Wissensökonomie*. München: Lehrstuhl für Raumentwicklung. http://www.raumentwicklung-tum.de/publikationen.php.

Thierstein, A., T. Held and S. Gabi. 2003. "'City of Regions' – Improving Territorial Governance in the Zurich 'Glatttal-Stadt'." In *The Real and Virtual Worlds of Spatial Planning*, edited by M. Koll-Schretzenmayr, M. Keiner and G. Nussbaumer. Berlin/Heidelberg/New York: Springer: 111-125.

Thierstein, A., C. Kruse, L. Glanzmann, S. Gabi and N. Grillon. 2006. *Raumentwicklung im Verborgenen. Untersuchungen und Handlungsfelder für die Entwicklung der Metropolregion Nordschweiz*. Zürich: NZZ Buchverlag.

Weichart, P. 1990. *Raumbezogene Identität. Bausteine zu einer Theorie räumlich-sozialer Kognition und Identifikation, Schriftenreihe Erdkundliches Wissen*. Stuttgart: Franz Steiner Verlag.

Weichart, P. 1999. "Raumbezogene Identitäten 4, Intensivkurs." Paper read at Alexander von Humboldt Lectures in Human Geography, 16.-17.09.1999, at Nijmegen, The Netherlands.

Christian Kruse

Mapping Hybrid Value-Added Landscapes

A Relational Landscape of Zurich's Creative Industries

The socioeconomic structures of mega-city regions are becoming increasingly complex. Patterns of economic behavior refer to a functional rather than a solely territorial logic. Subbranches, corporations and individuals of specific knowledge-based industries seem to show polycentric patterns in their business activities, which can also be described as an organizational structure of value-added networks. This paper introduces the concept of the relational landscape of the creative industry in the mega-city region of Zurich in order to propose a new approach to qualitatively and quantitatively analyzing and mapping functional patterns of business activities, networks and interactions. In this context, "mega-city region" is used as a term to specify a large-scale functional urban area that encompasses not only the city of Zurich and its immediate surrounding municipalities, but also a couple of closer functional urban areas.

Introduction

Take a large global service company requiring a strategy for a new brand with a view to supporting its global market position. This isn't just a small issue; the stakes are indeed quite high. Designing and applying a new-brand strategy needs the full range of specialized knowledge offered by a large community of service providers. And although there are world-famous brand companies, it is impossible to find a one-size-fits-all approach. The building of a new brand is the building of a value chain of competencies in the format of a value-chain network rather than just simply adding one service to another. It is about research, market analysis, brand recognition studies, legal advice, intellectual property protection, marketing, campaigning, communication, production, visualization, consulting, perception analysis, software development, information technology and a lot more. All of these services belong to high-end knowledge-based applications and can be easily found all over the world. Of course a lot of these specialized services cluster within the knowledge economies of mega-city regions.

From a regional economic point of view it is interesting to know whether those knowledge-based services develop certain spatial patterns, show structures of functional socioeconomic interaction and build the format of a structured value-chain network. If this is the case, one of the interesting questions is how those hybrid value-added landscapes could be identified, mapped and visualized. There are many more questions that apply to the same topic, but this paper will focus on the issue of mapping and visualization. In this article the example of the creative industry within the mega-city region of Zurich serves as a case study to explain the concept of relational landscapes, a tool which has been developed in order to systematically map value-added networks of urban economies. The mega-city region of Zurich refers to a definition discussed by Hall and Pain (2006) and specifically applied by Thierstein et al. (Hall and Pain 2006; Thierstein et al. 2006). Therefore, the authors argue, the socioeconomic structure of mega-city regions become increasingly complex. The political structure does not necessarily represent the functional-territorial logic of mega-city regions. Vertical and horizontal networks of corporations as well as individuals reveal a polycentric pattern of locations and business activities, which together in a complementary way form the structure and function of a mega-city region.

Zurich's Creative Industries in a Knowledge-Based Society and Economy

Since the 1990s, knowledge has come to play an increasingly centralized role in urban and metropolitan economies. For this reason, knowledge-intensive services take some of the responsibility for the transformation process of functional economic areas. According to Richard Florida (2002), a knowledge-based economy is primarily surrounded by a net of creative institutions, enterprises and individuals, initiating and implementing technological, economic, societal and cultural innovations (Florida 2002).

The creative industry of Zurich is the part of the cultural sector that consists of private enterprises. All creative enterprises that are on a private basis involved in creative/artistic production, its communication and/or propagation through the medium of goods and services, belong to the creative industry (see Held, Kruse, Söndermann and Weckerle 2005). The creative industry can be divided into seven submarkets: architecture, book and literature market, performing arts, design and communication, film industry (including TV productions), art market and music industry.

Creative industries, as defined, are a part of such creative networks, fulfilling an important function in the successful development of urban and metropolitan economic areas. It is not surprising that creative industries have established themselves as an element in the innovation or economic policy of many European countries. European cities and regions have also been launching related activities in recent years. Particularly from a regional economic perspective, creative industries play a decisive role in the structural change of urban or metropolitan economies. They are closely linked to an increased ability to compete in the form of increased entrepreneurship, innovation capability and value-added systems. Internationally, Zurich's mega-city region belongs to the few economically important locations to have developed practically no strategic approaches up to now in the area of creative industries.

If the Zurich City Region seeks to develop such strategies, it first needs to gain the necessary knowledge of its territorial specificities, i.e., the existing regional characteristics, perhaps even idiosyncrasies. This would include every potential, every ability, every form of human capital and each network that is specific to the region–elements definable as the relational assets of an economic area. These are characteristics which are difficult to mimic, i.e., transfer to any another location. They form a knowledge base that provides a resource for strengthening competitive ability, which in turn can then be put to strategic use. Economic policy measures would then need to be set in order to enable the establishment and development of the relational assets of the respective regions, providing the location with strong relative significance in global competition. This is critical because a location can still lose its standing despite its unique, regionally specific profile, for instance, if another location is better able to position its potential. Such a development could critically affect Zurich's location since not only the creative industries would suffer in terms of ranking and significance but also the related network branches, which could then lose one of the most important transformers of the innovative processes. For this reason, this complex of creative-industry branches is critical to Zurich's mega-city region.[1]

An Evolutionary Perspective on Urban Economies

With the traditional reflection of the development of urban economies, creativity has found its consideration often in the context of entrepreneurship. The economist Joseph Schumpeter introduced the notion of the creative entrepreneur. However, he basically described the innovative and production-focused actor, whom he claimed to be responsible for new impulses of regional economic developments of so-called technological innovation systems. The associated process has been described as "creative destruction" (Thierstein and Gabi 2004), which meant structures of regional economic transformation against the background of new organizational forms of entrepreneurship. This approach left its mark on generations of scientists, on their research for determinants and an explanation of regional and urban development.

However, since the 1990s the role of knowledge as a key factor of urban and mega-city regions became more important. Knowledge-intensive business services within a knowledge-based society seemed to be responsible for considerable transformation processes of the structure of functional economic mega-city regions.

The basic scientific understanding of the factor space and its relevance to research has undergone a fundamental change of paradigm in the regional economy and economic geography. The central field of research of the regional economic geography, which had focused on structures and developments of economic areas, regions or urban systems as "phenomena that need to be clarified" (Bathelt and Glückler 2002: 34, author's translation) has changed and focuses now mainly on the research of socioeconomic interactions between institutions, organizations (enterprises) and individuals from a special perspective.

Numerous papers – mainly English-language literature – developed a New Economic Geography in which, apart from economic approaches, socioeconomic concepts are used (see Scott 1988, 1989; Storper and Scott 1990; Martin and Sunley 1996; Martin 1999; Maskell et al. 1998). The primacy of describing entrepreneurial action mainly from the perspective of criteria of efficiency-optimized organizational structures and the minimization of transaction costs has been changed to a more complementary point of view. Due to the integration of socioinstitutional determinants, which influence the behavior of the actors, the concept of the enterprise, which acts without any influence from its surroundings, has been abandoned. The concept of "embeddedness" (Granovetter 1985), developed within the New Economic Sociology, especially maps out a position opposed to the atomistic concepts of action of Neo-Institutionalism, which are based on transaction costs (Coase 1937; Williamson 1975, 1985). The opposing position of embeddedness states that socioeconomic action is embedded in social structures, locally and culturally determined informal norms and rules.

In the traditional regional economic geography it was mainly the factor "space," believed to constitutionally influence economic and social processes, that had been the central object of research. Influenced by the neo-institutional and evolution-theory-based discourse within social and economic sciences, the new research programs of the New Economic Geography focused on structures of interaction as well as institutional and corporate learning and innovation processes. For some time the focus has no longer been on regions and the question of how existing locational advantages could lead to the settlement of companies. The center of interest concentrated on the question of how entrepreneurs and companies create and change their environment in order to use the best opportunities for their services and production (Bathelt and Glückler 2002; Storper 1997). In short, within the concept of relational economic geography the level of processes and interaction of individuals and companies as well as institutions occupy the foreground. In this context we need to examine corporate development, organizational structures, management decisions, the creation of corporate networks on the basis of the role of knowledge as the main driver of change in the global economy.

Traded and Untraded Interdependencies

The crucial responsibilities of knowledge for a reorganization of basic business processes have revealed a new perspective on the value-creation process and the way it is networked.

Creating value in our days is not an isolated process. Nobody is creating value on his own, but in cooperation with others, which results in a more or less complicated system of interdependencies. Therefore understanding a value-added chain means understanding the interdependencies of its participants. Storper (1997) has developed a concept, which is very useful in order to better understand those interdependencies, viz., the concept of traded and untraded interdependencies (Storper 1997).

On the one hand these interdependencies can be contractual and monetary relationships. They can be *traded* and therefore are called **traded interdependencies**. They are input-output-oriented factors of production.

On the other, **untraded interdependencies** is the term that applies to relationships that depend on personal networks. They are neither contractual nor monetary but depend on the communication between the involved persons and their evaluation of this communication.

The traditional economic perspective focuses primarily on traded interdependencies, whereas untraded interdependencies have been marginalized, as they are more difficult to describe and measure. Nevertheless the latter are of great importance within the boundaries of a company and even more from a perspective of cross-company cooperation.

For example, Cross (2004) has shown in his network analysis research that very often the official interdependencies within a company, as they are shown by formal organizational charts, have little in common with the informal structure of interdependencies, which describe the actual structure of how the work gets done and accordingly of how value is being created (Cross 2004). In a constantly changing economic environment, where knowledge has become a valuable factor of production, people work in fluid networks rather than under conditions of determined interdependencies. To be able to adapt to new situations very quickly, one has to generate knowledge quickly. This can be done much faster through a diversified network than through a few determined relationships. How you can act depends on what you know. What you know depends on whom you know. Those fluid networks do not primarily rely on contracts but on personal social relationships, on trust and reputation, and they are being influenced by social norms and traditions (Held and Kruse 2005).

Looking at cross-company cooperations, untraded interdependencies become even more important as they often precede and influence the traded interdependencies. When a company is searching for an external partner to complete the process of value-adding, there normally is more than one candidate. Which one of the potential partners the company will choose in the end depends not only on the offered price but also on trust and therefore personal relationships. A well-developed untraded interdependency can therefore lead to a traded interdependency.

Embeddedness – a Basic Concept of Relational Economies

Mapping the hybrid value-added landscape in functional economic regions requires a different perspective (described above) on evolutionary and relational business processes. As pointed out earlier in this paper, it is no longer the sole empirical analysis of a spatial economy and the detailed description of its location patterns, which today stands in the foreground. The focus lies on the analysis of processes, structures and dynamics of knowledge-based socioeconomic interactions as a matter of territorial (local) specificity.

In contrast to this, in neoclassical economics interactions have always been seen as a subject of transaction costs due to developing information asymmetries between two or more market participants. A basic perspective on entrepreneurial behavior, which is detached from social context and embeddedness, has dominated the analysis of economic structures of specific economic sectors within a given territory. Interactions of different actors are defined as the execution of a contractual relationship, of the connected interests and different status of information. But this approach is no longer sufficient if one wants to understand processes and determinants of relational interdependencies.

The concept of embeddedness marks a turning point in sociology. It opens a new landscape of academic terms that evolved from the central idea that economic interests do not solely drive relationships of exchange, but unfold in a context of dependencies on social structures, local and cultural norms, and the economic and social embeddedness of the actors involved (Burt 1980; Granovetter 1985). It is this context that not only influences the traded interdependencies but also helps to understand how untraded interdependencies come about and function. And in a broader perspective, investigating this context helps us to understand and describe value-added chains.

The concept of embeddedness distinguishes three major levels of perspective, viz., relational, structural and geographical embeddedness:
- Relational embeddedness describes the relationship between two singular actors who develop a high productive efficiency due to the creation of reciprocal trust in a long-term cooperation.
- Structural embeddedness describes relationships and interactions between many different actors and therefore is a precondition for the creation of networks.
- Geographical embeddedness integrates the local element of acting. It describes how the "region" factor influences acting and relationships.

The whole range of relationships cannot be described without taking into account the embeddedness of the actors in a social and cultural context. Our possibilities to interact depend on our social and cultural context. The better we can handle this context, the more power to act we gain. To describe this phenomenon two new forms of assets have been defined: Relational and social capital (Kruse 2005).
- Relational capital describes abilities, competencies and reflexive learning processes of actors and the possibility to integrate these into a collective system of interaction of many actors. It describes the potential of an actor to influence his social context in a way that allows him broader possibilities of putting his ideas into action.
- Social capital describes nonmaterial potentials of collective social interaction that build a framework of unwritten standards and socioeconomic values (Burt 1995; Granovetter 1992). From a social sciences perspective social capital lays the foundation of embeddedness because it affects the opportunities of market participants, creates stability within social systems, supports transparency of decision processes, and minimizes opportunistic behavior (Kruse 2005).

Taking a relational perspective leads to a different analytical approach to the landscape of market participants and its involvement in a value-chain network of (as described here) products and services of the creative industry. Landscape, used in this context, refers to a metaphoric use of the term in order to describe the heterogeneous structure of market participants who are involved into the creative industry of Zurich's mega-city region.

From Value Chains to Value-Chain Networks

The understanding of the value and strategic position of the creative industry within a functional mega-city region points to the need:
- to apply a concept of value chains, different from classical value chains in production systems;
- to develop a detailed understanding of functional interdependencies, which participants of the creative industry are exposed to;
- to analyze the self-awareness of market participants;
- to determine drivers of and hurdles in an optimized positioning;
- to research the relation between international connectivity and local embeddedness.

Within the aforementioned spheres the products and services of the creative industry are ordered, traded and executed in a functionally structured value chain. This paper argues that services and products of knowledge-intensive business services such as creative industries are organized within a concept of a value-added network rather than in a step-by-step structure.

How to Map the Hybrid Landscape of Value-Added Networks – the Concept of the Relational Landscape

How can something become visible that is still hidden and not tangible? The case of the creative industry in the mega-city region of Zurich is not a traditional topic of research; it has become complicated to find and assess existing data and build a clear image of the structural organization of the value networks of the creative industry. In order to solve this problem, we developed the concept of a "relational landscape." The relational landscape is a method that applies to situations where structured knowledge needs to be collected systematically in order to map and visualize value networks.

The advantage of this method is that within a short timeframe a qualitative plot of the relational structure of the sector can be generated, based on the knowledge and experience of those who design and represent the creative industry, i.e., the creative entrepreneurs. In a next step the qualitative relational landscape serves as a starting point for empirically testing and proving the value chain network – on the basis of quantitative web-based plots. The projected relational landscape (Figure 2) has been developed in a multistep process. A three-hour focus group workshop with representatives of the creative industry in Zurich concentrated on the production of a chaotic image of market participants, different segments of the creative industry and its connectivity, starting with the single artist and or creative entrepreneur. At the end of the workshop the chaotic image revealed systematic patterns, and different types of business activities. In cooperation with interaction designers this plot has been transferred to a 3-D relational landscape as shown in Figure 2. It now served as a tool to structure guidelines for interviews with creative entrepreneurs in order to learn and understand the relational socioeconomic interactions within the creative industry and adjust the relational landscape. In a third step the renewed relational landscape was the major subject of a full-day think-tank with 40 leaders of the creative industry of Zurich. A major part of the think-tank concentrated on the critical assessment, further development and completion of the relational landscape. The relational landscape thus has three major functions communication-tool, matrix-tool and analysis-tool as shown in Figure 1.

Communication-tool

The relational landscape helps structure a qualitative approach like an interview series as well as explain interdependencies within the economic sector to other experts.

Matrix-tool

The relational landscape is a product of self-perception and displays the economic sector's landscape from the perspective of the market participants beyond problematic statistical classifications.

Analysis-tool

It is a complementary approach to a statistical analysis, which can be used in interviews and workshops. It serves as the framework for a quantitative empirical analysis through web-based polls in order to prove, test and further develop the concept.

Figure 1:
Three major functions of the relational landscape.

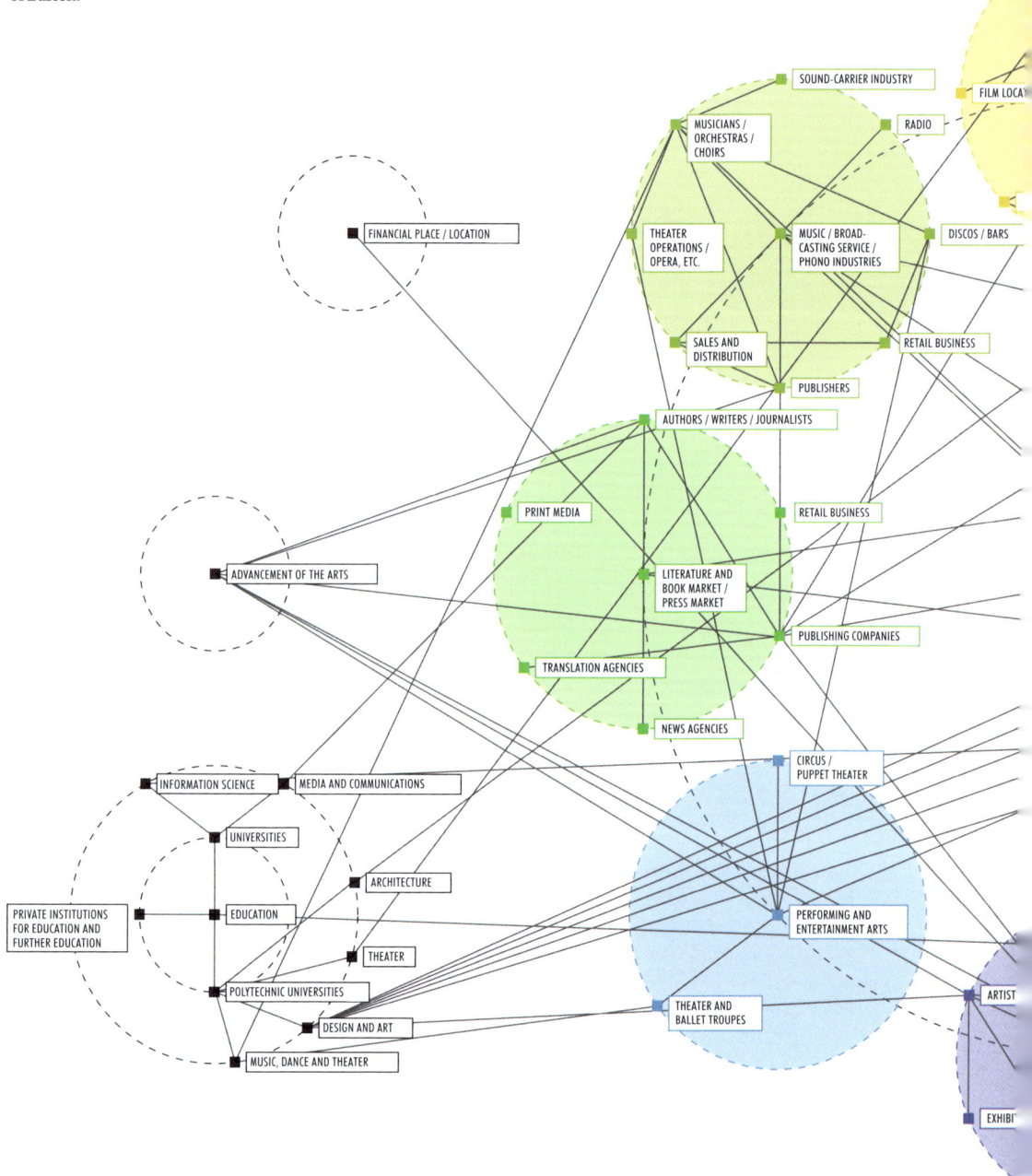

Figure 2:
The relational landscape of the creative industries of Zurich.

45 Mapping Hybrid Value-Added Landscapes

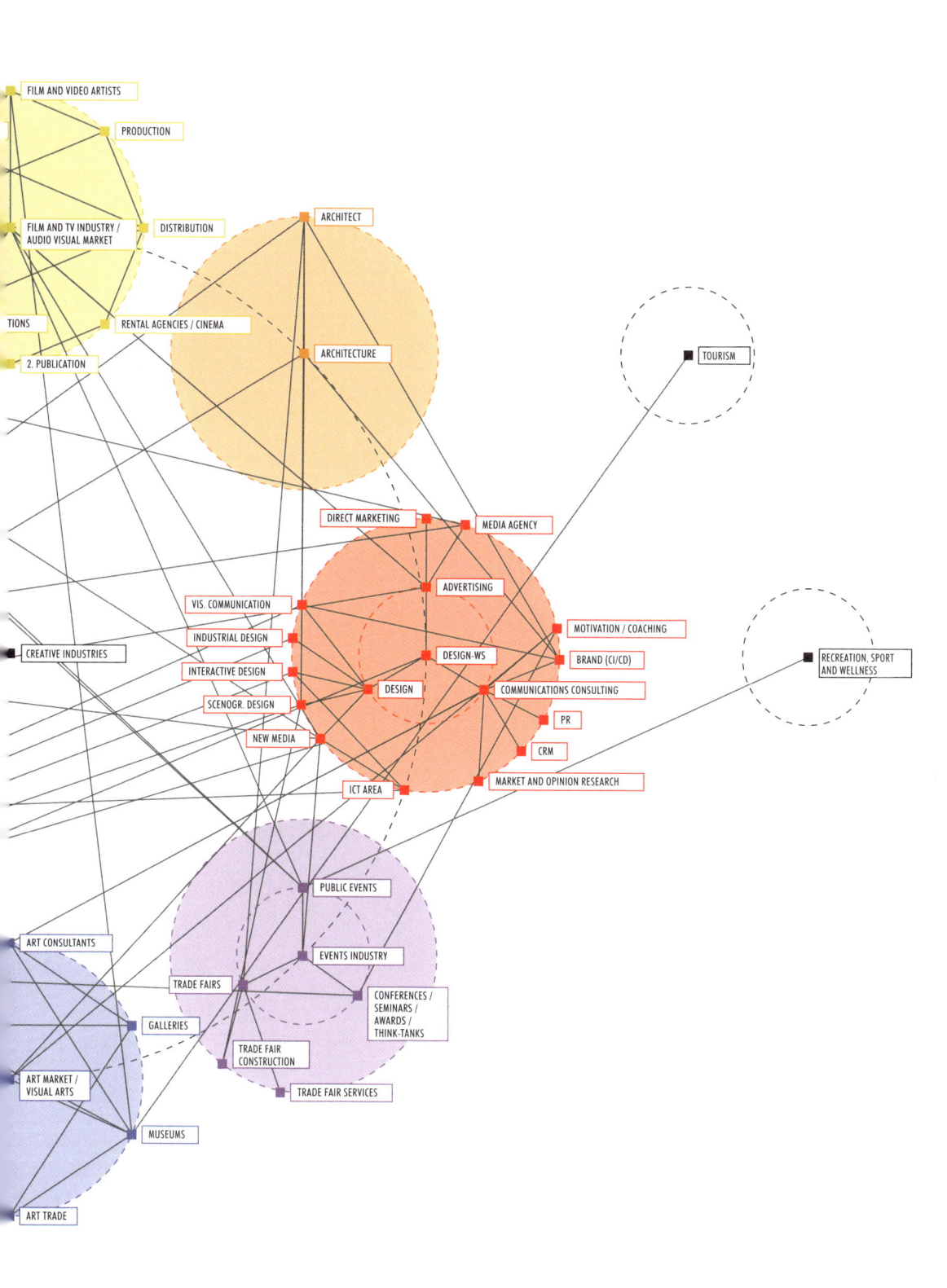

Figure 3:
Core activities of Zurich's creative industries.

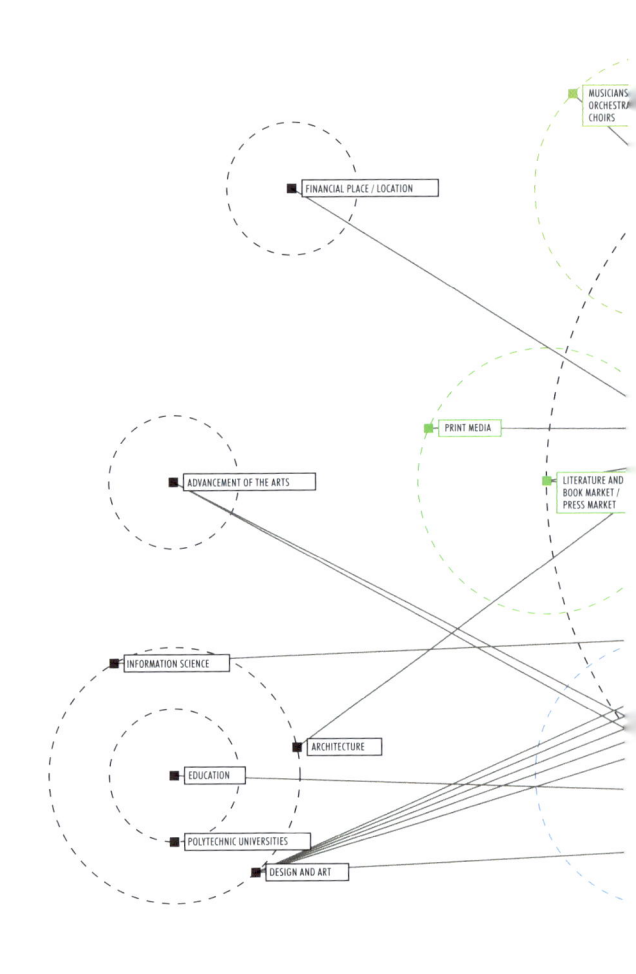

Figure 4:
Core Activities of Zurich's creative industries from the viewpoint of market participants.

Core Activity	Function
Design Industry	Innovation functioning in the form of "Swiss-Made Ideas" – interface of urban economies – education and research as the sustainable driving force of an internationally established design industry – supplier of employment
Architecture	Internationally renowned architecture functioning as a trademark – innovations function – leading-light function – interface in international networking
Events Industry	Platform – market place – quality and service awareness – trendsetter
Art Market	International art production – close ties to financial place – capital intensive

Mapping Hybrid Value-Added Landscapes

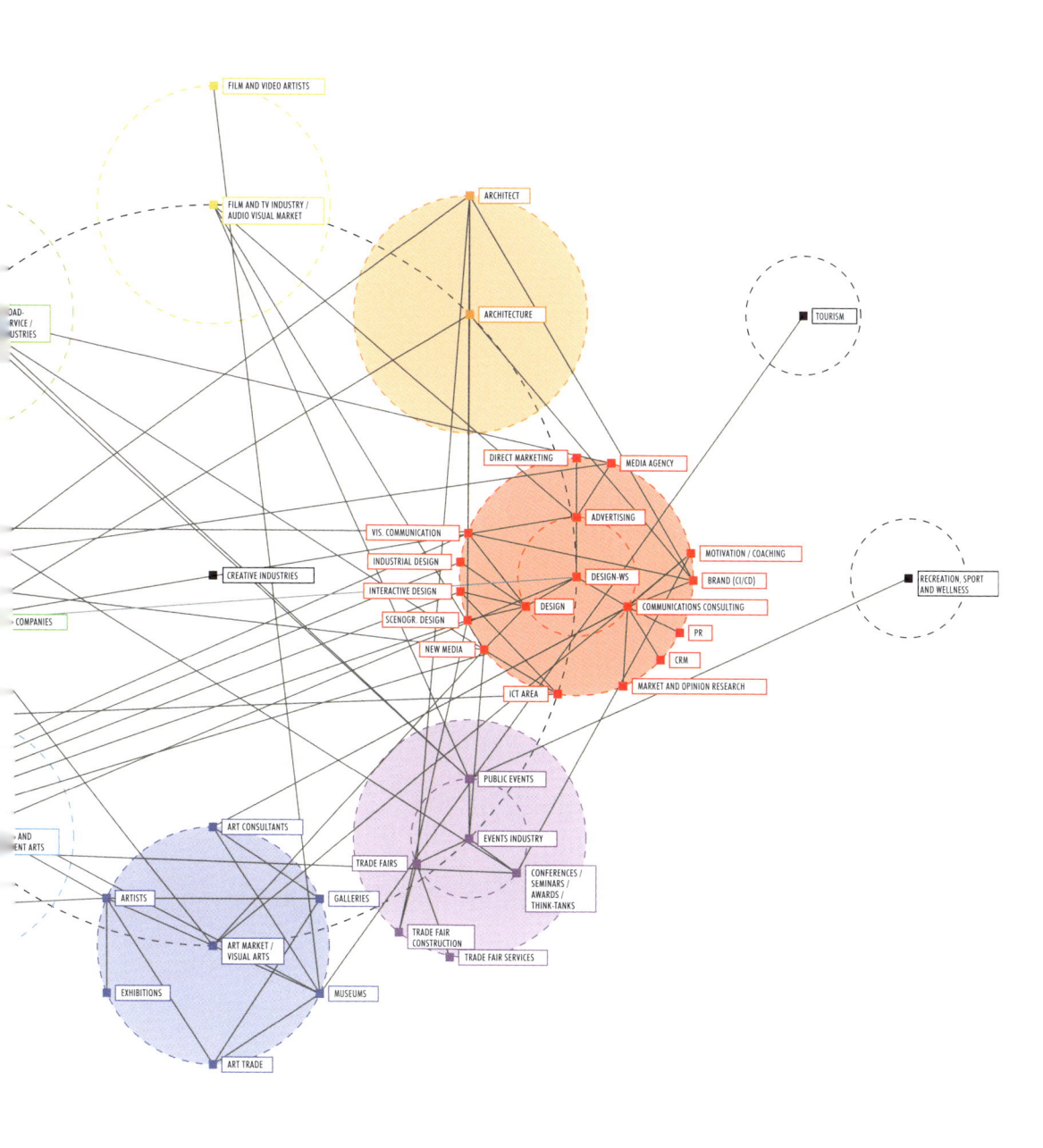

Figure 5:
Interaction axis of subsegments in Zurich's creative industries.

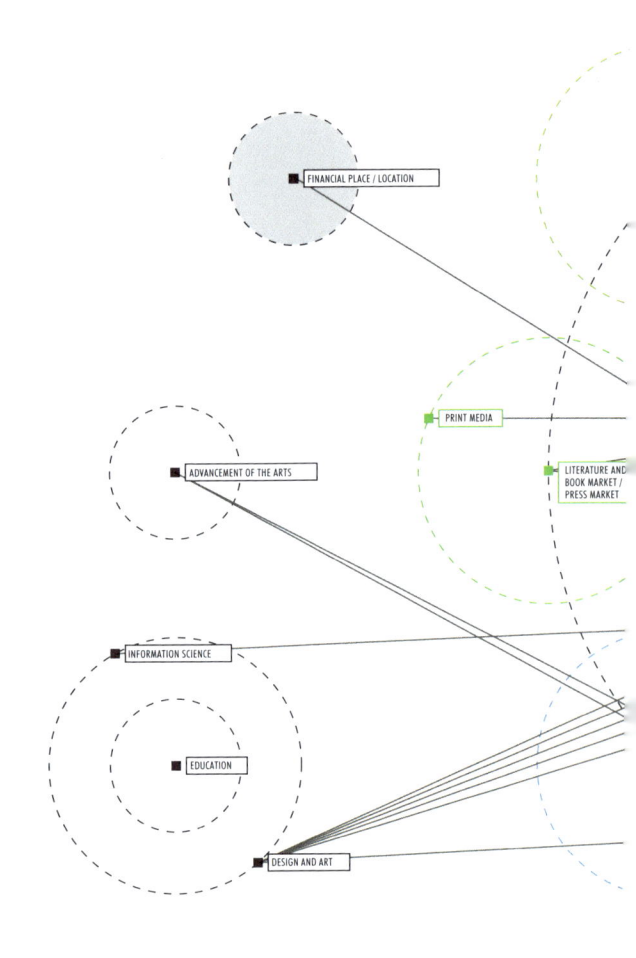

Figure 6:
Interaction axis of subsegments in Zurich's creative industries from the viewpoint of market participants.

Axis of Interaction	Subsegments
Axis of Interaction of the Financial Location	Design industry – art market – financial location
Axis of Interaction of Cultural Image	Art market/visual arts – performing arts – literature, book and press market – music, film and TV industries
Axis of Interaction of Visualization	Events industry – design industry – architecture – education and continuing education
Axis of Interaction of Knowledge	Education and higher education – architecture – design industry

Mapping Hybrid Value-Added Landscapes

Figure 7:
Strategic assets of Zurich's creative industries.

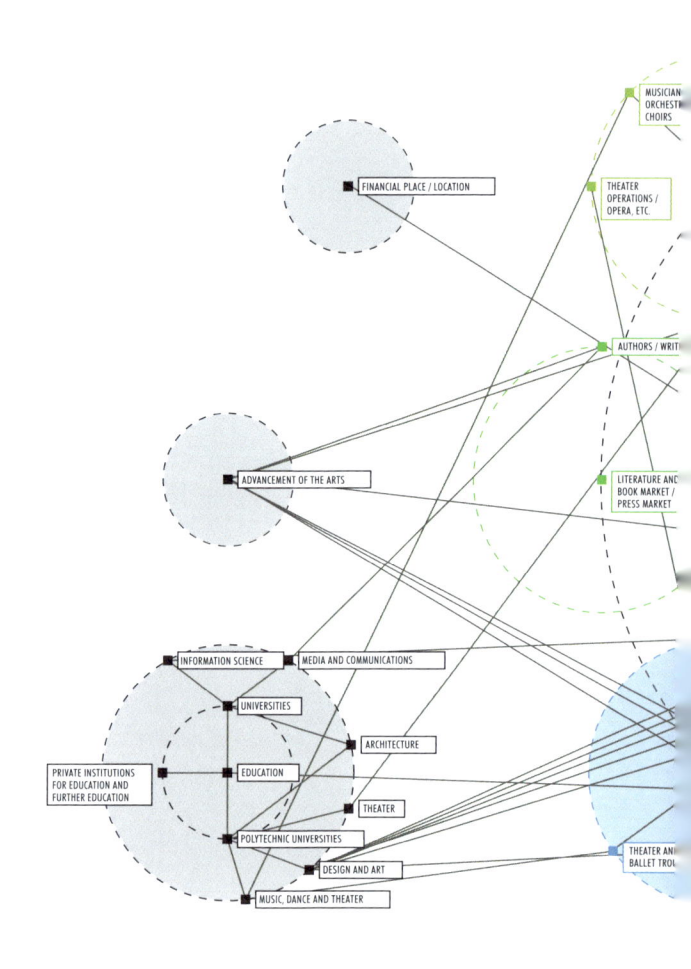

Figure 8:
Strategic assets of Zurich's creative industries from the viewpoint of market participants.

Strategic Assets	Function
Zurich's Financial Location	Host-city function – main buyer of knowledge-based services – important economic driver and intermediary facilitator within international networks
Education and Higher Education	Development of creative industries as knowledge-based economies – development of the relational equity – innovation – research
Events Industry	International positioning and visualization for Zurich
Art Market and Performing Arts	Sponsorship – attracting international clientele

Mapping Hybrid Value-Added Landscapes

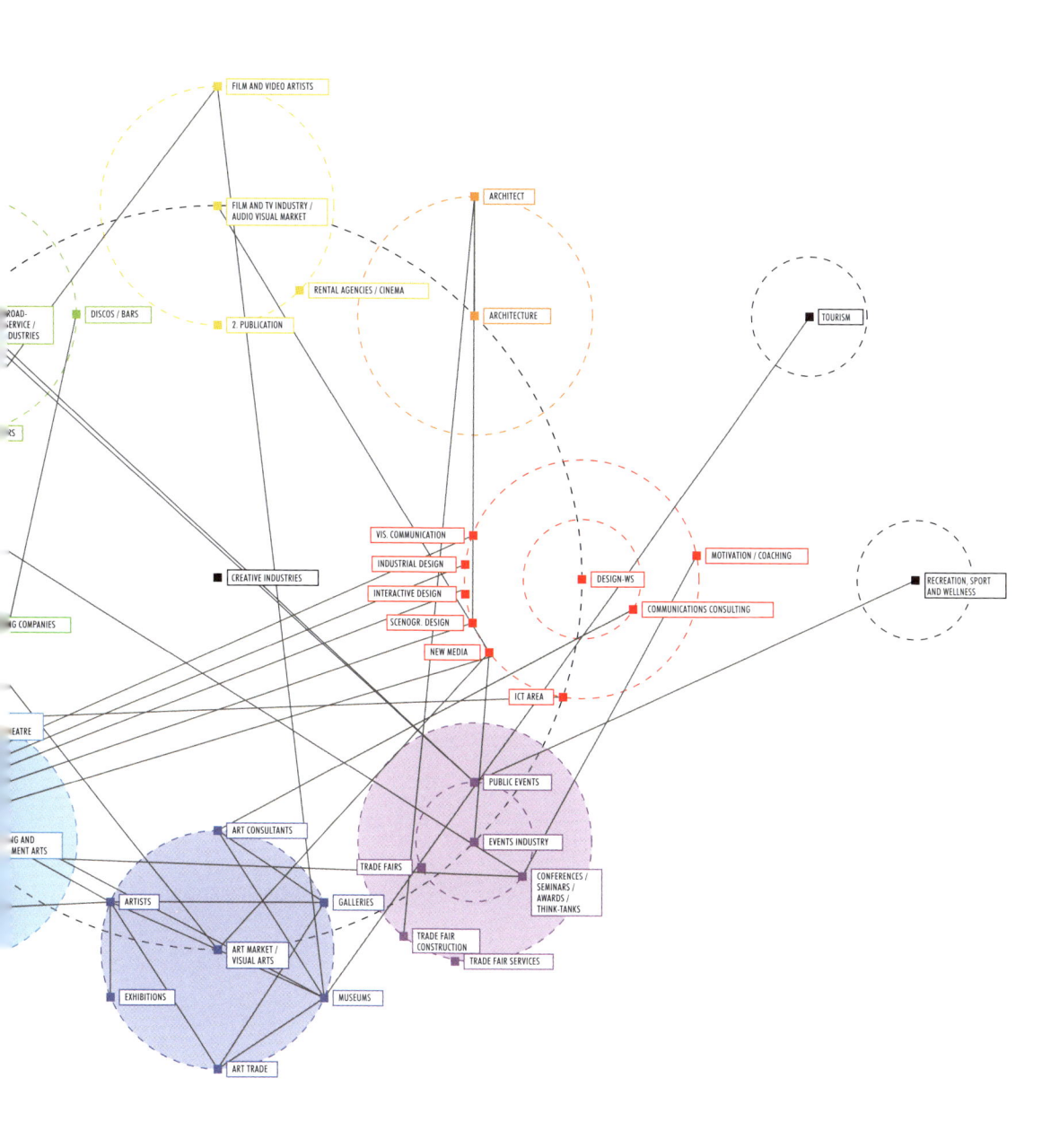

The Analysis of the Relational Landscape – Results and Findings

The term "creative industries" stands at the center of the model. The subareas are clustered around it. In this picture (Figure 2) the subareas are weighted neither in terms of their size nor their importance. Nine subareas, which can again be divided into further sub-subareas, have been identified:

- Design industry
- Events industry
- Fine arts
- Entertaining arts
- Market for literature/books/press media
- Market for music and radio
- Market for television, movie and audiovisuals
- Architecture

During the focus group workshop, the interviews and the full-day think-tank, it became clear that the existence of the creative industry in Zurich is closely attached to and embedded in

- other sectors of the economy (financial market and service sector, tourism, leisure, sports and wellness) of the economic area of Zurich and
- institutions like education and cultural promotion.

Numerous conclusions have been extracted from the tool "relational landscape" and led to the identification of necessary actions, obstacles, important potentials and networks, and to the development of scenarios. To enable a quicker understanding, the results of the relational landscape have been structured into four areas:

a) Core activities of the creative industry of Zurich
b) Central axis of interaction of the creative industry of Zurich
c) Strategic assets of the creative industry of Zurich
d) Connection of the subareas of the creative industry of Zurich

In order to formulate a qualitative portrait of Zurich's creative industries, the overall branch complex needs to be viewed as an interdependent networked system of subsegments which are often a part of functional division-of-labor value-added processes. In this context, the relational assets of Zurich's creative industries play a leading role, expressing themselves in different forms, i.e., in individual relationships, formal and informal cooperation among enterprises, important key persons and go-betweens among the different subsegments, as well as in the patterns of interaction within the branches. In analyzing the self-perception of creative-industry market participants, a qualitative portrait emerges of Zurich's creative-industries core activities, the central axis of interaction between the specific subsegments and the strategic assets. Independent subsegments display a superordinated structure, showing themselves to be an important economic driving force in their role as interface to the other service sectors, and important for the cultivation of a public and international awareness, as well as being responsible for knowledge production and education. The illustrations and tables in Figures 3 to 8 give an overview.

The creative industry in Zurich is predominantly a division of labor and networking system of interactions. Its qualities, internationalization and development depend on the structure and the embedding of its relational assets. Key to these competencies and networks are the people within the creative industries, i.e., the market representatives themselves.

In order to understand the relative importance of creative industries to a functional economic area such as the Zurich City Region, it is necessary to achieve a clear understanding of the functional interdependencies market participants in creative industries are subjected to. Creative industries in particular are strongly tied to the roles of key personalities – the creative industry is to a great extent a "people business." Market participants do not just engage at a purely economic level. Their interrelationships actually form, for the most part, out of the context of interdependencies, i.e., through the social structures, local and cultural norms, as well as the economic and social embeddings of an individual market participant. There are underlying contractual and monetary relationships, on the one hand, and individual and entrepreneurial business networks, on the other. The differentiation between the three types of embedding (relational, structural and geographical) should be mentioned here due to its importance in identifying the potential for a better positioning of creative-industry market participants. Relational embedding refers to a relationship between two market participants who develop a high degree of capability on the basis of the cultivation of mutual trust and long-term collaboration. Trust thereby reflects the social context within which market participants engage. This means that trust-building measures are of strategic importance to Zurich's creative industries. Structural embedding refers to relationships and interactions that are occurring simultaneously among a multitude of various market participants. It also establishes the conditions from which loose, unorganized as well as specific and organized, networks emerge. The key to these formations is primarily reputation, trust and social position. Geographical embedding explicitly integrates the local components of interaction. For entrepreneurs this is an important basis for operating within local, regional as well as international networks. This reinforces once again the reason why it is important to foster Zurich's creative industries as independent branches and content-carriers within Zurich's location.

System of Market Participants as Carriers and Driving Forces in the Creative Industries

From the individual subsegments and overall creative industries, a system of market participants emerges in the form of a three-tier structure. This system acts as the carrier and driving force of Zurich's creative-industries processes. Understanding this system of market participants is essential to analyzing creative industries:

Level 1: On the top level of the system of participants (see Figure 9), the entirety of the participants in the creative industries is mapped out in a loose, nonorganized pattern. Here it is important to note that Zurich's creative industries are to a large degree influenced by individual market participants – the empirical-quantitative analysis has already made this small-scale structure apparent. Single businesses, freelancers and students fall under this heading. Creative-industry products can be distinguished by a high job intensity. These are therefore correspondingly cost-intensive, on the one hand, while, on the other, based on a large pool of specific abilities, flexibilities and personalities. Collaboration among these market participants is based on personal networks and individual recommendations within a self-organized process. The services performed here range from professional acquisition and adequate financial compensation of performances to payments – which only cover a very small portion of the actual efforts. Particularly the small and smallest businesses – the empirical data point to a high share of single person operations in various subsegments – are reliant upon the development of more efficient networks. Often they lack the necessary competencies as well as resources to carry out a job. The classical small- and medium-sized enterprises (SMEs), which mainly carry out more complex and larger services for one or more big clients and buy needed services externally, are rarely seen. On the basis of this structure of market participants, specific strategic goals need to be developed in order to better position creative industries.

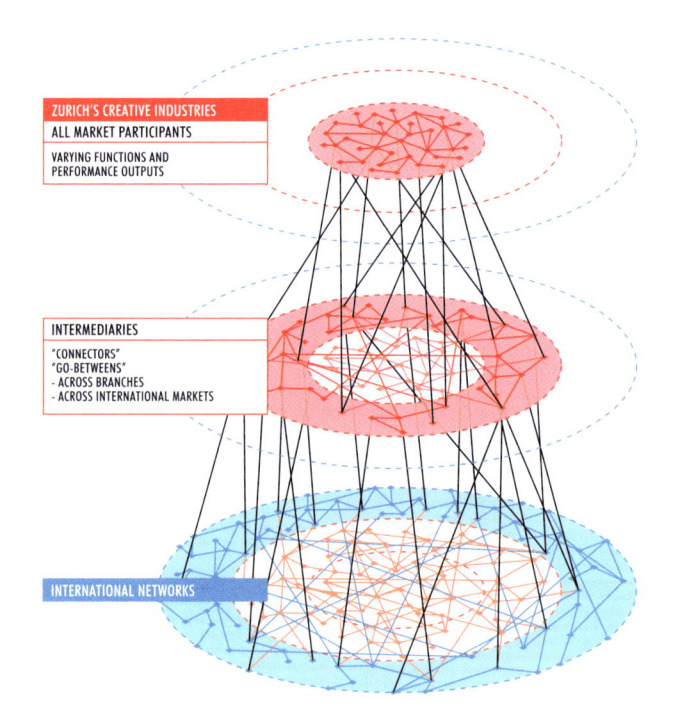

Figure 9:
Multilevel system of market participants within Zurich's creative industries.

ZURICH'S CREATIVE INDUSTRIES
ALL MARKET PARTICIPANTS
VARYING FUNCTIONS AND PERFORMANCE OUTPUTS

INTERMEDIARIES
"CONNECTORS"
"GO-BETWEENS"
- ACROSS BRANCHES
- ACROSS INTERNATIONAL MARKETS

INTERNATIONAL NETWORKS

Level 2: Well-known individuals, having their reputation and high profile at their disposal, are important in linking creative industries to varying content fields. They play the role of intermediary, facilitator and go-between across the individual subsegments of the creative industries, between established and nonestablished art and culture, between state and private institutions of the culture and creative industries, between creative industries and other economic areas (e.g., financial services), as well as between Zurich's creative industries and the international market. Without these key figures, the creative industry's embedding in a functional, urban economy would not happen.

Level 3: At the third level are the international networks. Zurich's creative industries will only gain international recognition if they are integrated into appropriate networks. This is reflected in the request of interviewed market participants to open regional and national markets.

How the Relational Landscape Can Become a Value Network Map of Mega-City Regions

The creative industry is understood here as a functional process and viewed from within the context of current development in urban economies. For this purpose, creative-industry market participants (organizations as well as individuals) and their interchange have been examined. What has emerged, among other things, is a relational landscape of the individual subsegments of the creative industries, granting novel insights into their structures as well as the geography of their self-perception. This approach has enabled key processes to be identified, conclusions to be reached and the need for action in the continued successful development of Zurich's creative industries to be expressed.

Of course the concept of the relational landscape possesses strengths and weaknesses. On the one hand, by using it in a first qualitative empirical phase such as expert workshops, structured interviews and one-day think-tanks, the concept allows one to structurally gather the views of a broad spectrum of market participants, document significant and related information and details and plot them visually in a relational model of the industry. It is therefore necessary to link the visual information scheme with the underlying background information and data, collected in interviews and workshops, which requires a connected database. The experience in this case showed that major insights and structures could be easily communicated to others and therefore be evaluated.

But of course from a scientific point of view, the real academic value of the relational landscape can only be achieved if the qualitatively collected picture with all its underlying information can quantitatively be assessed and underpinned with indicators of functional flows. However, this alleged weakness turns out to be a significant advantage in structuring an empirical survey, which at best should be web-based, thus trying to capture the interrelationship of companies, sub-branches and individuals. On the basis of a web-based poll as well as through a reconfiguration of statistical data about the creative industry in Zurich, the relational landscape will become a true value-network map of the interactions of the market participants who are involved in Zurich's creative economic sector.

Acknowledgement

This paper is based on an intensive working process with my colleague Thom Held, whose knowledge and passion helped equally to develop the insights and expertise found in the content. Special thanks also goes to Colina Frisch, who assisted in structuring the paper and gave input and comments.

Notes

[1] Paragraph quoted from Held, Kruse, Söndermann and Weckerle (2005).

References

Bathelt, H. and J. Glückler. 2002. *Wirtschaftsgeographie. Ökonomische Beziehungen in räumlicher Perspektive*. Stuttgart: Eugen Ulmer.

Burt, R. 1995. *Structural Holes. The Social Structure of Competition*. Cambridge: Harvard University Press.

Coase, R.H. 1937. "The Nature of the Firm." *Economica* 4: 386-405.

Florida, R. 2002. *The Rise of the Creative Class. And How It's Transforming Work, Leisure and Everyday Life*. New York: Basic Books.

Granovetter, M. 1985. "Economic Action and Social Structure. The Problem of Embeddedness." *American Journal of Sociology* 91 (3): 481-468.

Granovetter, M. 1992. "Economic Institutions as Social Constructions. A Framework for Analysis." *Acta Sociologica* 35: 3-11.

Held, T. and C. Kruse. 2005. *Kreativwirtschaft Zürich. Studie II – Raum für das Kreative. Konzeptionelle Ansätze für den Aufbau eines Clusters Kreativwirtschaft Zürich*. On Behalf of Wirtschaftsförderung des Kantons Zürich. Zürich: Museum für Gestaltung.

Held, T., C. Kruse, M. Söndermann and C. Weckerle. 2005. *Zurich's Creative Industries. Synthesis Report*. Zurich: Office for Economy and Labour of the Canton of Zurich.

Kruse, C. 2005. *Börsengänge am Finanzplatz Schweiz. Vernetzte Finanzintermediäre als Erfolgs- oder Risikofaktor für Börsenunternehmen?* PhD Thesis, ETH Zurich, Zurich.

Martin, R. 1999. "Critical Survey. The New Geographic Turn in Economics: Some Critical Reflections." *Cambridge Journal of Economics* 23: 65-97.

Martin, R. and P. Sunley. 1996. "Paul Krugman's Geographical Economics and Its Implications for Regional Development Theory. A Critical Assessment." *Economic Geography* 74: 259-292.

Maskell, P., H. Eskelinen, I. Hannibalsson, A. Malmberg and E. Vatne. 1998. *Competitiveness, Localized Learning and Regional Development: Specialization and Prosperity in Small Open Economies*. London: Routledge.

Scott, A.J. 1988. *Metropolis: From the Division of Labor to Urban Form*. Berkeley: University of California Press.

Scott, A.J. 1998. *Regions and the World Economy: The Coming Shape of Global Production, Competition, and Political Order*. Oxford: Oxford University Press.

Storper, M. 1997. *The Regional World. Territorial Development in a Global Economy*. New York: Guilford Press.

Storper, M. and R. Walker. 1989. *The Capitalist Imperative. Territory, Technology, and Industrial Growth*. New York, Oxford: Basil Blackwell.

Thierstein, A. and S. Gabi. 2004. "When Creativity meets Metropolitan Governance." *DISP* 40 (158): 34-40.

Thierstein, A., C. Kruse, L. Glanzmann, S. Gabi and N. Grillon. 2006. *Raumenntwicklung im Verborgenen. Die Entwicklung der Metropolregion Nordschweiz*. Zürich: NZZ Buchverlag.

Williamson, O.E. 1975. *Markets and Hierarchies: Analysis and Anti-trust Implications*. New York: Free Press.

Williamson, O.E. 1985. *The Economic Institutions of Capitalism. Firms, Markets, Relational Contracting*. New York: Free Press.

go

Simin Davoudi

Governing Polycentric Urban Regions
The Challenge of Collective Action

There is an increasing recognition among the research community and policy-makers that the existence of effective governance is an important prerequisite for developing and sustaining economically, socially and environmentally balanced urban regions across Europe. The capacity of urban governance can significantly influence the direction of economic potential and successful implementation of policy. This chapter aims to unpack the concept of governance and highlight the significance of developing "institutional capital" for meeting the challenge of collective action in the context of polycentric urban regions. It argues that effective governance relations depend largely on the development of intellectual, social, material and political capitals.

Governance Matters

The ways in which cities are governed both reflect and reinforce changes in social, economic and spatial structures of urban areas. In its 1997 Development Report, the World Bank demonstrated that the enormous differences between the performances of countries which act in the same global world economy can be explained, at least partly, by differences in governance (World Bank 1997). However, this was not a new revelation. Indeed, the recognition that the quality of life experienced by citizens depends largely on the quality of governance is as old as the civilization itself.

For example, seven centuries ago, in the city of Siena in Italy, Ambrogio Lorenzetti, painted two frescoes on the walls of the *Sala dei Nove* which was then the seat of government and is now Siena's Town Hall. One fresco represents the allegories of "good government" and the other is the symbol of "bad government." The result of good government is depicted as a society which lives in harmony, while the outcome of bad government is a society ridden with violence and destruction. While many of the virtues that Lorenzetti associated with good government, such as justice, fairness, fortitude and prudence, have remained valid in modern times, our understanding of the role and nature of government has changed considerably. Today, modern urban systems are characterized by complex patterns of interdependencies between actors, institutions, functional activities and spatial organizations. In the last two decades, the notion of *governance* has come to play a central role in explaining and conceptualizing these changing relationships.

The focus of my contribution is to unpack the concept of governance and the importance of capacity building in meeting the challenge of collective action. I will do this by reference to the theme of the conference yet with a specific focus on polycentric urban regions. But before that, it is important to remember two significant milestones that we have witnessed as we entered the 21st century.

An Urban Millennium

The first milestone is that the 21st century is the first urban century. Before 1850 there was no society that could be defined as predominantly urbanized and by 1900 only Britain could be so regarded. In 1975 only 38% of the world's population lived in cities. Today more than half of the world's 6.3 billion people are urban dwellers. Moreover, the developing countries are urbanizing more rapidly than the industrial nations did at the heyday of their urban growth. It took London 130 years to grow to a population of eight million. Mexico City reached that in only 30 years; Bombay is expanding even faster. Hence, we are witnessing an urban millennium where for the first time in history more people live in urban areas than in rural areas.

The second milestone is that for the first time the world's urban dwellers form part of a single networked globe. Cites worldwide are increasingly networked in complex systems of global interaction and interdependence. Informational revolution has led to what Manual Castells calls "time-space compaction" and the emergence of a "space of flows" (Castells 1996). However, contrary to the earlier predictions (such as Toffler 1980), this doesn't imply the "death of distance." On the contrary, advances in telecommunication have failed to reduce the significance of face-to-face contact and have not defused the forces of agglomeration. In fact population and economic growths continue to gravitate to major urban centers, leading to the creation of not only mega-cities of over ten million inhabitants, mainly in developing countries, but also to mega-city regions, or what, in 1957, Gottmann famously called a *megalopolis* to define a constellation of 600 miles of contiguous area along the east coast of America, running from Boston in the north to Washington in the south (Gottmann 1957).

Doxiadis, the modern Greek town planner, went even further in explaining the expanding scale of urban growth and the coalescence of metropolitan areas. He suggested that we would soon live in *Ecumenopolis* or world city (Doxiadis 1968). Although his vision was more of a poetic one, it was not far from contemporary realities. In

East Asia, for example, the Beijing, Seoul, Tokyo urban corridor transcends national boundaries, stretching almost contiguously along a 1500 km strip of highly networked and densely populated land with a maximum airtravel time of one and a half hours.

The Uneven Development of the European Territory

At the level of Europe, agglomeration forces have led to the uneven development of the European territory where a prosperous core stands against an underdeveloped periphery. This core-periphery conception of European space has been captured in a number of metaphors such as "European Megalopolis" (Gottmann 1957), "Golden Triangle" (Cheshire and Hay 1989), and "Blue Banana" (Brunet 1989). More recently, the European Spatial Development Perspective (ESDP) called it the "pentagon" (CEC 1999), referring to an area defined by London, Paris, Milan, Munich and Hamburg. Although this area covers only 20% of the EU-15 territory, it is home to 40% of its population, generates 50% of its gross domestic product (GDP), and receives 75% of its investment in research and development. This area is seen as the only economic zone which can compete effectively at the global level. Hence, the main thrust of the ESDP is to promote the creation of other zones of globally significant economic growth which would lead to not only a more competitive Europe but also a more socially cohesive one (Davoudi 2000).

ESDP and the Concept of Polycentricity

The spatial strategy that underpins this objective is polycentric development. By promoting polycentricity at the EU level, the ESDP aims to promote a more balanced spatial development in Europe and to change its image from a "blue banana" to a "bunch of grapes" (Kunzmann and Wegener 1991). Polycentric urban regions (PUR) can play a major part in this strategic vision. PUR is defined as a region with three or more historically and politically separate cities of more or less the same size, located in a reasonable proximity to each other with substantial functional interconnection and complementarities (CEC 1999).

Several examples can be found in Europe such as the Rhine-Ruhr city-region (Figure 1), which displays a sharp contrast to Brandenburg, where Berlin is clearly dominant (Figure 2). Other examples include the Flemish Diamond in Belgium and Northern Italy. Outside Europe, Southern California and the Kansai region in Japan are mentioned. The classic example of a polycentric urban region, however, is the Randstad in Holland (Figure 3), consisting of a ring of four large cities around an area of farmland and water called the Green Heart. Here each city thrives on a different, yet complementary, economic basis: Amsterdam benefits from the proximity to Schiphol airport, tourism and finance; Utrecht has the service sector and nice surroundings; The Hague is the seat of government, and Rotterdam lives off its port. The Randstad is not an administrative or political unit, but given the proximity and interactions among its constituent cities, it has been increasingly promoted and treated by the Dutch planning community as a single coherent region, branded as the European Delta Metropolis, capable of competing with London and Paris.

There are of course a number of definitional problems with the concept of polycentricity. Also, there are doubts as to whether polycentricity, as a specific spatial structure, is a panacea for resolving regional problems (see Davoudi 2003) or whether it offers a more sustainable form of urban growth. However, despite such ambiguities, the concept has offered a powerful strategic framework within the political discourse for promoting

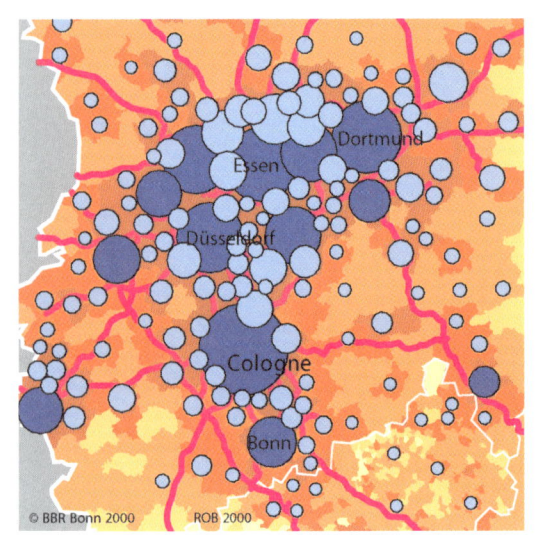

Figure 1:
Polycentric Rhine-Ruhr.

Figure 2:
Monocentric Berlin-Brandenburg.

spatial equity through balanced development. Indeed, at the EU level it has become the spatial manifestation of the concept of territorial cohesion (Davoudi 2005a).

At the national level it is used to challenge the polarizing effects of agglomeration economies and the resulting disparities. In the UK the concept of polycentric development underpins the recent Northern Way initiative, a coast-to-coast megalopolis, with the 130-mile M62 corridor, linking city regions of Leeds, Manchester and Liverpool, and also stretching from Sheffield in the south to Newcastle in the north. It underpins a spatial strategy which aims to close the 29 billion pounds productivity gap between the north and the rest of the country (Davoudi 2005b).

Similarly in Ireland the concept has been taken up by the National Spatial Strategy to address Ireland's highly monocentric pattern of growth in the last decade, which has led to the concentration of population and economic activities in the Greater Dublin Area. The concept of polycentric development has been drawn upon to maximize the potential of the regions outside Dublin by forging cooperation between neighboring cities of so-called "Atlantic Gateways" in such a way that they can expand their critical mass and comparative advantages by pooling their resources, complementing each other's functions and hence being able to compete more effectively in the world market (Davoudi and Wishardt 2005).

The Role of Policy Intervention

However, the critical question for policy-making is how to forge functional synergies between the constituent cities of polycentric urban regions. There are two key areas where policy intervention is particularly useful, viz., one is often obvious and relates to development of hard infrastructure, such as efficient transport and telecommunication networks between cities and with the outside world. The other, which attracts less policy attention, relates to development of soft infrastructure, notably governing capacity and institution building. The latter is crucial because in practice, the boundaries of local and regional governments do not match the evolving spatial configurations of polycentric urban regions. The administrative boundaries do not correspond with the functional interrelationships. Thus, if cities are to pool together their resources and create synergies and

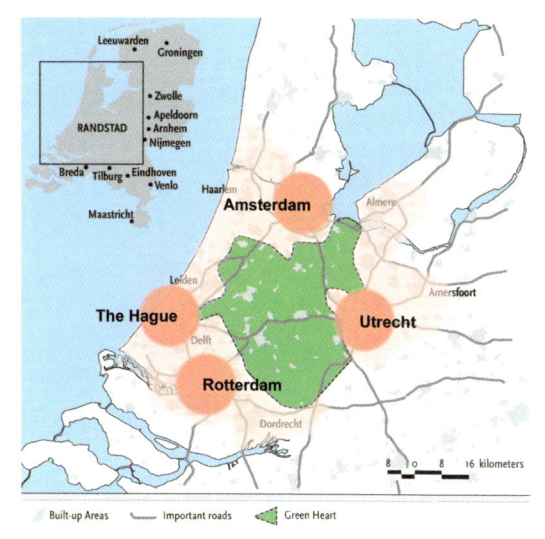

Figure 3:
Randstad in Holland.

functional complementarity, they need to develop effective governance at the level of the emerging polycentric urban regions.

This takes me back to where I started, that the direction of urban trajectory is to a large extent dependant on the quality of governance. But what is governance and how does it differ from government?

The Challenge of Governance

In its *descriptive* sense governance refers to the proliferation of agencies, interests, service delivery and regulatory systems (Healey et al. 2002). In its *normative* sense governance is defined as an alternative model for managing collective affairs. It is seen as a "horizontal self-organization among mutually interdependent actors" (Jessop 2000: 15), of which government is only one and enjoys only "imperfect control" (Rhodes 1997: 8). This contrasts with the notion of *Government*, which refers to the dominance of state power organized through the formal public-sector agencies and bureaucratic procedures, where there are neat and simple dividing lines between roles and responsibilities. The transition from government to governance represents the fading away of these simple hierarchical lines and their replacement with overlapping and complex relationships. As a result, there has been a:

- Relative decline in the role of the state
- Growing involvement of nongovernmental actors in a range of state functions, and
- The emergence of new forms of multi-agency partnerships and more flexible forms of networking at various spatial scales

The shift from government to governance has led to the expansion of policy-making space, the creation of new opportunities for wider participation in decision-making processes and the diffusion of the locus of power. However, it has also led to:

- Complex webs of relationships
- Institutional fragmentation
- Disparity of powers and responsibilities, and
- Increasing role of the market forces in the spatial distribution of economic activities

Controlling, managing or even steering these complex, fragmented and often competing societal interests is beyond the capacity of the state as an agent of authority. Governments are no longer the key locus for integration. They are one of many actors competing for access to resources and control of policy agenda. Hence, the challenge of governance is how to create new forms of integration out of fragmentation, and new forms of coherence out of inconsistency (Stoker 2000); and how to achieve collective action out of diverse range of interests, views and actors. Therefore, the capacity to govern depends on:

- Developing effective co-ordination of interdependent forces within and beyond the state, and
- Creating the condition that leads to collective action, i.e., getting things done

Building Institutional Capital

Building governing capacities which meet the challenge of collective action is more difficult in the context of polycentric urban regions, where the actors are not only drawn from outside the formal institutions of government and come from public, private and voluntary sectors. They also cut across the boundaries of different political and administrative jurisdictions and have overlapping competencies at various spatial scales. Within such arrangements, the focus is on governing mechanisms which do not rest on recourse to the authority and sanctions of government. In such flexible and voluntary arrangements the capacity to govern and to act collectively often depends on the quality of governance relations. This in turn depends on building or amplifying four types of capital: intellectual, social, material and political capital, as suggested by Innes et al. (1994). The following account will elaborate on these and outline the key factors affecting their development (for a detailed discussion of these see Davoudi and Evans 2005; Davoudi 2005c).

Intellectual capital refers to knowledge resources. Knowledge in this context is seen as a nonlinear, interactive and socially constructed resource, which is created over time and through a dynamic process of interaction between the actors. According to de Magalhaes et al. (2002), building up intellectual capital depends on:
- Firstly, the range of knowledge available to the actors; in the case of coalitions which aim to develop a coordinated spatial strategy, this includes knowledge of sociospatial processes that shape the trajectory of polycentric urban regions
- Secondly, free flow of knowledge and sharing of information between the actors in a process of collective learning
- Thirdly, the learning capacity of actors, which includes both willingness to learn and openness to new ideas
- Finally, frames of reference, which is about the underlying conceptions that enable multiple actors to make sense of the available knowledge

Building up *social capital* is critical in the formation of effective coordination and collective action, particularly given the voluntary and independent nature of governance coalitions. It is a crucial part of a shared sense of community, which allows the participants to respond flexibly and with one voice to multiple policy demands.

The concept of social capital links to the concept of "civic society" coined by Putnam (1993). His research showed that civic context matters for the work of institutions. Hence, creating and maintaining co-operation depends on setting up relations that are based on:
- Solidarity, trust and reciprocity rather than hierarchy and bargaining
- Mutual support for the actions that have been agreed, and
- A shared sense of purpose and recognition of mutual interdependency

The significance of *material capital* is self-explanatory. For a governing coalition to be viable, it must be able to mobilize resources commensurate with its agenda and program of action. This is the "iron law" of governing. Building governing capacity needs sufficient time and appropriate financial and human resources.

Finally, it is the *political capital*, which is about the capacity to mobilize all other forms of capital and depends on power relations. But, power in this context refers to power *to* act rather than power *over* the action of others (Stone 1989: 229). It is seen as a matter of social production rather than social control. The move away from a traditional model of hierarchical power to a system where power is shared and split between a variety of political and nonpolitical stakeholders has led to further diffusion of power and its multiple characteristics.

This dispersion of power among various actors means that although those with command power, such as government officials, may have an advantage in governance relations, they can only make use of their position if they turn that power into what may be called an *enabling power* which allows multiple and diverse participants to reach consensus on underlying issues, turn such strategic consensus into action, and act as a collective actor.

The Open Method of Coordination

One model which offers a potential in putting into practice some of these ideas is the Open Method of Coordination (OMC). The OMC was first mentioned in the Lisbon Summit of March 2000 as a way of implementing the European Employment Strategy. It was then publicized in the Commission's White Paper on European Governance in 2001 (CEC 2001), as a departure from total reliance on Community Method and its heavy-handed, regulatory approach to governing.

The OMC is seen as a softer mode of governing which is based on policy learning through information exchange, benchmarking, target setting, peer review, deliberation, voluntary cooperation, and naming and shaming of those who lag behind. The OMC has been applied in areas where the EU has no formal competence. In my view, it can also be applied in achieving collective action in the governance of city regions, because here the balance of power between the actors is much more subtle and diffused among diverse range of governmental and nongovernmental stakeholders at multiple spatial scales. The philosophy propagated under the concept of the OMC is that the rules of public life will increasingly be based on knowledge that is constructed and renewed in a process of collective learning.

Acknowledgments

This chapter is based on the text of the authors' presentation at the International Conference on "Making Mega-City Regions Visible!" Munich University of Technology, 2.2.2006. It draws on three published papers (Davoudi 2003, Davoudi 2005c, Davoudi and Evans 2005). These papers provide more detailed discussions on the issues raised in this chapter as well as an extended bibliography.

References

Brunet, R. 1989. *Les Villes Européennes: rapport pour la DATAR*. Paris: La Documentation Francaise.

Castells, M. 1996. *The Rise of the Network Society*. Oxford: Blackwell Publishers.

CEC (Commission of the European Communities). 1999. *European Spatial Development Perspective: Towards Balanced and Sustainable Development of the Territory of the EU*. Luxembourg: Office for Official Publications of the European Communities.

CEC (Commission of the European Communities). 2001. *European Governance: A White Paper*, Communication from the Commission, COM 920010 428 Brussels.

Cheshire, P. and D.G. Hay. 1989. *Urban Problems in Western Europe: An Economic Analysis*. London: Unwin Hyman.

Davoudi, S. 2000. "Making Sense of the ESDP." *Town and Country Planning* 68 (12): 367-369.

Davoudi, S. 2003. "Polycentricity in European Spatial Planning: from an Analytical to a Normative Agenda." *European Planning Studies* 11 (8): 979-999.

Davoudi, S. 2005a. "Understanding Territorial Cohesion." *Planning Practice and Research* 20 (4): 433-441.

Davoudi, S. 2005b. "The Northern Way, a Megalopolis." *Regional Review* 14 (3): 2-4.

Davoudi, S. 2005c. "Towards a Conceptual Framework for the Evaluation of Governance Relations in Polycentric Urban Regions of Europe." In *Beyond Benefit and Cost Analysis: Accounting for Non-Market Values in Planning Evaluation*, edited by D. Miller and D. Patassini. Aldershot: Ashgate: 275-277.

Davoudi, S. and N. Evans. 2005. "The Challenge of Governance in Regional Waste Planning." *Environment and Planning C* 23 (4): 493-519.

Davoudi, S. and M. Wishardt. 2005. "Polycentric Turn in the Irish Spatial Strategy." *Built Environment* 31 (2): 122-132.

Doxiadis, C. 1968. *Ekistics*, London: Hutchinson.

Gottmann, J. 1957. "Megalopolis – or the Urbanisation of the Northeastern Seaboard." *Economic Geography* 33 (3) (July): 189.

Kunzmann K.R. and M. Wegener. 1991. "The Pattern of Urbanisation in Western Europe." *Ekistics* 350 (September): 282-91.

De Magalhaes, C., P. Healey, and A. Madanipour. 2002. "Assessing Institutional Capacity for City Centre Regeneration: Newcastle's Grainger Town." In *Urban Governance, Institutional Capacity and Social Milieux*, edited by G. Cars, P. Healey, A. Madanipour and C. de Magalhaes. Aldershot: Ashgate: 45-62.

Innes, J., J. Gruber, R. Thompson and M. Neuman. 1994. *Co-ordinating Growth and Environmental Management through Consensus-Building, Report to the California Policy Seminar*. Berkeley: University of California.

Jessop, B. 2000. "Governance Failure." In *The New Politics of British Local Governance*, edited by G. Stoker. London: Macmillan: 11-32.

Putnam, R. 1993. *Making Democracy Work: Civil Tradition in Modern Italy*. Princeton, NJ: University of Princeton Press.

Rhodes, R. 1997. *Understanding Governance – Policy Networks, Governance Reflexivity and Accountability*. Buckingham and Philadelphia: Open University Press.

Stoker, G. 2000. "Urban Political Science and the Challenge of Urban Governance." In *Debating Governance*, edited by J. Pierre. Oxford: Oxford University Press.

Stone, C. 1989. Regime Politics: Governing Atlanta, 1946-1988. Lawrence: University Press of Kansas.

Toffler, A. 1980. *The Third Wave*. New York: Bantam Books.

World Bank. 1997. *The State in A Changing World, World Development Report*, Oxford: Oxford University Press.

ac

Maurits Schaafsma

Accessing Global City Regions
The Airport as a City[1]

"You can't participate in life via conference call" (United Airlines 2005). Globalization is about an information revolution and about a revolution in the transportation of people and goods, about "the physical Internet" (Markillie 2006). Globalization, network society, global shift, age of access: city regions are increasingly being faced with a highly dynamic global environment in which they have to compete internationally for economic activities, an internationalizing labor force, cultural facilities, leisure, shopping, sports, or international events in general. As global city regions they are competing with their individual regional qualities such as the business climate, quality of life, international and regional accessibility, business districts, technology parks, but also their regional identity, culture and creative environments (Scott 2001).

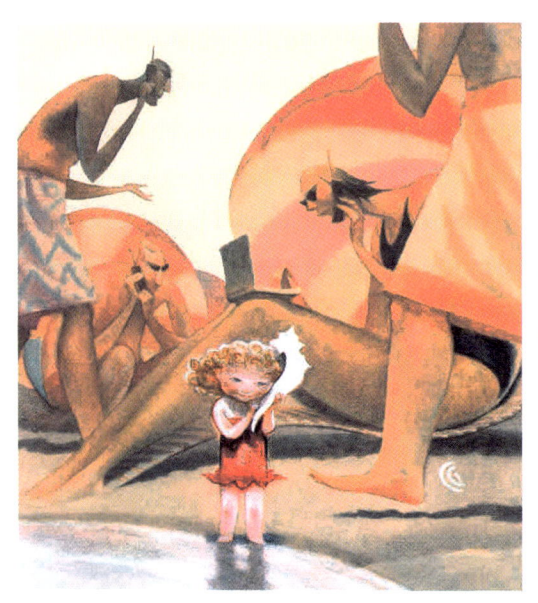

Figure 1:
United Airlines advertisement, 2005.

In the global competition of locations the physical connection of city regions among each other is of increasing strategic importance and is highly determined by the position within global airline networks. Airports as nodes between "the global" and "the regional" are becoming crucial locations within the city regions. In this context the airport city, the aerotropolis and the airport corridor are emerging urban concepts, integrating the airport in the city region. In a sense, the airports seem to be aiming at what the railway stations already have accomplished, i.e., being central places in the city. The case of Amsterdam and Amsterdam Schiphol Airport illustrates this development.

Railway Age

Transportation nodes historically are generators of urban development. In a modern sense the great railway stations from the early 20th century in the US may be considered the forerunners of airports. They are the birthplace of node-related commercial real estate. Between 1900 and the great depression of the 1930s a generation of railway-related real estate was developed throughout the country. The railways had become huge economic powers, aggressive companies dominating the New York stock exchange. The owners of the railway companies were nicknamed the "barons" (also "robber barons"). After the consolidation of the railways, real estate became an attractive secondary business for them: offices at the terminal stations and housing developments in the suburbs generated business for the core activity (selling transportation by train) *and* generated income from land and property development. In Los Angeles it was even the other way round. The development of the unprofitable network of regional interurban trains was merely to support the primary business of increasing the value of suburban land. In New York City the New York Central Railroad, then the second largest railway company in the world, created huge value by developing the air rights above their new Grand Central Station. For the old station at the same location, the company had acquired cheap land just outside the city for its marshaling yard. This area, located around the northern part of present-day Park Avenue between 42nd and 54th streets, Lexington and Madison avenues, was turned into a prime real estate location by developing a terminal city on top of the depressed railway tracks. The income from this development would more than compensate for the high costs of the new railway station. The terminal city included offices, apartments, a post office, hotels (the Commodore, the Biltmore, the Waldorf Astoria) and clubs (the Yale Club) and was developed between 1903 and 1930. The central business district phenomena had matured. Investment bankers J.P. Morgan and Company financed the whole development: building the new station with underground tracks in two stories and the development of the air rights. The

New York Central Railroad formed a separate real estate company, the New York State Terminal Realty Company, of which the Vanderbilts (founders and main owners of New York Central) were by far the most important owners, guaranteeing the control of the railroad over the real estate company. The new company developed the terminal city by constructing and renting out buildings, and by leasing air rights to other developers.

The railway station had become the main urban generator, Fifth Avenue the place to be, attracting other projects to the area, such as the Chrysler Building. The value of property in the area around Grand Central Station rose 374% between 1904 and 1930, against 175% in general in Manhattan (Schlichting 2001).

On a smaller scale other examples of integration of railway stations and commercial real estate are to be found in cities like Los Angeles, Dallas, Fort Worth, Detroit, Cleveland, Buffalo, Pittsburgh, Philadelphia and Montreal.

After World War II the railway companies lost their power, facing competition from airlines and private cars. Their main property development involved redundant yards at central locations. In Europe the situation was different but, except from London, new integrated commercial developments were exceptions. In London almost all major terminuses were turned into real estate developments in the 1980s and 1990s.

Creating Schiphol AirportCity

"Creating AirportCities" is Schiphol Group's motto. Is this AirportCity different from New York Central's terminal city? An important distinction is the separation between the business of air transportation and operating airports. But apart from that, there are interesting parallels.

Schiphol Group's AirportCity idea originated in the mid-1990s as a concept offering all kinds of amenities to passengers. Shops, restaurants, casinos, a branch of the Rijksmuseum, an in-terminal hotel (after passport control), passengers having to wait for their flight can spend their time in a useful or enjoyable manner. Another element of the concept was to develop commercial real estate on airport land. The idea was to stimulate air traffic growth by locating airport-related companies at the airport. Airport-related companies are those that have their business at the airport (such as airlines) or use the airport intensively (such as the head offices of international companies). The policy for development was coordinated with the governments involved.

With the experience gained in developing operational real estate and buildings for cargo, the step to developing commercial offices was not too big. Two organizational decisions together formed the framework for the development of airport-related real estate. In 1987 the Schiphol Area Development Company (SADC) was founded as a public-private partnership. Partners were the Province of North Holland, the City of Amsterdam, the municipality of Haarlemmermeer, the Nationale Investeringsbank (NIB) and Amsterdam Schiphol Airport. The main aim of the SADC was to develop the land *around* the airport in accordance with the "mainport strategy": the land should be available for airport-related European distribution facilities, combined with European head offices. The development was especially successful in attracting Japanese and American companies.

In the 1990s the real estate department of the airport itself developed the first commercial real estate at the airport, leading to the foundation of a semi-separate real estate company, Schiphol Real Estate BV in 1998. It is a fully owned Schiphol Group subsidiary. Schiphol Real Estate owns the commercial land at the airport (all land except land designated for airport operations purposes such as runways and terminals), and, like the New York State Terminal Realty Company, develops this land by constructing and renting out buildings, and by leasing land to other developers. So the activities are land development and ownership (the airport doesn't sell its land but leases it), property development (mainly office and cargo buildings), investment in property and management of property.

Figure 2:
Schiphol Center, AirportCity.

In this way the airport authority is involved in a public-private partnership developing the area around the airport and acts as a developer of land and buildings at the airport site itself.

Recently a new "mainport strategy" relates Schiphol to Amsterdam as a global city region. The strategy contains three interrelated levels: a worldwide airline network, a competitive airport and a competitive urban region. The AirportCity is also a contribution to a competitive region.

Business Model

Airports are in the process of undergoing dynamic changes. Deregulation and separation from governments is the trend both for airlines and airports, making aviation a more "normal" business. Deregulation of air traffic has led to the formation of worldwide alliances and mergers of traditional airlines. They have organized their networks in hub-and-spoke systems. This is the market for the airbus A380. For airports it is crucial to maintain their networks by having the status of a hub for one of the major alliances. In Europe the number of hub airports is decreasing as a result of this development. Each alliance tends to develop two European hubs only. In Asia the competition for hub status is fought by developing new mega-hub airports. In the US a wave of airline consolidation is expected, which will probably lead to new competition for hub status among airports.

On the other hand new, mainly low-cost airlines entered the market, operating more opportunist networks, not organized around (expensive) hub airports. The concept of by-passing the hub is another development which decreases the importance of hub airports. This is the market for the Boeing Dreamliner.

Schiphol is one of the two European hubs of the Sky Team Alliance, Paris Charles de Gaulle is the other. It is the policy of the airport to maintain that position.

Physical planning strategy	Business orientation and physical planning strategy	
Integration	City Airport *Washington National*	Airport City *Amsterdam Schiphol*
Separation	Protecting the Site *Denver*	Exploiting the Site *London Heathrow*
	Narrow	Broad
	Business orientation	

Airports are faced with two kinds of more direct competition, i.e., the competition between the airports of the different alliances (for a large part a competition between airline alliances) and competition within an alliance.

Airports, being in a process of deregulation, operate more and more like private companies. They are changing the nature of their operation from providing mainly infrastructure to also running a business. Profitability, the business model and business plans are of at least equal importance to the more traditional technical capacity-oriented airport master plan. Passengers are consumers. The business model has changed accordingly. In addition to the basic airport structure and the related aviation revenues, nonaviation revenues are growing in importance. Becoming a more "normal" company, Amsterdam Schiphol Airport has now been regulated by the Netherlands Competition Authority. There is a cap on aviation revenues, which prevents the airport from misusing its monopoly position. To obtain good profitability as a company, nonaviation revenues are essential.

Airport operators will have to optimize every link in the value chain (ground handling, retail, etc.). The question is which parts of the value chain will be outsourced. Schiphol has outsourced its ground handling operations, for example. Some airport operators are or will be "orchestrators" of their airport only. Choices made here will determine the business model of the airport operator (BCG 2004).

But these changes have not taken place in the same way everywhere. In Europe most airports are considered as national infrastructures but are organized as semi-independent companies. In the US the policy has been to make local governments (municipalities and states) owner and operator of the airport. Airlines have a more direct influence on investments made by the airport. As local governments outsource most of the operations (airlines often own the terminals), the drive for generating nonaviation revenues, often disliked by airlines, is much less. The business orientation of the airport operators differs accordingly.

The AirportCity as a "City"

The AirportCity is not a city in the traditional sense of the word. But which development is "urban" in this age of global orientation, gated communities and kinetic elites? The master plan for Schiphol of 1988 had created the space for landside development in the heart of the airport area, directly connected to the terminals and train station. Schiphol Plaza as an indoor and outdoor city square connects the two terminals, the train station and the prime landside real estate: the Sheraton Hotel, the World Trade Center and the Hilton Hotel. This central area is an integrated urban node where accessibility is of the highest level.

Schiphol as a "city" can be defined as an archipelago of areas. Apart from the central area (Schiphol Center), there is an ambitious development to be undertaken in the northern part of the airport: an office area of 200,000 m² floor space (Elzenhof) with an adjacent golf course and a hotel. This development will be a stepping stone in the direction of Amsterdam. At Schiphol East, the area where the airport's very first terminal was located, a concentration of aviation-related activities in the fields of management, research and development, aircraft maintenance and education is under development. Schiphol Southeast is the cargo area, or "Cargo World." The area is part of a larger development of airport-related multimodal logistics operations and other value-added economic activities ("Werkstad A4"), to be developed by SADC. Schiphol Northwest has been designated mainly for operational activities and serves as a long-term reservation of land for a new terminal area.

All these areas are being developed according to different urban designs by the offices of Benthem Crouwel, West 8, KCAP and Dominique Perrault. One of the themes in the plans is that all areas of the archipelago have their own central area, containing a concentration of public facilities.

In total 560,000 m² of offices (operational and commercial) and almost one million square meters of industrial real estate have been built at the airport. Almost 60,000 people have a job here (at all companies located at the airport itself). The rental prices of the offices are among the highest in the country.

The main issues for future development revolve around intensifying of land use, upgrading the "urban" facilities, developing new internationally competitive real estate concepts – the themes involve accessibility and efficiency, AirportCity quality and experience and (re-) combinations of functions – and a good physical integration into the surrounding areas.

Amsterdam and Schiphol

In the late 1990s an almost Asian plan for the future of Schiphol was masterminded. The airport would move to an island in the North Sea, leaving the present airport site available for redevelopment. Rem Koolhaas was invited to participate in a think-tank for the concept. He projected a double city. At the "former Schiphol site," which would retain the airport terminal as an entry point to the runways on the island, the spatial program for growth of the whole Randstad Holland for the 21st Century would be concentrated in a world city with the high densities the Netherlands lacks ("Hong Kong"). The city was to be the downtown area of the country, like a logo for the Netherlands. The second city was the airport city in the sea, a project of European dimensions. It was to become the meeting place of the "kinetic elite," offering facilities in the world's main time zones. A bridge would connect both cities with each other (Koolhaas 2000).

This "quantum leap," however, did not take place. The island plan was shelved for several reasons. The main ones were not concerned with the technique or cost of making the island as such; they involved operational and logistic complications and the long-term planning horizon that would cause great risk for the position of the airport vis-à-vis its competitors (Frankfurt, Paris, Brussels, Dusseldorf). The airport would be moved further from its market (catchment area). Schiphol instead studied the possibilities of further development at its present location. The airport was not to be a world city, but to continue its gradual pace of development, characteristic of an airport city. Meanwhile, the physical urban relationship between Amsterdam and Schiphol intensified. A major move was abandoning the idea to develop a Central Business District for Amsterdam adjacent to the city center on the banks of the IJ. The business community rejected the idea in favor of a location at the southern section of the ring road, close to the airport. ABN-AMRO Bank chose the Zuidas (literally South Axis in English) as the location of their new head office, and was soon followed by ING. The city changed its policy and is now developing the Zuidas as the Central Business District, connected by a new underground line to the city center.

Between the Zuidas and the airport a new office park called Riekerpolder was developed by Amsterdam. South of Schiphol, major office developments have taken place at Schiphol Rijk and Hoofddorp Beukenhorst. Thus, an urban corridor, an airport corridor, started to take shape. The core of it reaches from Amsterdam-the Zuidas via Riekerpolder to Schiphol and Hoofddorp. (In a wider sense, some consider the whole Haarlemmermeer-Amsterdam South-Almere development as the corridor.) The governmental parties cooperating in the SADC together took a first step in coordinating this development by preparing a planning document: the Ruimtelijk Economische Visie Schipholregio (REVS) of 2001 (Province of North Holland et al. 2001). One of the options is to extend the new metro line to the airport, serving the airport corridor.

Figure 3:
The Amsterdam Airport Corridor: Ruimtelijk Economische Visie Schipholregio, 2001.

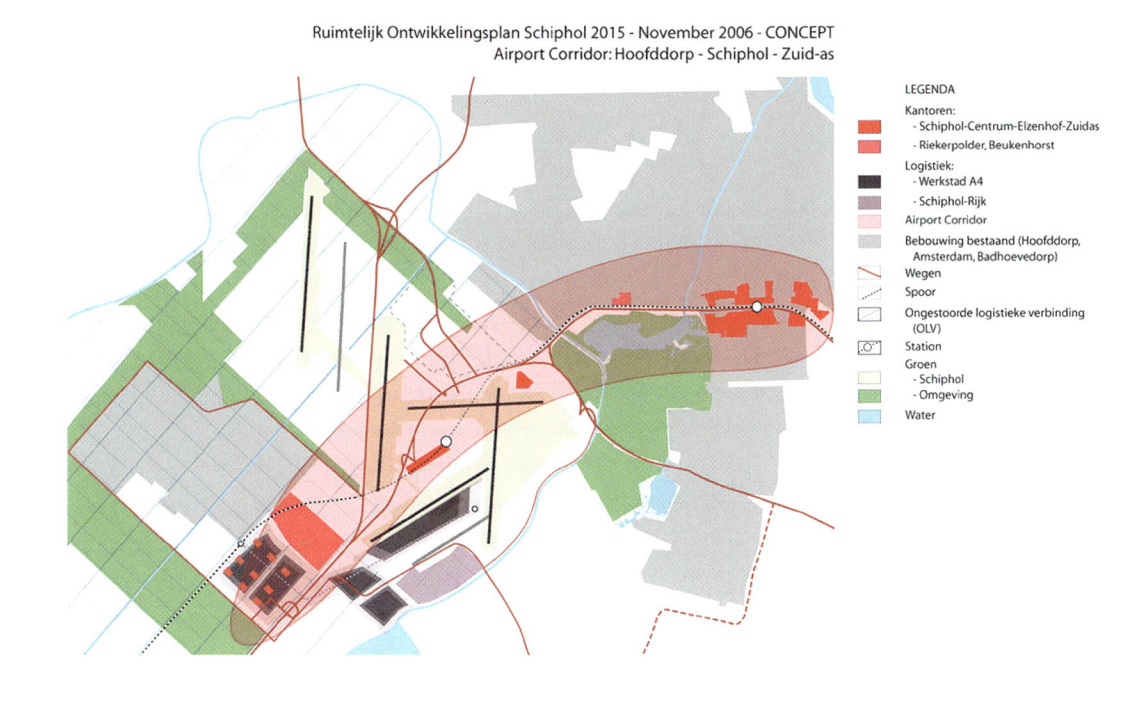

	Airport city	Aerotropolis	Airport corridor
Definition	Integrated development of airport and real estate	Separated real estate development near the airport	Integrated development of real estate and road/rail infrastructure
Location	Heart of the airport	Around the airport, between airport and city	Airport - city
Main actor	Airport authority	Private developers	Infrastructure developer
Scale	Local	Local +	City Region
Where	Europe, Asia	US	Europe, Asia, US

The Airport and the City

The airport corridor as an urban corridor between the airport and the city is not a unique phenomenon, nor is the airport city. The general movement of airports vis-à-vis the city can be summarized as follows:

- Airports tend to leave the city
- But the city "follows" the airport
- And the airport becomes a city

European airports have a different pattern of "urbanization" than those in the US. The airport city can be seen as basically European. In Asia, however, airport cities of much bigger ambitions are being developed, like Hong Kong Sky City, Bangkok and Seoul. In the US airport authorities have less drive for commercial real estate development. Having much more space available around the airport, private landowners and developers have developed real estate just outside the airport. These "Aerotropolises" are of considerable size and make use of the infrastructure that is available near the airport. Examples are Dallas Las Colinas, Denver Gateway and Stapleton, Washington Tyson's Corner and Detroit Pinnacle Aeropark (Kassarda 2000).

Both in Europe and the US, airport corridors, on the higher scale level compared to airport cities and aerotropolises, have developed more or less spontaneously, consisting of airport cities, aerotropolises, edge cities etc., bound by the road and rail infrastructure connecting the airport with the city. Typical developments within the airport corridor are office parks, technology parks, trade marts, conference centers, shopping centers, leisure parks and (gated) housing estates. In most cases there are no real planning concepts for the corridors (as yet), or at minimum they are running far behind actual developments. In Europe, apart from Amsterdam, examples are Zurich Glatttal and Copenhagen Orestad. Examples in the US are the I70 corridor in Denver, the Northwest Corridor in Dallas and the Edsel Ford Freeway in Detroit. In Asia, the new huge hub airports are often characterized by ambitious government-planned corridor developments. Examples are Hong Kong (along the new express railway and motorway), Kuala Lumpur (the Multi-Media Super Corridor) and Seoul (Inchon).

But not all successful airports have major real estate developments. Atlanta, being the busiest passenger airport in the world, has relatively very little aerotropolis development. Located on the "wrong," less affluent side of the city, the airport is in an area that is not liked by private investors. Office development is taking place in edge cities in the north, not the south of the city region.

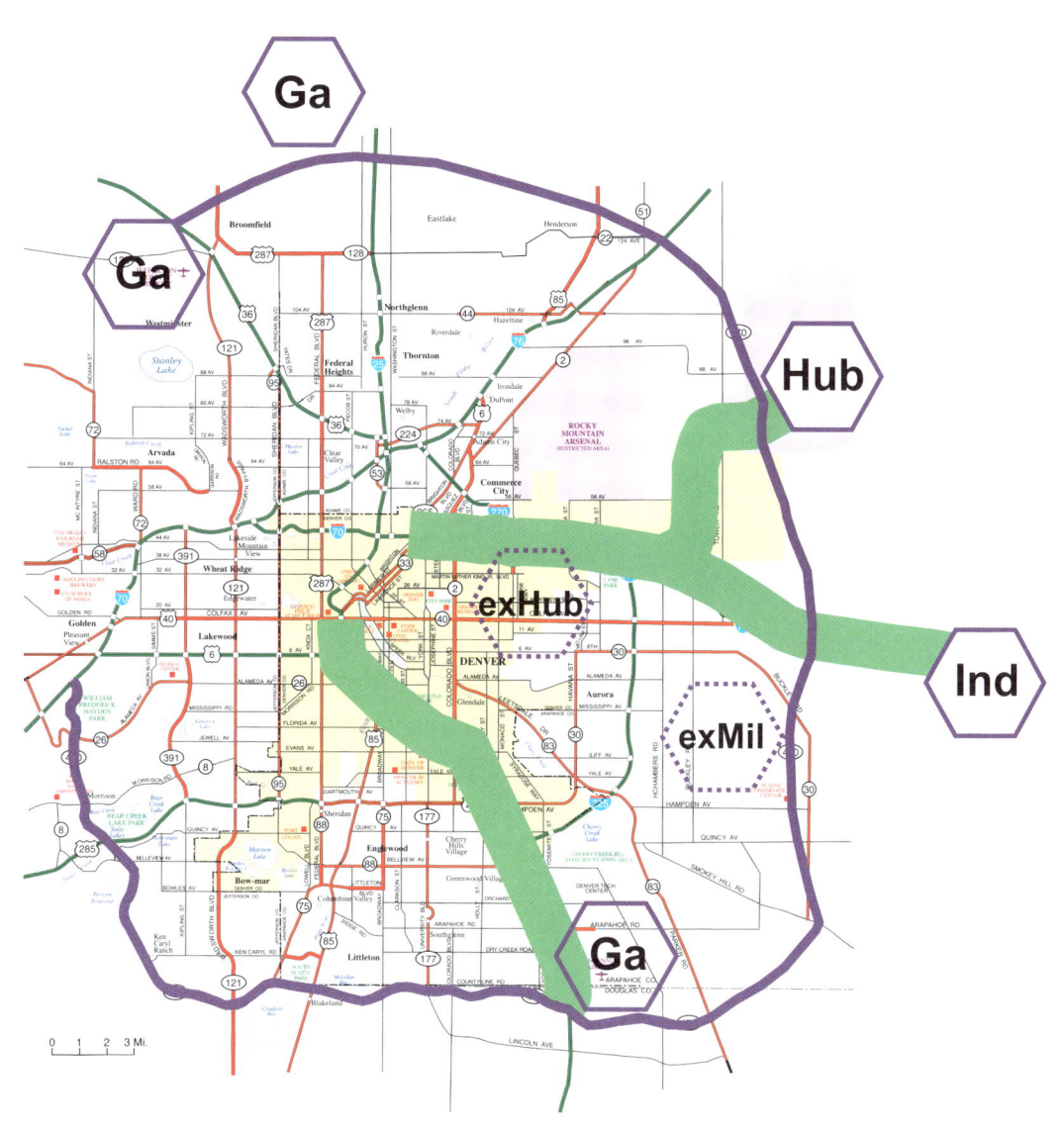

To conclude, factors determining the success and the nature of airport city/aerotropolis/airport corridor developments are:
- Status of the airport
- Ownership of the airport
- Location in the city
- Location in infrastructure networks
- Government / Planning tradition

Figure 4:
The interaction between city and airports in Denver.
- Green: economic development axis: East: I-70/Pena Boulevard; South: T-Rex Corridor
- Hub: Hub Airport
- Ga: General Aviation Airport
- Ind: Industrial Airport
- Ex: former airport, now closed

Dubai

Dubai shows the most extreme Asian approach. In Europe it is very difficult to develop urban airport concepts because of the many planning institutions involved, all having their own different interests. Governance is a necessary way out, but with rather weak results up to now; no Rem Koolhaas metropolism in Europe. In Dubai HH Sheikh Maktoum bin Rashid Al Maktoum was the man with the vision and the power. The huge metropolitan ambition for the city is centered around its position as a global hub airport. Dubai is an airport city in two senses of the word. First Dubai as a whole can be seen as an airport city. Accessibility is almost only by plane. The concept (business model) of Dubai is to become a world city as a regional metropolis in the Middle East, using its central position between Europe and the growing economies in Asia, so based on accessibility by plane. The main instrument in this policy is to become a global airline hub. For this reason Emirates was founded in 1985 and is becoming one of the world's largest airlines: Emirates has ordered 45 Airbus A380 mega-planes, which are deemed necessary in order to compete with other airlines.

Within Dubai a mega-airport city, the Jebel Ali Airport City is being developed. At the heart of this airport city is a new airport with a capacity of 120 million passengers and 12 million tons of cargo per year (In 1985 Dubai airport handled 4 million passengers; Atlanta, now the biggest passenger airport in the world handles almost 90 million passengers per year). Jebel Ali Airport City will have facilities such as a golf course, a Commercial City (850 office towers are planned), a multimodal Dubai Logistics City and an Aviation City. Dubai Jebel Ali is to be the mother of all airport cities.

Conclusion

Airports have taken over the position of railways in long distance travel and have become new focal points in urban developments, conceptually a combination of the central railway stations and edge cities. Their concept and business model show striking similarities to the model of the New York Central Railroad of the early 20th Century. The dynamic environment in which airports are today will change the business model, on the one hand increasing the importance of nonaviation revenues, and on the other hand outsourcing many activities. Airports will develop more airport city concepts. Private developers, however, have already recognized airports as hot spots in the urban region and are developing around airports and within the corridors between the airport and the city.

Airport cities, aerotropolises and airport corridors are a new reality, often overlooked still by planners and policy-makers. In Europe there are some attempts to coordinate the development between the airport and the city, as in the cases of Amsterdam and Zurich, but it is in Asia, in cities like Hong Kong, Seoul and Dubai, that the airport has become a main generator of metropolitan developments.

Notes

[1] This article reflects the author's personal ideas on the subject.

References

BCG, The Boston Consulting Group. 2004. *Airports – Dawn of a New Era. Preparing for One of the Industry's Biggest Shake-ups*. Munich, April 2004.

Kassarda, J. 2000. "Aerotropolis: Airport-Driven Urban Development." *ULI on the Future: Cities in the 21st Century*. Washington: Urban Land Institute.

Keur, J. 2003. *Airport City as Concept*, presentation.

Koolhaas, R. 2000. "Business & Velocity." *OMA@work.a+u*, Tokyo: A+U publishing.

Markillie, P. 2006. "The Physical Internet." Survey: Logistics. *The Economist*. 15 June 2006.

Province of North Holland, City of Amsterdam, Municipality of Haarlemmermeer and Schiphol Airport. 2001. *Ruimtelijk-Economische Visie Schipholregio (REVS)*. Report. Haarlem: Provincie Noord-Holland.

Schlichting, K.C. 2001. *Grand Central Terminal*. Baltimore: The Johns Hopkins University Press.

Scott, A.J. (ed.). 2001. *Global City Regions*, Oxford: Oxford University Press.

United Airlines. 2005. "You can't participate in life via conference call." Advertisement.

coop

Wilhelm Natrup

Cooperating and Competing

The Creation of Awareness in Polycentric Metropolitan Regions

From a normative perspective, polycentric metropolitan regions are the product of a vision guiding spatial planning policies at a European level; they are considered as potential motors of competitive ability within Europe. Within these large-scale regions, different actors from the political and economic spheres, from science and society, try for cooperation, while at the same time competition is flourishing. This article discusses the motivations and mechanisms involved in these processes of polycentric metropolitan development with reference to the metropolitan regions of Berlin-Brandenburg and Zurich; it also describes the difficulties and possibilities involved in such cooperation between different interests in the cores and peripheries of these areas. It is the peripheries and regional centers in particular that perceive an advantage in belonging to a region with a European dimension. There are no prescribed criteria for delimitation and classification of polycentric metropolitan regions. The growth of awareness regarding questions of advantage and disadvantage, of the opportunities and dangers inherent in the formation of these new categories of spatial development, is a process that is currently underway among networks of regional actors and political entities.

Polycentric metropolitan regions[1] represent a new category of spatial development in Europe. This category is seen as comprising closely integrated informal units that radiate an international character and that aim to compete at an international level by bundling their resources and potentials. The boundaries of these groups of cities and municipalities oriented toward one another economically, culturally and socially are not clearly defined, and the emerging conglomerates extend across existing borders as defined by regional authorities. This state of affairs presents these new extensive areas of cooperation with an opportunity but also the challenge of using the competitive situations and mechanisms operating between federal states/cantons, districts, cities and municipalities as a stimulant for further development within metropolitan regions. The new partnerships are based on cooperative relationships characterized by different levels of development and political legitimacy – depending on their remit they either comply or compete with the goals of the metropolitan region.

The Zurich metropolitan region, which is characterized by the small-scale, highly autonomous and self-assured structures of administrative responsibility typical of Swiss democracy, and the Berlin-Brandenburg metropolitan region, which consists of two federal states and is characterized by pronounced polarities between the core and its environs, provide examples here of the different experiences, opportunities and demands associated with polycentric metropolitan development.

1 Berlin-Brandenburg and Zurich: Comparing Two Metropolitan Regions

The polycentric metropolitan regions being discussed today are, on the one hand, units defined in geographical, socio-cultural, economic, political and spatial terms and, on the other, spaces in which local and regional political, economic and social actors network in an informal manner within organizations. The determination of membership and delimitation is dependent on different factors and interests.

The examples of Berlin-Brandenburg and Zurich are used here to illuminate certain facets of the process of consciousness formation. The perception and evaluation of the different parts of polycentric metropolitan regions are strongly influenced by the relationship between core and periphery. The motives behind delimitation, the division of functions and tasks and the value accorded to partners within the space will also be discussed. The findings detailed here are based on experience gained in both metropolitan regions in the course of some fifteen years of work and process management particularly in the field of spatial development.

1.1 The Berlin-Brandenburg Metropolitan Region

The federal states of Berlin and Brandenburg form one of eleven polycentric metropolitan regions in Germany as defined by the Conference of Ministers for Spatial Planning (MKRO) (BMBau 1995; BBR 2005).[2] Together they cover an area almost the size of Switzerland and have a total population of 5.95 million (2003).

In terms of cultural history the area, particularly as a former core area of Prussia, has a shared historical identity. However, the settlement and economic-geographical differences between the two states resulting from almost 40 years of political division are enormous and decisively shape the character of the area. This metropolitan region contains the highest and lowest densities of habitation and employment found in Germany as a whole. Brandenburg itself has few large urban centers, the biggest being the state capital Potsdam with a population of some 147,500 and Cottbus with a population of some 105,300 (2005) (LDS 2007). The largest section of the regional population is concentrated in Berlin and in the surrounding Berlin-Brandenburg area. The rest of the metropolitan area is extremely sparsely settled.

East Germany economic policy promoted the formation of industrial cores, particularly in what is today the federal state of Brandenburg. Following German reunification these industrial combinations, which had generally been central to the character of their locations, lost their signifi-

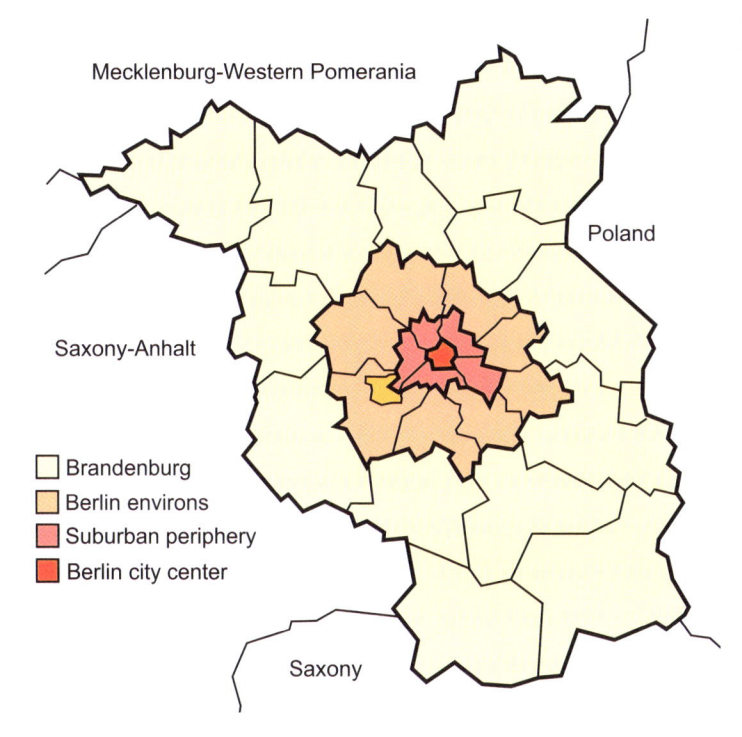

Figure 1: Berlin-Brandenburg metropolitan region: spatial types.

- Brandenburg
- Berlin environs
- Suburban periphery
- Berlin city center

cance and in some cases were no longer competitive. Government policy consequently attempted to shape the inevitable process of structural change by promoting new settlements and economic diversification. A number of areas located well away from Berlin were able to limit the drain on population and employment, while others suffered massive losses. The central dynamic influencing the two states was located in the area around Berlin. As a consequence of the suburbanization of inhabitants and employment, as well as the influx of new residents coming in part from the all over Brandenburg, Berlin experienced an increase in and a concentration of inhabitants and employment. The core city of Berlin was able to profit from this overall development in phases, although the population is now decreasing slightly.

A merger of the two states was discussed by policymakers in the 1990s but failed to come to pass when it was refused by the population in a referendum in 1994. However, prior to this, the states of Berlin and Brandenburg had already begun to coordinate their spatial planning policies directly after unification, creating a specific organization for this purpose, the Berlin-Brandenburg Collective Regional Planning Organization.

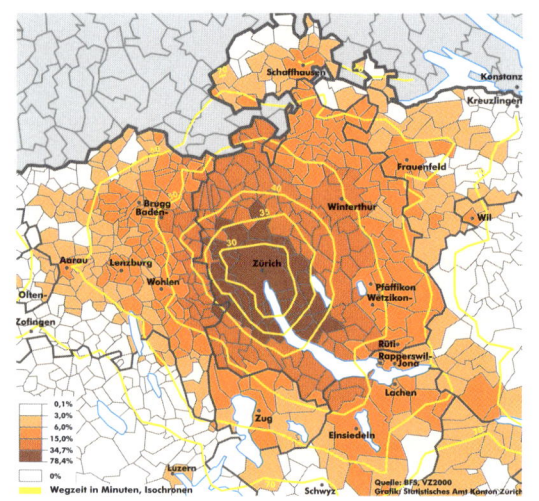

Figure 2:
Zurich within 60 minutes: the commuter area.

Figure 3:
The Zurich metropolitan region and the agglomerations included within it.

1.2 The Zurich Metropolitan Region

In Switzerland a discourse is currently being conducted both in political circles and among researchers in the fields of regional and economic planning concerning the definition and number of metropolitan regions that should be created as political and statistical-administrative entities. This process is still ongoing. A key dispute concerns the question of whether along with the Lake Geneva region (Geneva-Lausanne), the Zurich economic zone also constitutes a metropolitan region of European significance. However, how this area is to be defined is disputed and depends on whether it is seen as including the other Swiss-German centers of Basel, Bern, St. Gallen and Lucerne that are closely integrated with the Zurich region. The Federal Office of Spatial Development (ARE) recognizes five metropolitan regions in Switzerland as defined by the Federal Office of Statistics.

Against this background, the following comments regarding the Zurich metropolitan region[3] cannot be based on defined borders and established structures of cooperation in the same way as a discussion of Berlin-Brandenburg can. Indeed, this difference is fundamental to the characters of these two metropolitan regions and their self-conceptions.

The Zurich metropolitan region can only be defined in terms of commuter networks. As defined by the Swiss Federal Office of Statistics, it comprises 220 municipalities in 7 cantons and has a population of 1.68 million (BFS 2005: 14). The prosperity of this area has a significant influence on the economic life of Switzerland as a whole.

By Western European standards, the entire area is characterized by above-average population and employment growth. This is the result of the presence of high-quality knowledge-intensive service enterprises from the financial and insurance sectors and associated service providers. The quality of life offered by the region, which has been recognized by many rankings, and its excellent infrastructure have no doubt been decisive factors in shaping this corporate landscape.

The political structure, however, is multi-faceted and divided into small units. Apart from the city of Zurich with its population of 370,000, only the city of Winterthur, with just under 100,000 inhabitants, can be called a large urban center. All other municipalities, including those in the immediate surroundings of Zurich, have a population of 30,000 or less.

Figure 4:
Action space of the Greater Zurich Area.

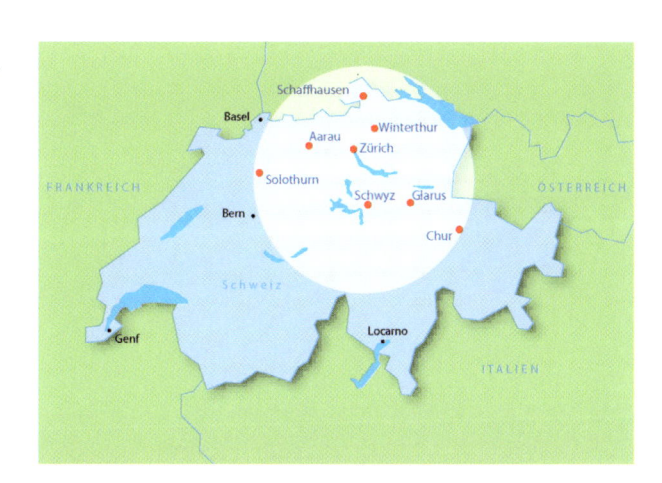

Figure 5:
Metropole Schweiz association: public discourse on the future of urban Switzerland.

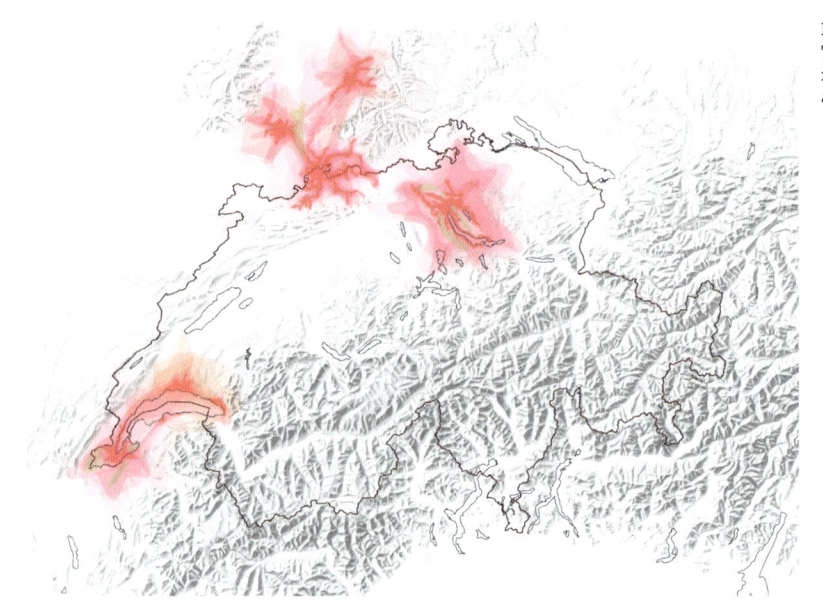

Figure 6:
The three metropolitan regions from *Switzerland – an Urban Portrait*.

2 Cooperation and Competition within the Two Metropolitan Regions

2.1 Zurich

The discourse concerning the Zurich metropolitan region was initiated by the Greater Zurich Area marketing organization founded in 1998 and its activities.[4] The organization links different cantons, cities and municipalities as well as leading companies that have helped shape the concept of Zurich as a desirable location, thus benefiting the extensive area linked with it. This extends from Graubünden in the south to Schaffhausen in the north and to Solothurn in the west.

This discourse has also been instigated by the activities of the *Metropole Schweiz* association, which was founded by a number of well-known figures as a forum for discussion about the future of settlement and society in Switzerland.[5] As a response to uncontrolled development, the association has drawn up a charter for the future of an urban Switzerland. Over recent years it has engaged in diverse forms of public relations work that have included symposiums and exhibitions such as the current traveling exhibition *Metropoly* and participation in the national exhibition EXPO 02.

The most recent contribution to this discourse has come from studies in the fields of urban development and regional economics. Following several years of analysis carried out in conjunction with students, professors and lecturers from Studio Basel, the Contemporary City Institute at ETH Zurich published *Switzerland – an Urban Portrait* (Diener et al. 2006). This extensive work maps the typologies of five Swiss spatial categories, ranging from metropolitan areas to disused Alpine areas. It was particularly the definition and delimitation of three large-scale metropolitan regions (Zurich, Basel/Oberrhein and Geneva-Lausanne) that gave rise to a political discussion concerning the preconditions for the further development of Switzerland's spatial structure with its orientation to regional cohesion. This discussion focused particularly on questions of urbanism and also drew on work by the "Avenir Suisse" think-tank, which was founded by Swiss companies in 1999 to critically analyze the development of Switzerland and formulate ideas for the future of the country. These activities and studies have led to different reactions to the question of regional formation, ranging from support to resistance and rejection. The issue of membership of the Greater Zurich Area and the formation of alternative interest-based and marketing coalitions such as "Espace Mittelland" in the Bern-Solothurn area have been discussed heatedly in the affected cantonal parliaments. These debates and their discussion in the media have extended beyond the economic sphere and led to an increasing identification within the population with a Zurich metropolitan region. However, the spheres of influence and the boundaries of this economic and residential zone have still not been clearly defined. The city of Zurich is currently inviting partners in metropolitan regions to conferences with the aim of identifying important themes and common interests. The intention is to create a platform for the exchange of information and experiences.[6]

Over and above this, for several years now collaboration between cantons and municipalities within the metropolitan region has been promoted by national policies related to agglomerations. In the face of transport bottlenecks and urban sprawl, incentives have been formulated to promote coordinated cross-border cooperation. Apart from the Zurich agglomeration itself, the Zurich metropolitan region includes a number of other, much smaller agglomerations as defined by the Federal Office of Statistics (see Figure 3). Agglomeration programs involving projects run by local actors have been developed in cooperation with municipalities and cantons for the dynamically developing parts of the canton as well as in the areas bordering the Schaffhausen canton in the north and in the Rapperswil-Jona-Freienbach-Rüti area referred to as "Agglo Obersee" (see Figure 7). Such programs and their *dirigiste* approach represent a new type of spatial planning instrument for urban areas in Switzerland. Their effect in terms of increasing awareness of integration within agglomerations and regions is highly significant. Established forms of cooperation within the framework of regional planning are thereby gaining a new dimension. Apart from the program focus "Settlement and Transport," no prescriptions have been set out relating to the themes and content of cooperation. The partners involved in these processes are using this scope to develop a broad range of intercommunal themes

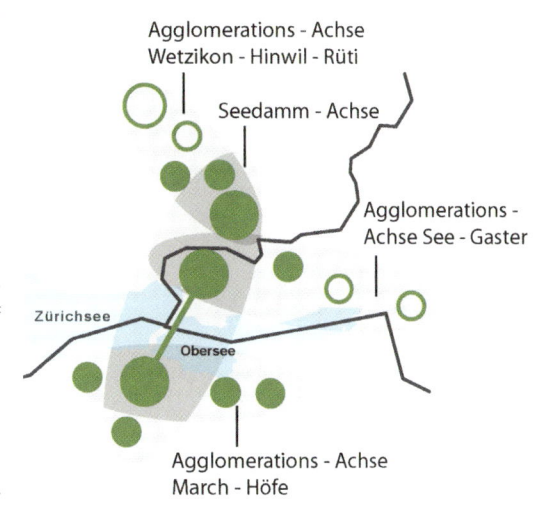

Figure 7:
Cooperation in the agglomeration: Agglo Obersee as part of the Zurich metropolitan region.

and tasks that include education and culture as well as questions of social and health policy.

Raising awareness in the Zurich metropolitan region is influenced, on the one hand, by a sense of local embeddedness and political responsibility within a federalist state structure and, on the other, by the lived realities and economic necessity of operating within larger spatial categories. Against this background, cooperation is particularly sought in the areas of infrastructural development and locational marketing. A particular role is assumed here by airport development, which, on the one hand, is accepted as being a motor of metropolitan development and, on the other, represents a disadvantage in terms of the quality of life of large parts of the population in the metropolitan area. Against this background, state legitimation of the metropolitan region framed in spatial planning terms tends to meet with a critical reaction from the cantons. When it comes to issues of cross-border cooperation, Switzerland, a confederation of states, traditionally relies on conviction and free choice. Given this background, a Zurich metropolitan region can be institutionally supported only with the involvement of a wide range of partners.

2.2 Berlin – Brandenburg

In the case of Berlin-Brandenburg, the issue of cooperation between the two federal states of Berlin and Brandenburg in one metropolitan space emerged immediately following reunification. In the mid-1990s this theme was also taken up on a national level in the context of the European discussion of spatial-planning policy. In this phase, Berlin-Brandenburg was confirmed as one of what were then seven metropolitan regions.

Following reunification, the Berlin-Brandenburg Collective Regional Planning organization (GL) was involved in the task of preparing for the integration of West Berlin with the former districts of East Germany, which today form the state of Brandenburg, and with the capital of East Germany, the former eastern part of Berlin. The first phase involved the elaboration of development scenarios and an overall collective spatial planning concept (see Figure 8). It was this phase which laid the foundations for the spatial planning concept of decentralized concentration that was later formulated (Brake et al. 1999).

The establishment of the GL planning organization was accompanied by a restructuring of functions and competencies in the regional planning area. The comparatively large administrative districts making up the state of Brandenburg were organized into five "regional planning communities" that stretch from the Berlin city boundary to the peripheral area of the state of Brandenburg. However, in terms of regional planning law the area was not structured to mirror these "slices." Based on the interests of Berlin, the area was divided into Berlin and the so-called "Berlin-Brandenburg Suburban Rim," the so-called "Further Development Area in the State of Brandenburg," the "Regional Development Centers" (REZ) and "Cities in the State of Brandenburg in Urgent Need of Action."

Following reunification a process of accelerated and dynamic growth was initially predicted for the region. A concentration and increase of jobs and population in Berlin formed the basis of forecasts. In order to curb uncontrolled development in the city's environs, it was envisaged that settlement development would be concentrated at particular points and generally limited. A declared goal of spatial planning was to channel any spillover effect above all into the regional development centers located 50 to 100 km from the Berlin city boundary. However, once the first realistic development prognoses based on demographic and generally stagnating economic development had been made and it became clear that the enormous demand potential of Berlin as the capital was not being realized as expected, this concept was questioned, particularly from the Berlin side. It became clear that stagnation or only mild growth could be expected. Against this background, the shared interests of Berlin and Brandenburg were progressively re-examined (Jähnke 1998).

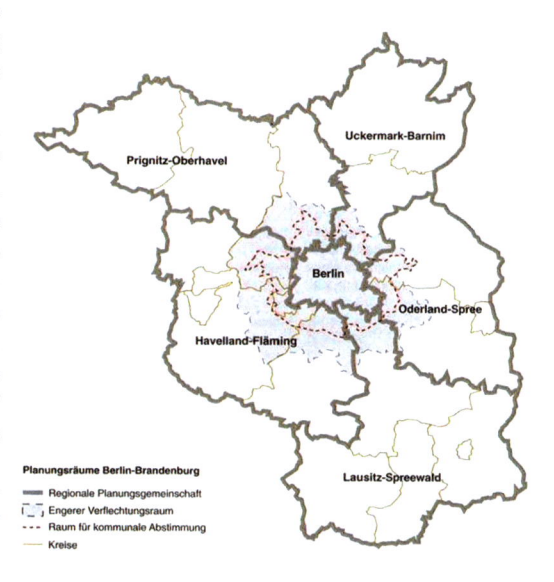

Figure 8:
Berlin-Brandenburg planning spaces: regional planning communities as "slices" extending from Berlin to the periphery.

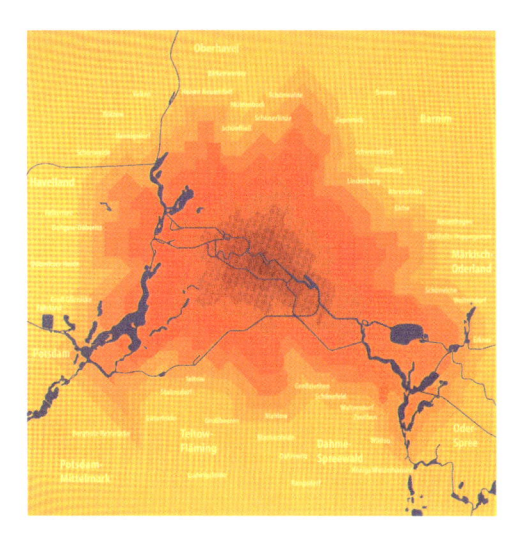

Figure 9:
The city and its neighbors:
cooperative projects
in the Berlin-Brandenburg
suburban rim.

Plans for the Berlin-Brandenburg international airport, which had initially favored locations in regions far away from Berlin, now focused on Berlin-Schönefeld with the aim of using the airport development to stimulate growth in Berlin. In other areas of functional division such as universities, Berlin was also given more weight. From the middle of the 1990s, following the failed attempt to merge the two states, it was clear that Berlin was favoring a more isolationist approach to economic and spatial planning issues. It was only slowly that Berlin began to refocus on cooperation in its immediate surroundings, particularly in relation to the long-term preservation of open landscape and recreational areas. For example, a Berlin initiative led to the formulation of a regional park concept involving cooperation between districts covered by the Berlin-Brandenburg Collective Regional Planning organization and affected municipalities. This concept aimed to establish a "wreath" of different natural areas to preserve open space and provide recreation in the surroundings of Berlin.

This joint planning involving Berlin and its neighboring municipalities and districts constituted a first step toward cooperation in the narrower metropolitan region. Further cooperation took place in the framework of INTERREG projects, including in particular the cooperation between Berlin and cities, districts and institutions in Brandenburg in the context of projects within the Baltic Sea region. These projects dealt with issues of large-scale urban development (Metropolitan Areas in the Baltic Sea),[7] the question of transmodality in the goods transport sector (ship, train, road) and urban development projects, e.g., for harbor areas/areas located on the water. These projects generally led to a better understanding and more intensive cooperation between Berlin and its neighboring municipalities. Moreover, different forms of concrete cooperation proved decisive for identity formation in the Brandenburg region. One example is the Working Group of Regional Development Centers in the State of Brandenburg (ARGE REZ), which is made up of the larger regional development centers situated around Berlin. Since 1994 they have been working together in the so-called "urban wreath" around the national capital. This network of cities has also cooperated with Berlin districts in the context of an INTERREG project. Further forms of cooperation (such as those between small and medium-sized cities with historic town centers) and regional collaborations (such as the integration of municipalities around a common developmental axis leading in the direction of Neuruppin) have fundamentally contributed to defining and positioning the metropolitan region. Apart from these instances of cooperation in the spatial planning sphere, it is also worthy of note that at the end of the 1990s "Schaustelle Berlin" (Venue Berlin), an initiative by the former Senator for Urban Development and Environmental Protection designed to draw attention to the changes taking place in the capital, was extended to cover the whole metropolitan region and renamed "Schaustelle Berlin-Brandenburg." This "venue" encourages residents of the area, particularly those from Berlin, to investigate spatial developments such as the restructuring of the coal mine area in Lausitz and the construction of large infrastructures such as the Cargo Lift Hall in Spreewald and to comprehend them as part of their environment.

Within the general framework of locational and business promotion, individual firms have also contributed to the collective marketing and positioning of the area. A further factor fundamental to identity formation has been the establishment of the Berlin-Brandenburg Transport Alliance (VBB).

In general it can be seen that the identity of a Berlin-Brandenburg metropolitan region has not yet been clearly defined. Awareness has grown in Brandenburg that a suburban-ring concentration of employment, enterprise and population represents an alternative to a spatial-planning concept of decentralized concentration. This concept is being presaged by population movements and concentrations of business and corresponds to a metropolitan outlook. Such an outlook assumes that the strongest stimuli to growth must be concentrated in Berlin and the suburban ring around it and that the advantages deriving from the agglomeration can be used for the benefit of the entire area.

3 Cooperation and Competition

Polycentric metropolitan regions offer the chance to build synergies between different partners. At the same time, such forms of collaboration compete with existing local and regional interests, organizations and cooperative enterprises. From the point of view of polycentric metropolitan development it is nevertheless clear that there is an awareness of the need to use the advantage of cooperation in these areas (Behrendt and Kruse 2001).

In both Berlin-Brandenburg and Zurich the responsible parties have recognized that the development of an airport can only proceed with the agreement of all affected partners within a metropolitan region. For example, all partners have an interest in a high-quality link with international networks. In both metropolitan regions, all partners accordingly support in principle the upgrading of infrastructures. They are also looking to cooperate in the area of locational marketing.

A further area of cooperation involves representing the interests of the area in relation to other parts of the country and the state. The representation of the interests of metropolitan centers and agglomerations takes on a particular national significance in Switzerland, which is oriented to achieving a high level of cohesion between the different parts of the country. Moreover, cooperation can also offer advantages in the development of strategies and projects. In certain fields, cooperation within metropolitan regions can be advantageous for all participants, as seen in the case of the federal agglomeration programs.

However, areas of competition persist alongside these different forms of cooperation. It would not make sense for collaboration in the metropolitan regions to aim at leveling out individual locational advantages. It is precisely the degree of diversity and individual features of locations that strengthen a metropolitan region in relation to other cities and regions and thus enable it to establish its own particular profile.

In this sense, there is a danger in the case of Berlin-Brandenburg that Berlin as a powerful metropolitan center will not recognize the manifold opportunities and possibilities presented by the rest of the metropolitan region. By contrast, the polycentric character of the Zurich metropolitan region means that municipalities and subregions place a high value on their autonomy and as a result can quickly lose sight of their shared interests. For example, shared infrastructural elements such as the opera house and other central facilities in the city of Zurich are supported and in part co-financed. A fundamental feature of the situation in Switzerland is the existing competition with regard to taxation. Within the scope of their self-administrative powers, municipalities can set their own levels of municipal income tax for natural and juridical persons. This constitutes a fundamental element of the competition between municipalities within an economic zone, and this also applies to the Zurich metropolitan region. In the case of Berlin-Brandenburg, the relationship between different areas, particularly between the core of the metropolitan region (Berlin) and agricultural parts of Brandenburg situated a long way from Berlin, is determined in a different way. Apart from infrastructural aspects and geographical situation, it is subsidies and other *dirigiste* measures rather than the tax burden that constitute a key determinant of locational quality.

The discussion of polycentric metropolitan regions primarily refers to innovativeness and competitiveness. Far less attention is paid to the way in which these regions can be steered and monitored. It is thus above all the economic question that is emphasized, and a broader understanding of integrated spatial development is not yet sufficiently informing debates. The relationship between regional development and existing cooperative relationships is also not being comprehensively covered in discussions. As yet, we seldom see attempts to establish further institutional dimensions in this context. It is in this area that the regions concerned will face their most fundamental challenges in the future. In the Zurich area there are some signs of a reorientation of regional planning. However, initial attempts in this regard have failed at a political level. Since 1958 the "Regional Planning for Zurich and Environs" (RZU) association has worked to strengthen regional cooperation and integrate the activities of neighboring regions. As yet, the association's activities only cover the city of Zurich and these neighboring regions, which is a far cry from including the entire agglomeration, let alone the Zurich metropolitan region. This state of affairs points to a need for new sponsors for projects particularly within the framework of the agglomeration program introduced by the federal government. By contrast, in Berlin-Brandenburg, the Collective Regional Planning organization (GL) is already working to meet these challenges. This constitutes a fundamental difference between the two metropolitan regions being considered here.

Extending cooperation into other fields will constitute a further challenge. The limitation of the Zurich metropolitan region to the fields prescribed by the federal agglomeration program, i.e., an emphasis on the areas of "settlement and transport," is not viable as a long-term strategy. The interests of municipalities would be far better served if cooperation included areas such as culture, education, health, social integration, etc.

As yet, cooperation has been focused above all at the political level of municipalities and regions. The future of spatial development will decisively depend on the extent to which business and scholarship as well as civil society can be integrated into these cooperative processes.

4 Factors of Successful Cooperation in Polycentric Metropolitan Regions

The following findings are based on experience in the regional planning field, including work on the concept of decentralized concentration in Berlin-Brandenburg, the provision of support for the Working Group of Regional Development Centers in the State of Brandenburg and diverse regional studies for diverse local authorities in this area. In the Swiss context our findings are based on work on the fundamentals of spatial planning in the 1990s and on federal agglomeration policies, as well as the provision of consultation to agglomerations and cantons on questions of spatial development.

- Institutionalization

Cooperation needs to be learnt in stages. If questions regarding institutional collaboration and sponsorship are raised at the beginning of the cooperation process, this can lead to a collapse of the partnership involved. It is only after the successful initiation of a project, when the prospect of shared success and political viability are clearly in view, that sponsorship and cooperation models can be developed appropriately.

- Regard for boundaries and jurisdiction

Discussions concerning polycentric metropolitan regions raise questions of administrative and thematic boundaries and institutional jurisdiction. If these issues are raised at the beginning of a cooperative venture, there is a strong chance that it will fail. The primary focus should thus be on creating a functioning partnership rather than questions of fusion or incorporation. This does not rule out the possibility of changes to boundaries in the longer term, but these should not be a condition of cooperation.

- Leveling out locational advantages

Diversity and complexity, particularly in polycentric metropolitan regions, should be used as a starting point for the further development and strengthening of a region with its own distinctive profile. The attempt to level out locational advantages represents a particular stumbling block in the Swiss system.

- Thematically oriented cooperation

Cooperation should accord with the principle of "variable geometries." This means that along with collaboration between partners within a polycentric metropolitan region, other forms of cooperation should also be possible. The advantages for the region of such an approach are shown by INTERREG projects, city networks, etc.

- External collective marketing – internal competition

Metropolitan regions require effective external presentation of their locational and settlement policies. Marketing organizations such as Greater Zurich Area and the *Wirtschaftsförderung Berlin-Brandenburg* can be enormously helpful in this respect. However, care must be taken that such institutions do not obstruct or exclude competition within metropolitan regions. Competition between locations strengthens metropolitan regions, and the competitive ability of regions is dependent on the vitality of their individual parts. This means that competition among partners within the region should be accepted and should form the basis for cooperation.

- Cooperation in fields that offer a strong chance of success

Cooperation within metropolitan regions is a decisive factor in the formation of regional awareness and identity. Particularly in initial phases, it is therefore important that fields be chosen for cooperation that offer a good chance of success, and those areas with a potential for generating tension between partners be avoided. Concepts for the creation and design of open spaces, the cultural sphere and in particular the public transport area lend themselves to successful cooperation. By contrast, projects involving the distribution of economic resources or facilities intensively used by the public can easily lead to conflict. This does not mean that such areas of cooperation should be excluded in metropolitan regions. However, they tend not to be suited to initial cooperative projects, which should focus on areas of common interest.

- Exponents of the metropolitan region

It is extremely important that key figures promote the metropolitan region and are personally associated with it. The Zurich City President is an important regional figure in this respect, and other business and political representatives are also working to promote the region. As yet, a similar development has not been evident in Berlin-Brandenburg.

- Allowing time for development

Establishing cooperation as a self-evident feature of polycentric metropolitan regions and thus building regional awareness and identity are processes that need time. Efforts to foster cooperation within Berlin-Brandenburg have been going on for fifteen years and are only now showing the first signs of success. Other examples in both Germany and Switzerland also confirm the fact that cooperative ventures given adequate time to develop have a greater chance of success than those oriented to results in the short term.

- Cooperation on a voluntary basis

Cooperation in a polycentric metropolitan region should not be dependent on shared location. It is far more important that partners are united by their shared interest in the area of cooperation in question.

5 Concluding Remarks

Polycentric metropolitan regions could see themselves as conglomerates of political, economic and civil-societal actors with different locational advantages. Indeed, it is this potential that constitutes their major strength when compared with entities defined in concise legal terms and by institutionally anchored administrative structures and spatial-planning categories. The collective marketing of locations within a framework of international competition is a goal that needs to be recognized and pursued. Metropolitan regions will be successful when they recognize and use their synergetic potentials while at the same time being able to refrain from interfering in areas lying within the sole competence of individual local authorities.

Building awareness and thus identity in polycentric metropolitan regions opens up new possibilities for the cooperative management of spatial development. However, such forms of management are only now beginning to be developed and tried out. Further processes of experimentation and evaluation are required in order to gain an adequate understanding of the opportunities and risks that these informal types of cooperation existing outside established processes of democratic decision-making entail.

Notes

[1] In this article the term "metropolitan region" and the more specific term "polycentric metropolitan region" are used as the normative equivalents of the basically analytical concept of "mega-city regions."

[2] The MKRO resolution of 8 March 1995 named seven European metropolitan regions. Four more were added in 2005.

[3] As defined by the Swiss Federal Office for Statistics, the Zurich metropolitan region comprises 2,104 sq. km and has a population of 1,675,000.

[4] See www.greaterzuricharea.ch.

[5] The *Verein Metropole Schweiz* was founded in 1994, see www.metropole-ch.ch.

[6] On 22 May 2007, the city of Zurich organized a conference held in Rapperswil entitled "Giving Economic Zones a Face and a Voice."

[7] See www.baltmet.org.

References

BBR, Bundesamt für Bauwesen und Raumordnung. 2005. *Raumordnungsbericht 2005*. Bonn: BBR.

Behrendt, H. and C. Kruse 2001. "Die Europäische Metropolregion Zürich – die Entstehung des subpolitischen Raumes" *Geographica Helvetica* 56 (3): 202-213.

BMBau, Bundesministerium für Raumordnung, Bauwesen und Städtebau. 1995. *Raumordnungspolitischer Handlungsrahmen: Beschluß der Ministerkonferenz für Raumordnung in Düsseldorf am 8. März 1995*. Bonn: BMBau.

Brake, K., R. Danielzyk and M. Karsten. 1999. "Dezentrale Konzentration – ein Leitbild mit besonderen Herausforderungen für interkommunale Kooperation." *Archiv für Kommunalwissenschaften* 38: 88-103.

BFS, Bundesamt für Statistik. 2005. *Die Raumgliederung der Schweiz. Eidgenössische Volkszählung 2000*. Neuchâtel: Bundesamt für Statistik.

Diener, R., J. Herzog, M. Meili, P. de Meuron and C. Schmid. 2006. *Die Schweiz – ein städtebauliches Portrait*. Basel: Birkhäuser.

Jähnke, P. (ed.). 1998. *Komplementarität statt Konkurrenz – Regionale Entwicklungszentren und ihr Umland in Brandenburg*. Dokumentation einer gemeinsamen Fachtagung der ARGE REZ und des IRS am 10.02.1998. Erkner: IRS.

LDS, Landesbetrieb für Datenverarbeitung und Statistik Brandenburg. 2007. Bevölkerung des Landes Brandenburg nach Verwaltungsbezirken 1990 bis 2005. LDS, 16.11.2006. Available from www.statistik.brandenburg.de.

m

Reinhard Frei

Managing Reputation

The term reputation encompasses ideas of standing, kudos, and the appraisal of an individual or group. Reputation also constitutes capital – cultural, societal and entrepreneurial. If one's reputation is damaged or tarnished, then it is very difficult to regain the prestige one previously enjoyed. This applies to regions just as much as it does to firms. Indeed, in the case of the region, the significance of reputation has now shifted to center stage. Today a region without kudos finds it extremely difficult to compete with other regions. Locational reputation management involves a long-term process that is connected to both hard and soft factors. It is a "head, heart and hands" process that must be initiated and sustained by regional stakeholders.

"The design of a political system can only be successful if it includes consideration of the citizenry's emotional attachments, which are defined by boundaries of all types" (Matt 2006).

Reputation generates trust and vice versa, and both fall into the category of soft locational factors. To what extent is trust in regions and locations connected with their image and reputation? A region with a good image radiates a positive quality and exerts a certain force of attraction, particularly for firms and entrepreneurs. A region with an attractive image is accorded competence as a matter of course. For example, it is assumed – and trusted – that Silicon Valley generally offers a good climate for innovation even though many firms and entrepreneurs there fail.

Until now it has tended to be hard factors such as taxes, duties and transport access, etc. that have determined the reputation of a region for enterprises. However, with many locations now offering comparable conditions in terms of hard factors, it seems that soft factors such as image, profile, quality of life, trust in local authorities, cultural activities and regional organization are becoming increasingly important to regional reputation.

Region Versus Metropolitan Region

Henner Kleinewefers (2005) argues that the creation of increased competition due to the expansion of the EU means that robust regions within a country – in Switzerland these include the regions around Basel, Zurich and Geneva – will flourish even more in the future, while peripheral regions will increasingly face problems (Kleinewefers 2005).

What are referred to here as robust regions are in fact so-called metropolitan regions. However, these metropolitan regions are themselves made up of a large number of regions, subregions and microregions. Metropolitan regions consist of at least one major city as well as several agglomerations of different sizes. Definitional criteria of metropolitan regions include competitive capacity, connectivity and critical mass (Thierstein 2005). In my opinion, attractive subregions – understood as elements within or on the periphery of a metropolitan region – are distinguished above all by their proximity to decision-makers in the political and administrative spheres as well as other institutions in the realm of civil society. The particular strength of "embedded," as opposed to isolated, subregions is their strong network of stakeholders (i.e., people know one another), lean and simple structures, spatial proximity to major cities and a high level of accessibility due to a high-quality transport infrastructure. I would therefore argue, in contrast to Kleinewefers, that subregions that are "embedded" in this sense have a good chance of asserting themselves within the framework of larger metropolitan regions, above all when they network with one another and work on their external presentation (image, profile) and "internal fitness" (taxation and infrastructural conditions).

This background informs the following considerations, which are intended as a guide for action above all by stakeholders in embedded and networked subregions.

The Reputation of the (Sub)Region

A region is often preceded by its reputation in the sense that it is associated with an image that has been formed over a period of years and that has become fixed in our minds, whether this image is in fact accurate or not. The most famous example may well be *Silicon Valley*, which tends to be seen as a "land of milk of honey" when it comes to ideas, capital, a highly qualified workforce, access to research and development, etc. For a long time the *Swiss Jura* was regarded as just the opposite, a region of dying (clock) industries and depopulated valleys and villages. But then, like a phoenix from its ashes, the clock industry flourished again and rapidly improved the reputation of the region. By contrast, the *Alpine Rhine Valley* has no reputation to speak of. Indeed, it is hardly perceived as a region at all and thus, as a conglomeration of subregions and microregions, is unable to generate a unitary image.

A region without a clear, unitary profile, without a good reputation, has difficulty being heard and seen within the wider regional framework. It is therefore important to identify the actual reputation that precedes a region, i.e., how that region is perceived, externally and internally. Representative surveys of relevant groups provide quick results in this respect, and the results often show that external and internal perspectives, self-perception and outsiders' perception significantly diverge. Once an image has been identified, it can be cultivated, corrected and even changed. Professional locational reputation management can make a valuable contribution to this process.

Several years ago the reputation of Switzerland was tarnished above all in the USA; the debate concerning the dormant accounts of Holocaust victims cast a shadow over the whole of Swiss politics and damaged Switzerland's image abroad. The effects were also felt by Swiss firms, whose products were in part boycotted, an experience shared in the past by Shell, Nestlé, Sandoz and many other enterprises. Once a reputation has been blemished the process of "repairing" it is a very arduous and expensive one that involves intensive communication with all relevant reference groups. However, a better approach is to cultivate these relationships "in advance" and, in terms of the present subject of discussion, this is best achieved by means of professional locational reputation management.

Locational reputation management involves the management of relationships with the significant stakeholders, the goal being to strengthen and increase the "good-will factor" – the non-monetary value attached to cities, regions, countries and their administrative and political entities – over the long term. In this sense, locational reputation is actually an intangible "asset." The reputation of a country or a region and thus its attractiveness for firms and HNWI (high net worth individuals) or for intermediaries such as journalists, analysts, rating agencies, etc. is fundamentally dependent on how effectively this reputation is fostered. Taxes can be rapidly lowered everywhere – a good reputation needs care and time.

The "reputation value" of a region can and should be measured from time to time. This process can involve a range of indicators: surveys, media resonance, rankings, etc. While different service enterprises (banks, insurance firms, etc.) rank regions on an annual basis, it is often only hard factors that are taken into consideration. It would seem that such rankings now also need to take reputation value into account.

The Problems Created by the "Uprooting" of Enterprises

The fact that regions now seem suddenly to have become more active as entities of course has its reasons. The transition from a stable, predictable world to a more complex, networked world has dissolved or dislocated structures and boundaries. Much that was previously taken for granted has been called into question. Many enterprises have not comprehended the necessity of adapting to these changes. In this time of upheaval, which can be attributed specifically to the internationalization of enterprises and generally to economic globalization, the economic sphere has increasingly distanced itself from the political sphere. Enterprises have "uprooted" themselves and the region has become a "mere" location for them rather than a home. At the same time, (sub)regions have been drawn into the orbit of metropolitan regions, and new enterprises that had no previous ties to regional actors and little sense of regional identification have impinged on such regions from the outside.

Today managers – there are almost no traditional "bosses" anymore – often live a long way from the enterprises they work for. A process of locational decoupling is taking place. The relationship between these managers and regional actors is now often only marginal, and there may be no personal contact whatsoever.

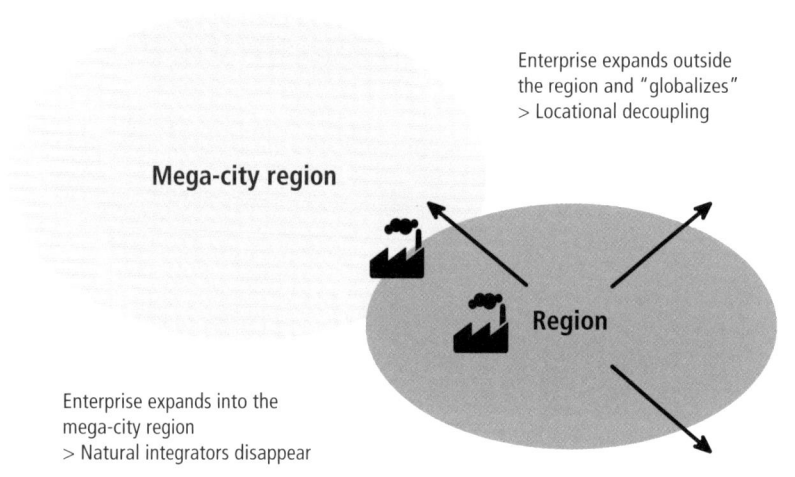

Figure 1:
Problems for subregions and peripheral regions and locational decoupling.

Enterprise expands outside the region and "globalizes"
> Locational decoupling

Mega-city region

Region

Enterprise expands into the mega-city region
> Natural integrators disappear

The Example of Wild/Leica

One example that can be used to illustrate locational decoupling is that of Leica Geosystems, an amalgamation of Wild Heerbrugg and Wild Leitz. This company, which has existed for some 80 years, was founded by the Schmidheiny family, a business dynasty with strong regional ties, in Heerbrugg in the Swiss Rhine Valley, which is part of the Alpine Rhine Valley. The success of the firm also brought prosperity and prestige to the Rhine Valley region, in part due to the generosity and patronage of the firm's founding family. However, during the 1980s and 1990s the founders increasingly withdrew from their leadership role, selling their shares in the company and floating it on the stock market. As a result, from 2004 onwards the company's fortunes were left in the hands of investors and analysts. Decisive in this context was the timely rationalization of the firm by a farsighted management, which enabled it to compete globally. However, this process was accompanied by one of "locational decoupling" – suddenly managers no longer came from the Rhine Valley but from Holland, China, England, etc. They also no longer lived in the Swiss Rhine Valley but commuted from Zurich, St. Gallen and other cities to Heerbrugg. The takeover by the Swedish firm Hexagon in 2005 meant that the existing management was also completely replaced and that decisions were now no longer made in Heerbrugg, but in London or Sweden.

Relations between regional associations, institutions, etc. and Wild/Leica once functioned at the level of personal acquaintances. Management was aware of regional and local concerns and, when requested, help was provided quickly and directly. Today the situation is different. The intensification of competition and the orientation to the global market have meant that it is often difficult to find an attentive ear for regional and local concerns. It has to be said that a company is of course justified in focusing more on its most important stakeholders (its customers, employees and proprietors) than on the concerns of local municipalities, associations and institutions. Nevertheless, this decoupling entails a loss in terms of natural integrators, local actors who also have a keen sense of the welfare of the region and the location, who are able to network, sustain contacts with political and economic actors and thus contribute to regional identity.

It is unarguably positive for the image of a region when it provides a location for firms with a good international reputation, since this "rubs off" on the reputation of the region. Yet it is surely also in a company's interest that the reputation of its location is strengthened and that the surrounding region has a good image, above all in a time when highly qualified workers are in short supply. In the future, firms will thus need to engage with local and regional concerns.

Growth is increasingly a feature of metropolitan agglomerations, above all population growth. Well-trained workers are increasingly also moving into the peripheral areas of metropolitan agglomerations. It is thus important for subregions to cultivate their attractiveness for such potential residents. This phenomenon also impacts on firms in the sense that a firm which sees its responsibilities as including its role in the region and endeavors to position itself there in a positive way will also be attractive for workers.

It is thus very much in the interest of firms to cultivate and invest in a good regional reputation, whether in relation to a metropolitan region, a local or regional environment or an agglomeration.

Coordinating and Orienting Activities

This means that regions and firms (the political and economic spheres) need to come together again, that they must work in concert to cultivate regional identity. It is important that all stakeholders are included in regional development. Moreover, regions must coordinate their activities in this context with those of other regions and take into account their most important "neighboring" metropolitan regions.

However, the example of the Alpine Rhine Valley also shows how difficult it is to win the support of these stakeholders for such a collective project. It is here that regional political actors are required to play a role. Municipal leaders, parliamentarians and government representatives need to initiate and sustain dialog with representatives of business. Furthermore, it is imperative that businesses understand that although the world may be their market, that world begins in the region.

How does successful locational reputation management function? The reputation of a location depends on both hard and soft factors. Managing this reputation entails a long-term process of dealing with internal and external reference groups with the goal of strengthening the region's "goodwill factor."

Just as it is the CEO or upper echelons of management that fundamentally influence the reputation of an enterprise, so in the case of the region it is political decision-makers who are most readily identified with the region and who embody it for the outside world. The identity of a business is often associated with a charismatic leadership figure, and it is often a charismatic political figure that can give a region a "face." This "regional face" needs to be incorporated in the locational reputation management process and also guide it. Regional reputation relies crucially on its credible representation by regional actors, which contributes fundamentally to building trust. Such actors need to be aware of this if locational reputation management is to be effective.

Locational Reputation Management as Process

When we look into the "toolbox" of locational reputation management, it is important to note that these are not tools that we can merely avail ourselves of in a crisis situation. Reputation management should not be equated with crisis management. If the reputation of a region has taken a battering, only time, persistence and a certain amount of luck can lead to its improvement. A new prospectus or a new campaign cannot obliterate the mistakes of the past from one day to the next. Indeed, a change in strategy or image correction can even create additional problems for a region in the sense that, burdened by a poor reputation, it is now faced with the task of projecting a new, unfamiliar image.

It is thus perhaps instructive to turn to a positive example, an example of an unknown region with an outmoded image, a region located in the center of Europe and yet on the edge of its respective nation states: the Alpine Rhine Valley region and the Swiss Rhine Valley embedded within it.

In the early 1990s the Swiss Rhine Valley commissioned a study of its reputation. The survey that was conducted as a result produced very different results in terms of the way the region was perceived externally and internally. Outsiders'

Legitimation	Organisation	Conception	Implementation	Evaluation
· Legal legitimation	· Structure · Sequence · Development	· Vision · Goals · Project environment analysis · Concept	· Reputation management · Measures	· Controlling · Feedback

Figure 2:
Locational reputation management as process.

image of the region was more positive and the Swiss-German view clearly more negative than the view of Rhine Valley residents, who identified strongly with their region.

It was evident that while Rhine Valley residents strongly identified with their region, among Swiss-Germans, above all Zurich residents, the image of the Rhine Valley region was poor. Those who had commissioned the study, the employers' federation and the Rhine Valley municipalities, saw this as a warning. Something had to happen – and indeed it did. A process was initiated.

A Valley of Opportunities – Regional Actors Team Up

A working group made up of business and political representatives was formed and initiated the project *Chancental Rheintal* (Valley of Opportunities), initially a working title and later adopted as the project's official title. The study referred to above showed that the Rhine Valley had certain potentials that were either not being grasped or were underused. These potentials (an attractive location in the center of the Lake Constance region, a well educated workforce, favorable wage levels, excellent residential and recreational possibilities, etc.) formed the basis of a process organized by the working group under the former employer's association president Dr. Karl Stadler with the help of professionals from the location-marketing and communications fields. This process was structured as follows:

1. Image-analysis
   Representative survey of the population regarding the image of the Rhine Valley.
2. "The Image of the Rhine Valley"
   Open-space workshop based on the image study and involving over 400 Rhine Valley citizens with the aim of launching a wider discussion in the valley.
3. Structural analysis
   Shedding light on the Rhine Valley and its potential by means of in-depth interviews and analysis of data.
4. Perspectives seminar: "The Rhine Valley under scrutiny"
   Some 40 opinion leaders and policy-makers discuss the accumulated data and elaborate perspectives for the future.
5. Vision and action
   Elaboration of visions and possible projects for the Rhine Valley.
6. Round tables
   Round tables involving different groups analyze the individual projects and formulate concrete measures to realize them.
7. Implementation of four to six projects
   The working group agrees on the implementation of a small number of projects, which are then launched.
8. Conversion into location-marketing organization
   The *Chancental Rheintal* working group is converted into an independent organization (*Verein St. Galler Rheintal* – www.chancental.ch).

While the *Chancental Rheintal* project was not actually created as a locational reputation management process, following several setbacks it had a considerable degree of success. This success was based on two important pillars. On the one hand, the project had a significant driver in the person of the former president of the Rhine Valley employers' association, which all the important enterprises such as Leica Geosystems, SFS Stadler AG, Jansen AG, etc. belonged to. On the other hand, political decision-makers recognized the importance of the process and supported it from the outset in financial, conceptual and organizational terms.

The open-mindedness and preparedness to act found in St. Gallen's Rhine Valley is not found everywhere. Nevertheless, this brief description illustrates the importance of collaboration between businesses and political decision-makers in a process of this kind. At the time the project was initiated, the St. Gallen's Rhine Valley region had an image problem, and it has still not solved all of its problems in this respect. However, the process is continuing. Moreover, the example of the St. Gallen's Rhine Valley provides a basis for charting the way in which a process of professional locational management can function.

Legitimation in legal terms is an important initial step. Ideally this involves the establishment of regional development organizations (association, consortium, etc.) that include all stake-holders. The example of the Rhine Valley shows that a loose working group is quite capable of initiating this process, but it is important that this process quickly acquires a level of legitimacy. Such legitimation can be based on financing from municipal or city budgets or on a poll, although the latter requires intensive prior communication with regional residents in order to convince them of the necessity of the process. Ideally, an association will be founded that brings together all relevant actors.

Once the *organizational structure* has been established, a specific "regional development concept" must be elaborated. This involves a range of commonly used instruments such as open-space workshops involving residents, visions workshops involving opinion-leaders and policy-makers, analyses, etc. Of particular importance is a project environment analysis of regional stakeholders:

The larger the circle, the more important the stakeholder.
The closer to the project, the greater the degree of influence.

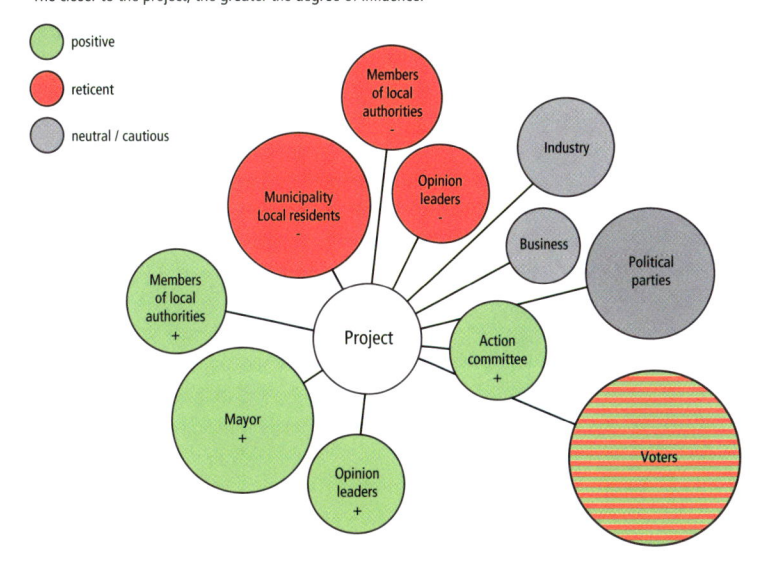

Figure 3:
Example of a "stakeholder" project environment analysis.

The stakeholder analysis shows how involved stakeholders are in the project, what influence they have, how important they are, whether they have a positive or negative attitude to the project, whether efforts need to be made to involve them more in the project, etc. The regional development concept needs to take into account opportunities and potentials as well as problems/risks and misgivings associated with the project.

Implementation with "Head, Heart and Hand"

Implementation marks the beginning of the actual process of locational reputation management. This process must proceed on three levels: objective, emotional and processual.

The actual locational reputation management process takes place on the *objective (head) level* in particular. Relevant measures involve above all communication by way of advertising, public relations and general marketing, the cultivation of relationships with all stakeholders, innovations in locational development and in the field of human resources both in relation to existing staff and the acquisition of highly qualified new staff, etc. This level requires the constant adjustment of instruments to the prevailing situation and the results of implemented measures. It is also important that data be presented that convince regional actors of the importance of locational reputation management.

The *emotional (heart) level* involves the engagement of people living in the region by means of projects and events. Regional organizations tend to do a lot in this area, although their efforts in this respect are often derivative and ineffective. What needs to be understood is that a region has to "live" in the sense that its inhabitants associate particular "images" with it in their minds. Many cities and regions are now attempting to establish themselves as centers of popular culture, above all by hosting musicals. However, genuinely novel approaches to regional identity formation are rare. While drawing inspiration from established models can be helpful, focusing on the specific strengths of a region and taking a different route is a far more productive approach.

The emotional level also involves cultivating relations with relevant actors, particularly those from the business sector. Sponsoring and sponsoring events can help to integrate businesses in the process and promote their sense of obligation to a region without making excessive demands on management's time. An active, lively region is something that business leaders can also take pride in.

The *processual (hand) level* involves making affected parties into participants. In this context it is above all important that the region, like a business, is capable of change. In contrast to businesses, where processes of change must be initiated and realized from one day to the next, regions are subject to slower processes of decision-making. It is therefore important that relevant decision-makers are repeatedly reminded that change is necessarily ongoing. It does not suffice to work out a locational development concept as a fixed plan. The initial situation that forms the point of departure for such a concept is also subject to constant change, however gradual this may be.

Public Relations and Calculability – Oiling the Regional Engine

Many regions include areas associated with industrial pollution – Basel has Schweizerhalle, Germany's Ruhr area has its disused coal mines and Italy has Seveso. Such areas damage a region's reputation and may necessitate the type of costly process of "image correction" that can be seen in the Ruhr area. Unlike businesses, regions cannot change their location; they must in effect "live" with their reputation. However, by means of locational reputation management this reputation can be shaped and improved.

Two aspects are of overriding importance in this context: an intensive cultivation of relations with all stakeholders by means of locational reputation management and calculability. Calculability generates trust, strengthens relationships and creates a sense of security. Public relations and calculability are the oil of regional reputation management. Identities and images are difficult to alter, as seen in the case of commercial

	Goals	Possible measures

Objective level	· Factual information
	· Argumentation
	· for / against
		· Image studies
		· Information events
		· Reputation management mix
		  · Communication
		  · Public relations
		  · Innovation
		  · Human resources

Emotional level	· Appealing to emotions · Generating enthusiasm for the region · Facilitating encounters · Promoting trust in authorities	· Cultural events · Sporting events · Sponsoring · Regional club · Regional festival (e.g., Slow down, One-eleven etc.)
Processual level	· Making affected parties into participants! · Enabling change · Developing a vision collectively · Project elaboration	Process of regional change · Strategy · Concept · Realization · Controlling

Figure 4: Implementation/measures in locational reputation management process.

brands. It takes several years for a new name or brand to become imprinted on consumers' consciousness, and this process takes even longer in the case of regions.

Once a region has embarked on a process of strengthening, improving or changing its image, it is imperative that it maintains its course in the face of any initial criticism. Calculability also requires consistency and effective public relations require competence and appeal. Competence without the capacity to appeal to a target group has little chance of long-term success. Regional actors and regions themselves must radiate competence and appeal if success is to prove sustainable. A region, whether small or large, can only assert itself if it projects an air of authenticity and distinctiveness.

References

Matt, P.v. 2006. "Behagen und Unbehagen im Föderalismus. Über die seelische Wirklichkeit der Grenzen." Presentation to Swiss government seminar on the Future of Federalism/Regional Politics, 05.01.06, at Interlaken.

Kleinewefers, H. 2005. "Basel, Zürich ziehen davon." Interview by R. Thöny. *SonntagsZeitung*, 10.4.05.

Thierstein, A. 2005. "Raumentwicklung 2." Lecture on spatial development, 6th semester, Chair of Spatial and Territorial Development, TU Munich, at Munich.

Wil Zonneveld

Visioning and Visualizing

Experience from the Northwest European Mega-City Region

Mega-city regions can be conceptualized on different spatial scales, from the regional on up. The northwestern part of the European continent, with its dense pattern of cities and urban regions, has traditionally been regarded as one large, spatially integrated metropolis. Half a century ago professionals developed depoliticized images of the spatial structure of this metropolis, focusing mainly on the pattern of urban areas and open spaces. However, neither these images nor the related pleas for a European Community approach to spatial planning landed on the desks of politicians. From the 1990s onwards the urban and economic structure of Europe has become increasingly important in the political domain. Visual representations of this structure need to break free of the professional domain and become an integral part of every future (European) spatial planning exercise.

I Introduction

Mega-city regions come in different shapes and sizes; that is to say, over the years, planning researchers and practitioners have introduced concepts and images suggesting that mega-city regions exist at various levels ranging from regional to global. This paper discusses visioning and visualizing the urban structure of Northwest Europe. The main focus is on transnational cooperation in spatial planning, in which "transnational" refers to a level beyond cross-border but below the European Union. Efforts to organize policy cooperation at transnational level were launched at the very moment that spatial planners "discovered" the concept of the Northwest European megalopolis in the late 1950s. As images form a key element in spatial planning communication, we are particularly interested in the way urban structures in Northwest Europe have been visualized over the years. Essentially, what sets planning apart from other policy fields is its focus on spatial dispositions and activity patterns – which are best depicted visually. "The most common way in which this is articulated is by means of a plan in the classic sense: a map" (Faludi 1996: 96; see also Zonneveld 2005a). So maps and visualization are the main concern of this paper. Which issues are brought to the fore by visualizations? What were the purposes of the images developed over time? Why does visualization on a transnational scale suddenly become so difficult when cooperation leaves the domain of planning practitioners and enters the domain of politics, as happened at the turn of the century? And finally, how can these difficulties be overcome? These are the four key questions addressed in this paper. We start with some early examples of visualization at the Northwest European level. We then examine some of the highly political images of Europe's territorial structure that appeared in the 1990s. In the next section we move back to the transnational level, focusing on Northwest Europe in particular. In the final section we present some major conclusions and some ideas on transnational visualization.

II Early Images of the Northwest European Mega-City Region

An Emerging National Planning Agenda

About half a century ago, in 1957, Jean Gottmann published his landmark essay "Megalopolis, or the Urbanization of the Northeastern Seaboard." Looking at the east of the United States, Gottmann coined the term "megalopolis" for the Boston-Washington corridor (or BosWash): a continuous stretch of urban and suburban areas, the result of a process of polynuclear urban growth, with a main axis some 600 miles long. Gottmann cheered the megalopolis, saying that it "heralds a new era in the distribution of habitat and economic activities" (Gottmann 1957).

In Europe the question was posed whether the European continent might be hosting an urban structure similar to the BosWash. The answer was positive. At the end of the 1950s Dutch, Belgian and German planners claimed that a megalopolis had emerged on both sides of the North Sea (Klerkx 1998; Zonneveld 2005b). This area was duly christened the *North Sea Board*, echoing Gottmann's Northeastern Seaboard.

Very little data was available to underpin the European megalopolis hypothesis. This is where images came in, simple images borrowed from atlases, as there was nothing else on hand. Figure 1, which appeared in the Dutch government's first ever national report on spatial planning, was taken from a school atlas and shows the population distribution in Europe in 1935(!) (MVB 1960). Dutch planners used one of the simplest drawing techniques to demonstrate the existence of a megalopolis: they added a circle with a radius corresponding to 600 km. Other pictures (see Figure 2), comparing North America and Europe, were borrowed from the 1951 Oxford Atlas and were presented as the ultimate proof that the European continent was also hosting a megalopolis. Such ideas were used to construct a spatial planning agenda at national level and also at the level of the – newly established – European Economic Community.

Figure 1:
A simple method of spatial positioning: putting a country at the center of a large concentration of population.

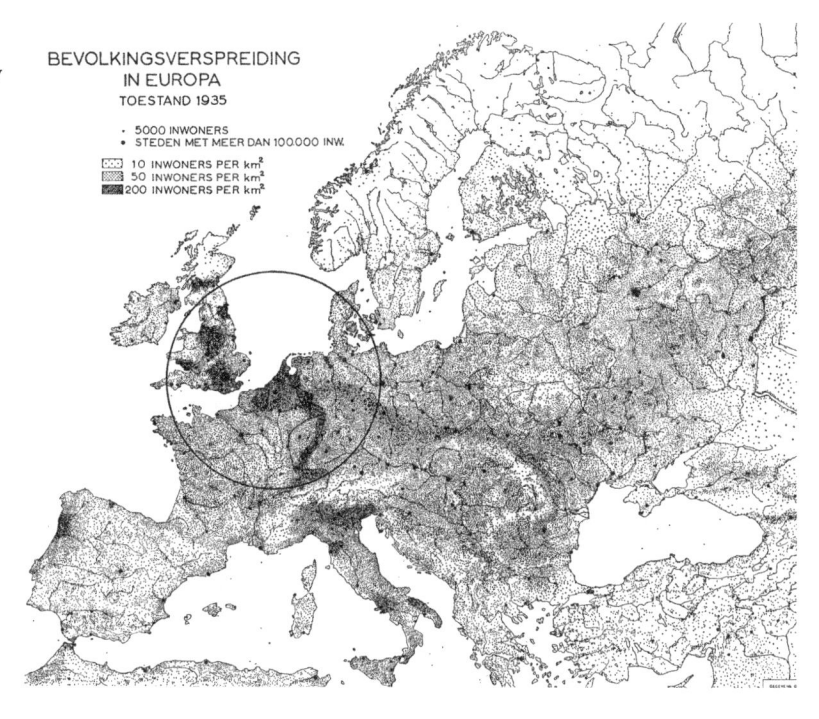

BEVOLKINGSVERSPREIDING IN EUROPA
TOESTAND 1935

- 5000 INWONERS
- STEDEN MET MEER DAN 100.000 INW.

- 10 INWONERS PER km²
- 50 INWONERS PER km²
- 200 INWONERS PER km²

In contrast with the decades to come, the Netherlands did not have a national spatial planning policy in the late 1950s. Figure 1 was used to identify what was later considered the main driving force of spatial development in a country in urgent need of government intervention. If one looks carefully, the point of the compass is on the harbor of Rotterdam. The 1960 report on spatial planning claimed that 150 million people lived inside the circle and that the Netherlands was the major gateway to the European continent. This would necessitate not only the constant expansion of harbor areas but also the development of vast terrains for heavy industry, all in the west of the country. In effect these findings all constituted major arguments for a deconcentrated mega-city region called Randstad, a "planning doctrine" that would characterize Dutch national planning for decades to come (Faludi and Van der Valk 1994).

Other images were used to underpin the arguments. Figure 3 shows an early effort to unravel a kind of Northwest European spatial structure. The various amoeba-type figures represent the Dutch Randstad, the Belgian "ABG city" (Antwerp-Brussels-Gent) and the Rhine-Ruhr, plus some smaller interjacent urban clusters, like the Brabant cities ribbon. All these mega-city regions were given a name – a clear indication that they were perceived as the successors to individual freestanding cities and that spatial planning had to focus on regional and subnational structures instead of separate cities.

Transnational Visioning Mark I

The megalopolis hypothesis and the accompanying images prompted what might be called the first stage of transnational planning in Europe, a period dominated by informal networks of planning professionals who came together at conferences and bilateral meetings. In these years (the second half of the 1950s) crucial negotiations were also taking place, which would eventually culminate in the treaty to establish the European Economic Community. Planners from the Low Countries were especially active and were so worried about the course of urbanization that they

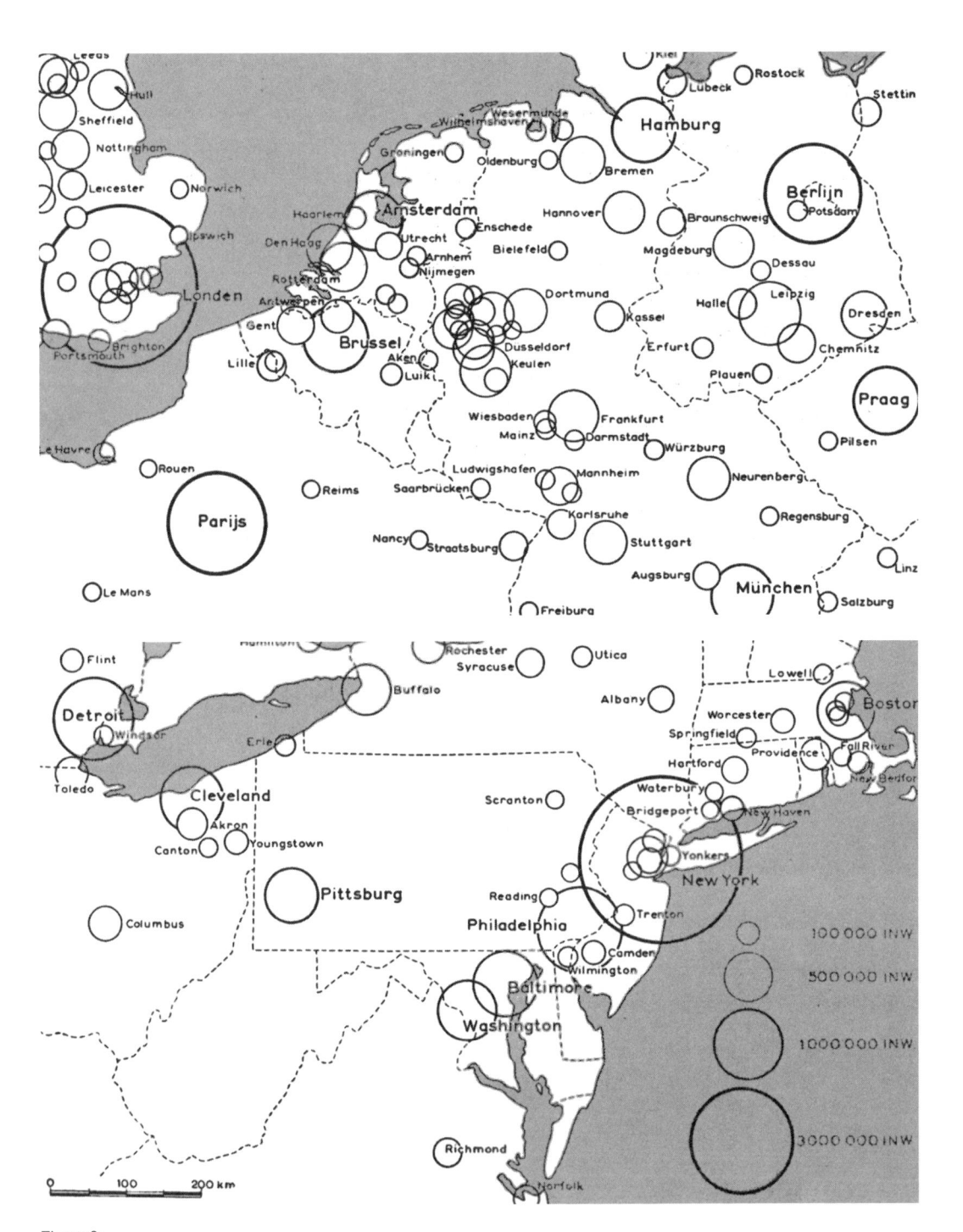

Figure 2:
Images of a megalopolis based on the 1951 Oxford Atlas.

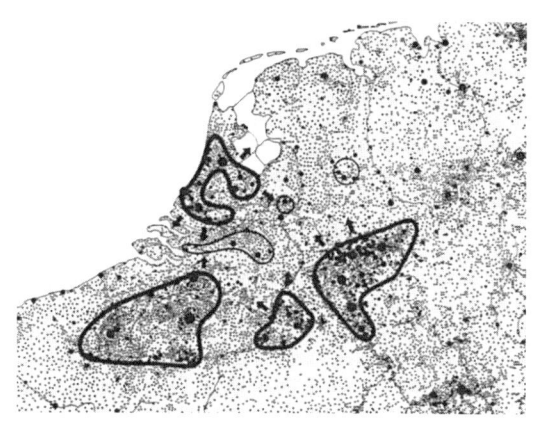

Figure 3:
An early effort to unravel the urban structure of Northwest Europe.

maintained that spatial planning had to become part of the high politics of the emerging EEC. They claimed that the expansion of the steel and coal industries would create vast urban conglomerates, together forming a gigantic European megalopolis which would need a powerful planning program. In simple terms, spatial planning had to enter the EEC treaty because European cooperation would precipitate the emergence of a European megalopolis!

However, these transnational planning professionals seriously overestimated the importance of their agenda. European spatial planning was a nonstarter. Ultimately, in 1959, planners from the Netherlands, Belgium, Luxembourg, France and Germany (mainly North Rhine-Westphalia) resorted to the establishment of an NGO, the (standing) Conference of Regions in Northwest Europe, known by several acronyms depending on the language (CRONWE, CRENWE). Senior government officials attended the regular meetings of CRONWE. The content of the talks trickled down to domestic planning polices, so CRONWE functioned to a certain extent as a kind of proxy for a genuine European planning subject.

Initially, CRONWE focused on industrial and mining regions. As industry was the prime economic sector in these years, and in line with dominant geographic location theories, urban development was seen as the result of a pattern of industrial development. The main concerns of the members of CRONWE related to the *pattern* of urbanization. There was a genuine threat, so they believed, that cities would coalesce and form vast conglomerates. This prospect had to be nipped in the bud by the maintenance of green belts on various scales. This strategy was visualized in a map developed by a German administrator which was published in 1967 (see Figure 4) and which indicates that spatial planners were beginning to develop a visual language of their own and were no longer dependent on the cartographers of atlas publishing houses.

In a way this map might be regarded as the high point in this early stage of transnational thinking on the development of mega-city regions. In the late 1960s and early 1970s, planning agendas were changing and were focusing almost entirely on local and regional issues, such as urban renewal and social integration and transport in urban regions. Trying to understand Europe's spatial structure, and especially the potential formation of a megalopolis, was a matter of concern only to a small fraction of the professional community who attended meetings of CRONWE and Council of Europe working groups. Transnational visioning remained firmly ensconced in the domain of professional practice, research reports and conference proceedings. The maps being produced were about population distribution and the fabric formed by urbanized areas, green belts, large leisure areas and nature reserves. The focus was on morphology and urban structure rather than the pattern of economic development and spatial relations, as was the case in the 1990s and later. The political sensitivities surrounding the latter concerns were much greater than the former. As we shall see below, it proved almost impossible to insert maps on these topics in political documents.

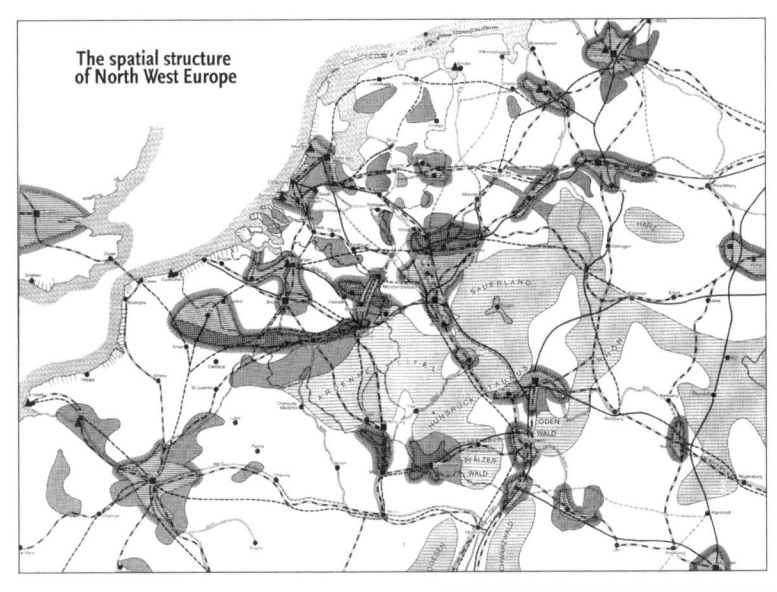

Figure 4:
An intricate visualization of the desired spatial structure of Northwest Europe.

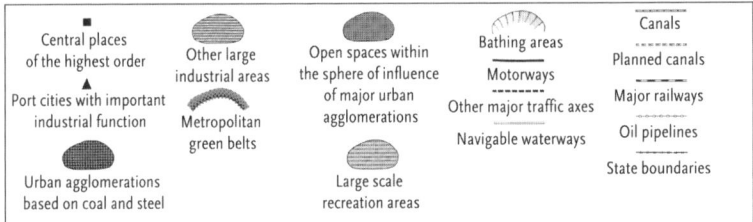

III Politicized Visualizations of Europe

EU-wide discussions on spatial development involving the EU member states and the European Commission started in the late 1980s. The EU/EC was finally prodded into action largely as a result of the course taken by the "European Project," especially the steps leading to a single market. It was widely acknowledged that the single market had the potential to make a strong territorial impact, especially in terms of economic competition between cities and regions. The Dutch and other staunch advocates of a European approach believed that the time had come to mobilize other countries. Representatives of France, Portugal and the Netherlands put their heads together and agreed that the very first EU/EC meeting of spatial planning ministers would be held in Nantes (France) in 1989. After that, such meetings took place regularly and ultimately led to the European Spatial Development Perspective, which was finalized in 1999. While this intergovernmental effort was crystallizing out, the European Commission produced its own series of research reports, known as Europe 2000 and Europe 2000+ (Faludi and Waterhout 2002; CEC 1991; CEC 1994). It was beginning to look as if the European Union/European Commission was taking on the type of planning role, which the planning professionals had envisaged in the late 1950s, even though progress was seriously hampered by the issue of competence (for a detailed account see Faludi and Waterhout 2002).

The problems were caused by serious clashes involving researchers and planners, which had repercussions at the EU level, not only thematically as these discussions were almost exclusively on the spatial pattern of economic development instead of just urban development, but also in terms of spatial images. Visualizations of Europe's spatial-economic structure formed the epicenter of discussions. With hindsight we may conclude that maps became such a sensitive issue over the years that their insertion in political documents became taboo, with the exception of maps considered as evidence-based, such as those produced by ESPON, the European Spatial Planning Observation Network.

The clashes were triggered by a report commissioned by the French agency DATAR (*Délégation à l'aménagement du territoire et à l'action régionale*).[1] This is the well-known report by a research group headed by the geographer Roger Brunet, classifying European cities on the basis of a large set of indicators (Brunet 1989). The report would probably have been more or less forgotten nowadays if it had not contained a synthesis map in its final pages (Figure 5). Though this map was presented as being firmly based on evidence, it turned out to be a cartographic *deus ex machina*.[2] Brunet et al. position Paris outside the banana-shaped European economic core region. As we know from Lipietz (1995), the map was primarily produced for domestic reasons, to interfere in the national policy debate on the priority to be accorded to the competitive position of the Paris capital region and on whether central government investments and subsidies should be shifted from the regions to Île de France (Lipietz 1995).

The map was readily picked up in a wider, European debate on what was in fact the very same topic, the spatial pattern of economic development across Europe and the question whether to bet on the strong horses or to start from the potential of all cities and regions. The ultimate visual expression of the latter stance is the well-known image of the bunch of grapes in a publication by Kunzmann and Wegener (1991) – in fact, not a map but a cartoon (see Figure 6) (Kunzmann and Wegener 1991). Published somewhat later and also destined for some measure of fame – but no less cartoon-like – was the image known as the "red octopus," which visualizes the developmental expansion along trans-European transport and ICT networks towards the north, south and east of the enlarged EU (Stockholm–Copenhagen–Helsinki, Ruhr–Hanover–Berlin–Poznan–Warsaw, Prague–Vienna–Budapest) (Van der Meer 1998).

The 1999 European Spatial Development Perspective presents yet another image of the core of Europe, this time with the inclusion of the French capital region. Again a metaphor is used, although this time it is not organic (banana, grapes, octopus), but neutral and geometric, viz., the pentagon defined by the metropolises of London, Paris, Milan, Munich and Hamburg. This pentagon could have been depicted very easily, but obviously a spatial image would have emphasized a core-periphery division of the EU, so the makers of the ESDP refrained from using it (CSD 1999). Instead, a verbal alternative was proposed called polycentricity. Besides the pentagon, other areas had to become economic core regions, able to compete at European and global levels. This policy scenario was not visualized either, although in a later stage

TISSUS DE VILLES

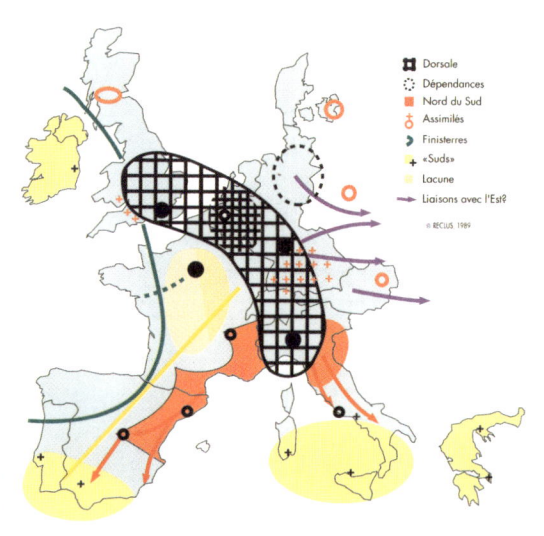

Figure 5:
A highly manipulative image of Europe's spatial pattern of economic development.

Figure 6:
The cartoon-like representation of an alternative for economic concentration.

(see Figure 7) a proposal was mooted by the Conference of Peripheral Maritime Regions of Europe (CPMR 2002).

Polycentricity is, in fact, a neat political term for the bunch of grapes. Nevertheless, the bunch of grapes was the most powerful metaphor and spatial image of the 1990s. No wonder one of its makers contends that visualization can be extremely powerful and help to overcome language barriers (Kunzmann 1996). Kunzmann (1993) classifies images like the bunch of grapes as geodesign, a type of cartographic representation which combines minimum information with maximum effect (Kunzmann 1993). This explains why geodesign maps are used as a rhetorical device in spatial planning discussions. However, the associations conjured up by such maps (or any map for that matter) cannot be controlled by their advocates. Some even think that they are much too powerful, that they lead too much to hegemonic discourse by pushing aside alternative visions and concepts. This is why map-making sometimes meets with opposition (Van Eeten and Roe 2000).

The makers of the ESDP clearly understood such messages (Zonneveld 2000; Dühr 2003, 2007). The ESDP contains only analytical maps, meant to represent the current situation, devoid of predictions, let alone images of a desired situation. As we shall see below, the same happened in nearly all cases of transnational visioning produced in the wake of the ESDP. Apparently, the makers of these documents did not endorse the viewpoint that visualization is an intrinsic part of spatial planning.

Clearly there are huge differences between this state of affairs and the course of events traced in the previous section. The discussion arena of the 1990s is densely packed with "stakeholders," researchers and planners. The debate also became pan-European or at least pan-EU and attention shifted from the low politics of land use and urban development, generally considered the exclusive domain of national and regional governments, to the high politics of economic development and its territorial distribution. It is against this background that the efforts to envision Northwest Europe's spatial structure can be understood.

IV Transnational Visioning Mark II

Megalopolis Revisited: the "CCC Area"

As explained above, the European Commission carried out several studies in the early 1990s. These formed the building blocks for a possible future development perspective for the European territory, as they were formally grounded on Article 10 of the European Regional Development Fund regulation (although it turned out later that this article did not suffice as a basis for a development perspective by the Commission; see Faludi & Waterhout 2002: 32). Europe 2000+, the second report published by the Commission, was written partly on the basis of a range of transnational studies. For this, the EU territory was carved up like a jigsaw puzzle (CEC 1994).

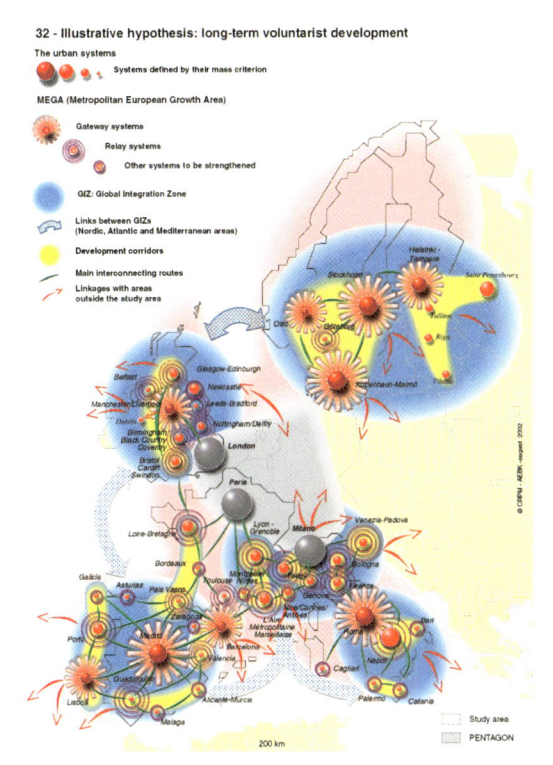

Figure 7:
An image of what polycentric economic development could look like.

One of the study areas was Central and Capital Cities (CCC), a compact region formed by the southeast of England, the southern part of the Netherlands, Belgium, Luxembourg, and parts of northern France and Germany – in fact almost exactly the same mega-city region as studied by CRONWE about three or four decades earlier and hence suggesting that we are dealing with some sort of "natural" region with common characteristics like a dense pattern of cities and a high degree of internal integration.[3] The CCC study culminated in two scenarios, i.e., a "trend" scenario and a "policy" scenario. In both cases a key role was played by visualization; the main issues are summarized cartographically (CEC 1996).

In view of the developments described above, it will come as no surprise that neither of these scenarios was about the pattern of urbanization.

The CCC study, like all other transnational studies, is dominated by the issue of the territorial distribution of economic development. The key spatial concept of the CCC study is the Euro-corridor. According to the authors, economic development is concentrated along the main infrastructure traversing the CCC area. Economically some cities and urban regions perform far better than others; the latter are not part of the system of Euro-corridors. Spatial trends can make no fundamental changes to this pattern. The challenge is therefore to create various new Euro-corridors so that all city regions can be fully integrated in the CCC economy. It is a matter of dealing properly with the strengths and weaknesses of the respective city regions and of improving their connectivity.

The end result is a map (Figure 8), which is far more schematic and symbolic than the maps of a few decades earlier. This map tries to capture the *position* of city regions and their relations. Cities and city regions are no longer defined with sharp contours. Their immediate sphere of influence is depicted with more or less fuzzy boundaries. The relational aspect is visualized schematically through faint lines symbolizing the corridors. Figure 8 also shows the world outside the CCC area as a blank space, although it is suggested that some of the Euro-corridors stretch beyond the perimeters. All the same, the impression conveyed by Figure 8 is that the CCC area is a system of islands, especially when one looks at the way the southeast of England is depicted. The objectives of the study and the way the results were discussed obviously encouraged an inward-looking attitude. The imaging and visualization of the spatial structure of the CCC areas were only partial, not just because the pattern of economic development dominated the discussion but also because spatial positioning did not go beyond the confines of the CCC area. Following on from Williams (1996), we can describe positioning as the capacity to conceptualize or think about one's location or situation within the spatial structure of Europe as a whole (Williams 1996: 97). The ability to do this has to be learned; planners and politicians are, on the whole, not used to it. On the one

Map. 9.2   Development possibilities

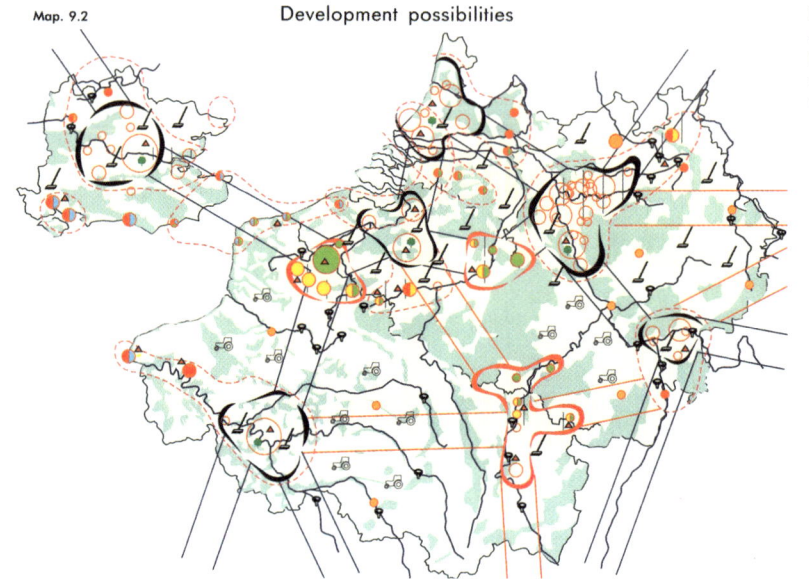

Figure 8:
An abstract image of the desired spatial structure of the Central and Capital Cities area.

hand, Figure 8 signifies a huge leap forward as it prompts people to consider the position of cities and regions on a transnational scale. On the other hand, the known world more or less ends at the margins of the study area.

Another conclusion is that imaging the effects of policy only produced one map, suggesting not only that there was a consensus on the future of the CCC area but also that: 1) policy could be effective in creating an integrated system of Eurocorridors; and 2) policy could lead only to one "future." That said, the CCC report presents the last effort in planning history so far, to analyze the spatial structure of the Northwest European mega-city region or megalopolis. Although certain parts of the CCC underperform economically, the entire area obviously has the characteristics of a European core region. In terms of territorial development the prime concern of the European Commission, the initiator of the CCC report, is territorial cohesion, i.e., the realization of comparable levels of economic development across the EU. So, there is no real interest in the fate and fortune of a dominant core region like this. In INTERREG the CCC was absorbed in a far wider area, its name becoming extinct, although every now and then efforts are undertaken to put it back on the map, albeit with different names, as we shall see below.

INTERREG Visioning

At a very early stage it was acknowledged in the European Community that national borders have negative consequences for the directly adjoining areas. This is exemplified by the Community Initiative INTERREG, which was set up in 1990 to stimulate cross-border cooperation. Gradually a realization grew that the geographic scope of this program needed to be widened to include a transnational level, encompassing major parts of groups of countries. In 1996 this resulted in a new "panel" in the INTERREG II program and explains the designation IIC. The INTERREG IIC Guidelines published in 1996 use the division of Europe into transnational areas as a starting point. The Commission was opting for new patterns of governance based on cooperation. The transnational studies of a few years earlier were meant to contribute to this. It was hoped that dividing Europe in a way which seldom corresponded with national borders would lead to a new approach to the framing of policy issues and strategies.

Participants in most INTERREG IIC projects were expected to cooperate at a practical level and collectively learn to realize policy innovations. Part of the INTERREG IIC strategy was to continue the search for new conceptual frames for space and territory. This is why the European Commission attached such importance to vision-making, in particular "…to encourage new ways of thinking about spatial prospects which are not limited by national boundaries and to stimulate a bottom-up approach to the development of links between regions" (CEC 1994: 69). The Commission did not hand out terms of reference for what constitutes a "vision." As INTERREG is a community initiative, a (firm) directive was not deemed appropriate. As there was no common and explicit understanding of "vision" or "visioning," one could justifiably ask whether the INTERREG spatial visions which have been produced are genuine visions, and what is the position on visualization.

Shipley and Newkirk (1998, 1999) observe a steady rise in the use of visions and visioning in politics through the 1980s and 1990s (Shipley and Newkirk 1998, 1999). They also claim that the term "vision" is often used in a misleading way. It should be left with its classic and literal connotations, i.e., the act or faculty of seeing (Shipley and Newkirk 1999: 590). In reality, "vision" is used in a wide range of policy documents and processes with reference to, among others, goal-setting and the identification of values and decision criteria (Shipley and Newkirk 1999: 589). If this is the case, then why not say so, they ask rhetorically. In the eyes of Shipley and Newkirk this practice leads to a watering-down of the concepts of vision and vision-making. This is exactly what happened during the transnational visioning exercises in INTERREG IIC areas.

Visioning in the context of INTERREG was only a partial response to the Commission's call for spatial visions. For, a vision was produced for only three of the seven transnational cooperation areas, with the vision-making processes running more or less parallel, beginning in 1998 and ending in the first half of 2000. Two of these three visions focused on the northwest of Europe, i.e., NorVision, the spatial vision for the North Sea Region (NorVision Spatial Vision Working Group, 2000) and the Spatial Vision for the Northwest Metropolitan Area (NWMA Spatial Vision Group, 2000).[4] Both were developed in a similar way, drafted by small groups of experts, although NorVision was the subject of wider consultation during the vision process (Zonneveld 2005a, 2005c; Stumm and Robert 2006). Only the NWMA Spatial Vision meets Shipley and Newkirk's criteria as it alone contains spatial images.[5]

Interestingly, the groups that made NorVision and the NWMA Spatial Vision differed widely in their perception of a vision. According to the makers of NorVision, any sort of visualization involving the use of maps to illustrate a desired spatial structure implies the compilation of a comprehensive (master) plan. So they opted for a purely verbal interpretation for the presentation of policy through what is called "verbal visionary pictures" – surely an oxymoron (Thornaes 2000: 61). The maps in NorVision are all descriptive, inventory maps. Thus NorVision is a kind of framing exercise without images. Following on from Nadin (2002a), the term "vision" is obviously a "misnomer" in this case (Nadin 2002a).

The makers of the NWMA vision seem to have been less afraid of map-making, as the centerpiece of this document is a so-called Vision Diagram (see Figure 9). However, its very title reflects the delicate nature of mapping exercises since "vision" implies the policy-driven imaging of space, while "diagram" refers to a more neutral, analytical and descriptive unfolding of spatial characteristics.

The Vision Diagram is, according to Nadin, not a master plan but an agenda. It was hoped that it would begin "…a process of establishing a common spatial development 'identity' for Northwest Europe" (Nadin 2002b: 33), and stimulate thinking about the international positioning of cities and regions (Nadin 2002b: 35). The Vision Diagram depicts the spatial structure of Northwest Europe as a system of networks and nodes. Worthy of note are the indication of numerous corridors and axes which should be strengthened and the designation of various polycentric urban regions as "counterweight global gateways and economic

A VISION FOR NORTH WEST EUROPE
An agenda for a sustainable and balanced development

Open Zone — Extensive high quality natural environments, threats from depopulation, decline and intense tourism in certain locations. Poor links to urban services. Priorities are to strengthen role of regional towns, links with strategic centres, maintain low environmental pressures and build on indigenous potential.

Island Zone — Generally urbanised and industrial areas with pressure on surrounding natural enviroments. Important urban centres have capacity for expansion but with strong barriers and relatively weak links to global cities and gateways. Priority to strengthen global functions and corridors/links with central zone.

Central Zone — Global powerhouse Extreme environmental pressures from agriculture and traffic exceeding capacities of natural systems. Open spaces and accessible rural areas threatened. Water management issues are critical, especially the Rhine-Scheldt-Meuse. Priorities to maintain competitiveness of global cities and internal and external accessibility, whilst containing physical growth and relieving pressure on environment.

Inland Zone — Diverse landscapes in a predominantly rural area with threats of depopulation and important urban centres. Major opportunities to develop recreation and cultural assets, and to play a role in improved connections to the east and south.

Cooperation zones.

- Inland Zone
- Central Zone
- Open Zone
- Island Zone

- **Global cities and gateways** cities of major economic importance for north-west Europe/rest of the world with high level of access to and from them
- **Strategic polycentric areas** cluster of cities, high level of economic activity, key role in inward investment to north-west Europe
- **Strategic centres** monocentric, high level economic activity, key national/regional role and focus for inward investment
- Eurocorridors.
- Corridors/transport axes to be strengthened.
- Communication bottlenecks.
- Enhanced external connections.
- Counterweight global gateways and economic centres.

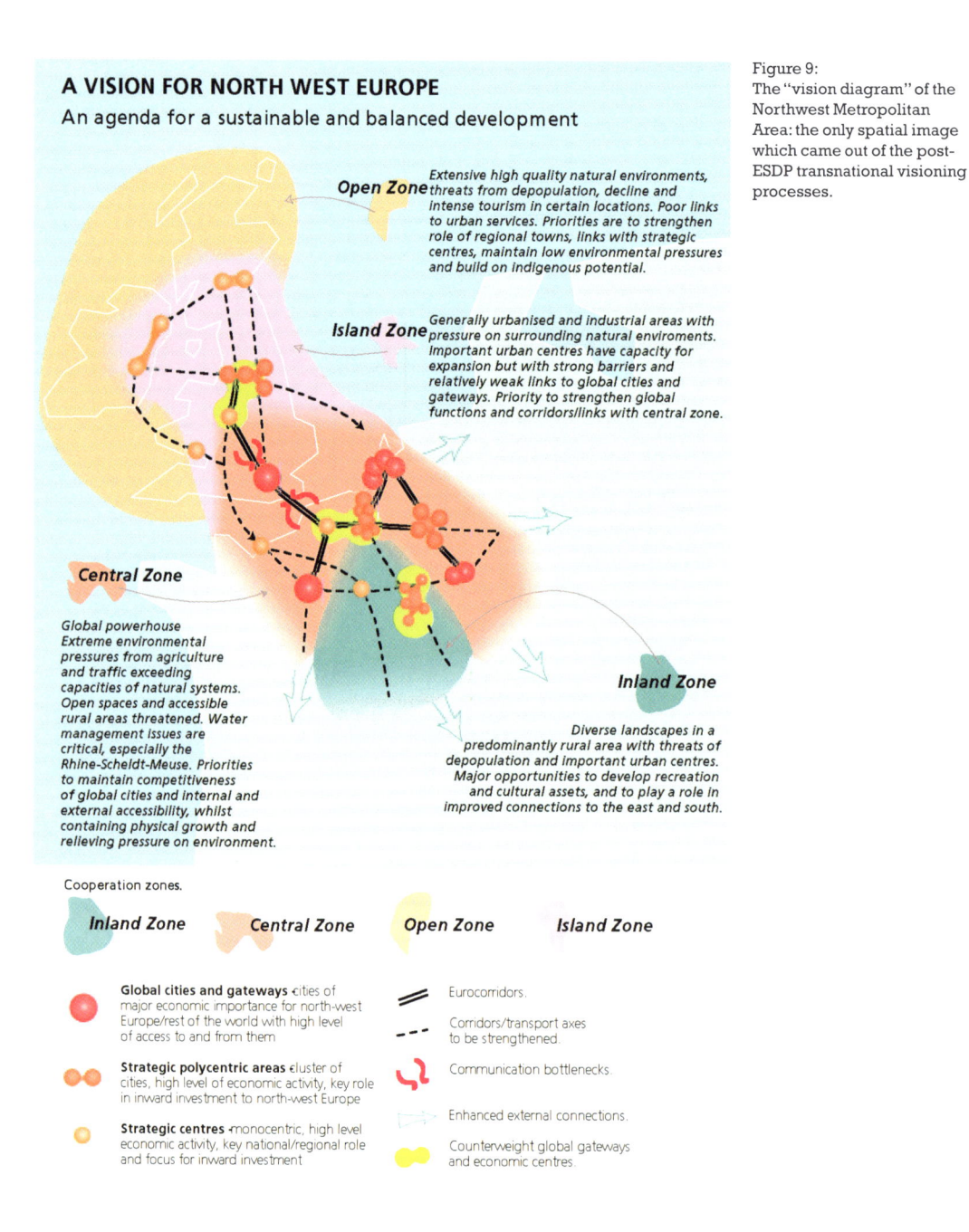

Figure 9:
The "vision diagram" of the Northwest Metropolitan Area: the only spatial image which came out of the post-ESDP transnational visioning processes.

centers" – a clear echo of the CCC study. Very much like the CCC study, a key assumption is that adequate infrastructure is a precondition for economic development. The same goes for geographical position, i.e., cities and city regions that have a central position in Europe or Northwest Europe have more potential than more remote areas, such as central Scotland. Essentially, the counter-strategy entails altering the time-space continuum of Northwest Europe by improving the connections between peripheral areas and the so-called Central Zone.

The consultation phase, which started after the publication of the first draft, raised some important considerations in terms of the vision process and its main outcome, the Vision Diagram. To start with the former, the lack of consultation and cooperation with a wider range of interests was seen as a drawback by most of the respondents (NWMA Spatial Vision Group 2001: 7). Hence, in order to take proper account of issues of transnational relevance, the Vision Document needs to take on board the wide range of regional interests and the use of alternative scenarios to stimulate a visionary approach to the Vision exercise. Basically, this means that the Vision cannot be confined to the presentation of just one image of a desired spatial structure. In fact, many commentators on the Vision Diagram came to this conclusion, thereby suggesting that the vision process had descended into a kind of hegemonic discourse. Some argued that most of the attention focused on the metropolitan areas of the central zone (NWMA Spatial Vision Group 2001: 15), while others stated that the urban hierarchy presented in the Vision relied too heavily on financial and economic decision-making powers, thus understating the international position of some cities (NWMA Spatial Vision Group 2001: 10). The focus on the economic potential of cities and regions has marginalized the importance of the natural and cultural heritage of Northwest Europe (NWMA Spatial Vision Group 2001: 12).

During the process leading up to the Vision Diagram other interpretations of the NWMA spatial structure were, however, visualized. Figure 10 presents two striking examples, part of a set of four maps. Although the key to these maps is missing, the logic can be deduced from the imagery. The image on the right presents the northwest of Europe as an area of waterflows, interconnected landscapes, green belts and major ecological relationships. The image on the right seems to capture the cultural significance of major landscape units. Images like these were not taken on board in the final NWMA spatial vision, the prime reasons being that the empirical base was too feeble and that there was not enough time or money left to improve the images in these respects (Wiersma 2004).

Figure 11 shows an image that comes closer to the final printed Vision Diagram. Its spatial language is somewhat sketchy and rough compared with the sleek language of the definitive version. There is a striking difference between the two maps in terms of content, meaning and connotations. In the sketch the outermost zone to the northwest, west, southwest and southeast is portrayed in bright green and bold pencilled lines. It is known from other vision trajectories, such as the Benelux Structural Outline from the late 1990s, that there is often an aversion to denoting areas as just "green," especially if the discourse is dominated by socio-economic issues (see Zonneveld 2005a). "Green" is associated with a green desert. Not many politicians and government administrators are likely to accept that the prime characteristic of "their" area is its openness, its emptiness, its nothingness. The indication chosen in the diagram is "open zone," with the emphasis on issues such as depopulation, decline and poor links to urban services and not just the splendid characteristics that urban dwellers from the highly congested "central zone" are seeking in areas like Scotland and the west of Ireland.

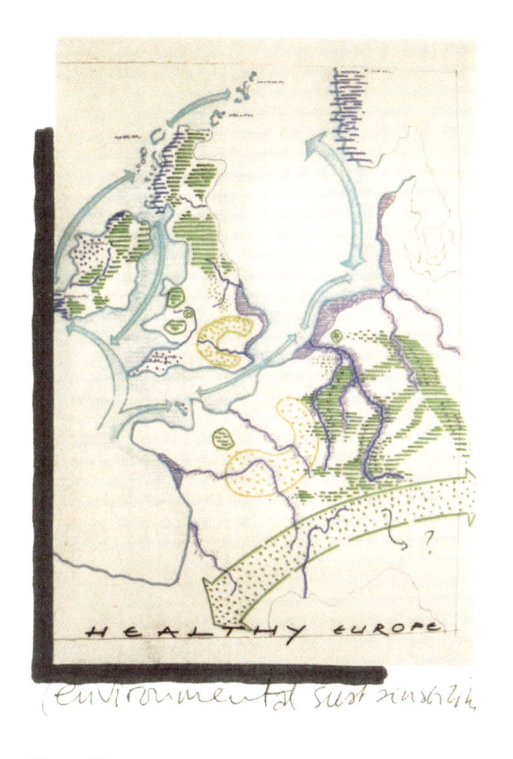

Figure 10:
Images of the structure of the Northwest Metropolitan Area which did not reach the final document.

V Conclusion: Visioning without Visualization?

In this paper we have discussed the spatial planning discourse on Northwest Europe – still Europe's only megalopolitan area as Jean Gottmann defines the concept. We have shown that, over the years, planners and researchers have produced maps and images of the spatial structure of this mega-city region and that the idea of a European mega-city region on such a grand scale has been politically controversial because its very existence is sometimes envisaged as a threat to European territorial cohesion. Nevertheless, up to the present day, there are staunch advocates of the concept of a Northwest European mega-city region, using concepts like *UNICITY* (Boelens 2005), *Interconnected Metropolis* (Modder 2004), *Urban Delta* (Lambregts and Zonneveld 2003) and *Eurodelta* (RV&W 2005).

As the boundaries of the Northwest European mega-city region are fuzzy, not all conceptualizations refer to exactly the same area. On the whole, the "delta" concepts are about mainland Europe and include the Randstad, the Flemish Diamond and the Rhine-Ruhr region. Other concepts include the southeast of England and the "development corridors" stretching in more or less every direction. This is where visualization comes in, i.e., to unravel an area's spatial structure and its relations with the outside world and to determine whether it is legitimate to speak of a Northwest European mega-city region. And, if so, for which regions and for whom?

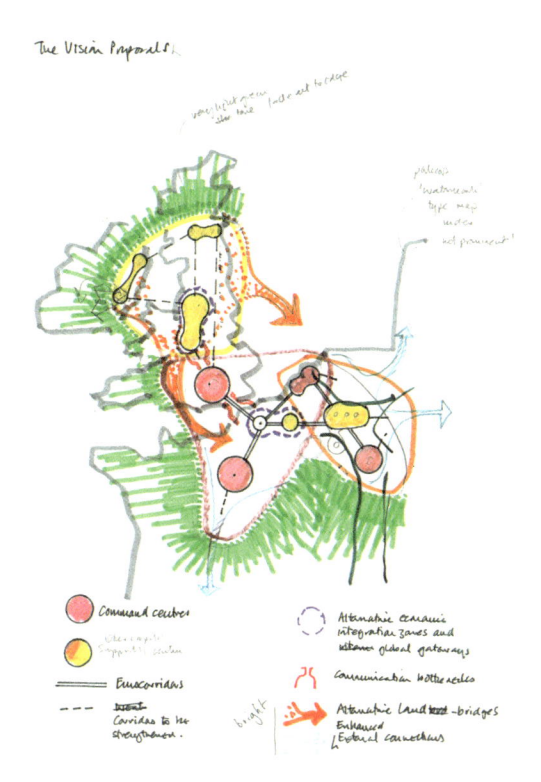

Figure 11:
A draft version of the NWMA Vision Diagram.

The future of visualising the Northwest European mega-city region still looks rather bleak. There seems to be a prevailing view that visualizing space and territory at the transnational level can derail political debates (Stumm and Robert 2006). Indeed, the making of spatial visions, perspectives and outlines (more or less equivalent terms given the way they have been used) has been surrounded by controversies in cases where the making of maps on the future situation has been a central issue (see, for instance, Dühr 2007 on the European Spatial Development Perspective and Zonneveld 2005a on the 1996 Benelux Structural Outline).

In the North Sea Region and Northwest Europe (since 2000 the designation of an enlarged NWMA) new visioning processes have been started along more pragmatic lines. The goal is not to develop images of space and territory but to identify and explore priority themes for future transnational cooperation (Davoudi et al. 2006). Across Europe this seems to be the dominant view on the purpose of visioning at the transnational level.[6] Although this pragmatic approach is understandable in view of the often lengthy discussions on visualization and the uncertain outcome, the term "vision" does not seem appropriate. We believe that spatial visioning without any sort of visualization is a *contradictio in terminis* and that spatial planning should reserve the term "vision" for documents that actually contain visualizations of space and territory, and that other documents should be differently designated, for instance, as a "strategy" or a "program." Spatial planning is about structure, relationships and position. These can, of course, be discussed verbally but some key issues cannot be addressed properly without some sort of visualization.

We have seen that visioning at the transnational level does not automatically produce visualizations of the internal spatial structure and relationships of an area and its external position. Of all the transnational spatial visions produced around the turn of the century only the so-called Northwest Metropolitan Area contains a visualization of the future outlook of the territory. As this vision was prepared by a small group of professionals, its political and mental appropriation and application by others was rather limited – in fact it was largely absent (Zonneveld 2005c; see also Stumm and Robert 2006). All the same, the NWMA spatial vision is an interesting case, as its makers have tried to capture the meaning of spatial structure in words as well as in images.

The repertoire of visualization methods is large. This book contains an impressive range of techniques. At transnational and European levels, maps are a key method of visualization. They have a relationship with a concrete space or area and can convey rather complicated issues. Icons and diagrams can be used to illustrate policy objectives, as in the case of the 1999 European Spatial Development Perspective, arguably the mother of all transnational visions. But such images are devoid of direct links to concrete spaces and areas and are therefore only partially useful for unraveling spatial structure and relationships.

This brings us to the thorny question of how to develop transnational spatial images and visualizations. As pragmatism appears to have the upper hand in current European and transnational discussions, there does not seem to be much room for visualization. On the other hand, many participants in transnational cooperation projects do try to understand the characteristics of their area on a higher scale. We therefore believe that at least a latent need exists for visualization. It is our considered opinion that future programs on transnational cooperation (from 2007 onwards as part of the new third objective of the EU structure funds) should allocate a small budget to enable a better understanding of the spatial structure and the external position of the area in question and the forces that influence them. This can only work if there is a loose coupling or no coupling at all with operational decisions on, for example, the allocation of budgets to project proposals, because, of all its connotations, such an exercise should not be referred to as developing a "vision." A handy term might be "territorial state," as in "The Territorial State and Perspectives of the European Union," a document that lays the foundations for the so-called "Territorial Agenda," to be decided by the EU ministers responsible for territorial development in Spring 2007 (see Faludi and Waterhout 2005; Waterhout and Faludi forthcoming). This document will draw heavily on the findings of the ESPON research program. The same could be done when preparing a territorial state for a transnational area like Northwest Europe.[7]

In an ideal world the preparation of a territorial state would precede the implementation of transnational cooperation programs. This cannot happen since the future programs will probably start in 2007. As we believe that there should be a loose coupling with operational decision-making, this does not have to be a bad thing. As projects will be started and carried out over a period of seven years, each new-style visioning process has the potential to support and enrich ongoing projects, providing it is open. When undisturbed by policy-makers and decision-makers, small groups of researchers and designers will certainly be very creative in developing images of a transnational area. The question is whether this will have any impact. Visioning and visualization must break out of the professional realm and enter the mindsets of others in order to become and remain relevant.

If the visualization exercises sketched above could not, for one reason or another, be carried out in the context of the future transnational cooperation programs there are still other possibilities. The ESPON 2013 program could play a role. The new research program will be more directly linked to ongoing policy discussions than the current program. Adding a transnational "panel" would support European territorial cooperation enormously. Another possibility is for a country or a region to take the lead. For example, in the past, the Dutch spatial planning agency conducted a vision exercise called "Perspectives in Europe" and discussed the outcome with representatives from other countries (NSPA 1991). The process fizzled out mainly because it was a one-agency job. However, a collective exercise by the Netherlands Institute for Spatial Research (RPB), the German *Bundesamt für Bauwesen und Raumordnung* (BBR) and the French *Délégation interministérielle à l'aménagement et à la compétitivité des territoires* (DIACT) could probably have a considerable impact. This would also make sense from another perspective. The transnational cooperation area of Northwest Europe (NWE) is so large that it forms a kind of little Europe on its own. A focus on subareas showing a certain degree of integration and communality in spatial planning issues would be a legitimate approach. The CRONWE has disappeared and has not been replaced by anything else. A new platform for the Northwest European mega-city region could bring about the sort of visioning and visualizations that are needed to enrich policy-making.

Acknowledgements

The author wishes to acknowledge the financial assistance of the Dutch government through the Habiforum Innovative Land Use Program and Delft University of Technology through the Delft Center for Sustainable Urban Areas.

Notes

[1] In 2005 DATAR was replaced by a new agency: DIACT (Délégation interministérielle à l'aménagement et à la compétitivité des territoires). Compared with DATAR the emphasis is less on regional economic development and more on the competitiveness of the country as a whole (www.diact.gouv.fr).

[2] The 2003 update of this study does not contain such a synthesis map (Rozenblat and Cicille 2003)!

[3] The original CRONWE area did not include (parts of) England. As soon as Great Britain became a member of the Economic Community the CRONWE area was extended to include the southeast.

[4] VISION PLANET was the third vision involving CADSES: Central European, Adriatic, Danube and South Eastern European Space. In a later stage – September 2003 until mid-2005 – a "spatial development perspective" for the Atlantic Space was also drawn up (Stumm and Robert 2006).

[5] The spatial vision for CADSES is not a spatial vision according to the criteria used by Shipley and Newkirk.

[6] This perception of spatial visions emerged during discussions at the ESPON-INTERACT seminar on spatial visions and scenarios on 27–28 March 2006, Milan, attended by participants in INTERREG projects from all parts of Europe.

[7] Under the new third objective of the structure funds, the division of Europe in transnational cooperation areas will not change, with the exception of CADSES ("Central European Adriatic Danubian South-Eastern European Space"), which will be divided into two areas ("Central Europe" and "Southeast European Space").

References

Boelens, L. 2005. *Van planologie naar fluviologie? Queeste naar een nieuwe benadering van de ruimtelijke ordening* [From "planology" to "fluviology"; the quest for a new approach towards spatial planning]. Inaugural speech, University of Utrecht. Utrecht: Universiteit Utrecht.

Brunet, R. 1989. *Les Villes "Europeennes"*; Rapport pour la DATAR: Délégation à l'aménagement du territoire et à l'action régionale. Paris: La Documentation Française.

CEC, Commission of the European Communities. 1991. *Europe 2000: Outlook for the Development of the Community's Territory*. Luxembourg: Office for Official Publications of the European Communities.

CEC, Commission of the European Communities. 1994. Europe 2000: *Cooperation for European Territorial Development*. Luxembourg: Office for Official Publications of the European Communities.

CEC, Commission of the European Communities; Directorate General XVI. 1996. *The Prospective Development of the Central and Capital Cities and Regions, Regional Development Studies* No. 22. Luxembourg: Office for Official Publications of the European Communities.

CPMR, Conference of Peripheral Maritime Regions of Europe; Peripheries Forward Studies Unit. 2002. *Study on the Construction of a Polycentric and Balanced Development Model for the European Territory*. Rennes: CPMR.

CSD, Committee for Spatial Development. 1999. *European Spatial Development Perspective: Towards Balanced and Sustainable Development of the Territory of the EU*. Luxembourg: Office for Official Publications of the European Communities.

Davoudi, S., P. Ellison and N. Evans. 2006. *Study no.4: Synthesis Report Towards a Strategic Framework for Action*. Lille/Leeds: INTERREG IIIB Secretariat North-West Europe/Leeds Metropolitan University.

Dühr, S. 2003. "Illustrating Spatial Policies in Europe." *European Planning Studies* 11 (8): 929-948.

Dühr, S. 2007. *The Visual Language of Spatial Planning. Exploring Cartographic Representations for Spatial Planning in Europe, RTPI Library Series*. Abingdon, Oxon: Routledge.

Eeten, M. van and E. Roe. 2000. "When Fiction Conveys Truth and Authority: The Netherlands Green Heart Planning Controversy." *Journal of the American Planning Association* 66 (1): 58-67.

Faludi, A. 1996. "Framing with Images." *Environment and Planning B: Planning and Design* 23: 93-108.

Faludi, A. and A. van der Valk. 1994. *Rule and Order: Dutch Planning Doctrine in the Twentieth Century*. Dordrecht / Boston / London: Kluwer Academic Publishers.

Faludi, A. and B. Waterhout. 2002. *The Making of the European Spatial Development Perspective; No Masterplan. The RTPI Library Series* No. 02. London: Routledge.

Faludi, A., and B. Waterhout. 2005. "The Usual Suspects: The Rotterdam EU Informal Ministerial Meeting on Territorial Cohesion." *TESG, Tijdschrift voor Economische en Sociale Geografie* 96 (3): 338-342.

Gottmann, J. 1957. "Megalopolis, or the Urbanization of the Northeastern Seaboard." *Economic Geograph* 33: 189-200.

Klerkx, E. 1998. *Plannen met Europa; Nederlandse pleidooien voor een bovennationaal ruimtelijk beleid* [Planning with Europe; Dutch pleas for transnational spatial planning], Master thesis, University of Nijmegen.

Kunzmann, K.R. 1993. "Geodesign: Chance oder Gefahr?" *Informationen zur Raumentwicklung* 7: 389-396.

Kunzmann, K.R. 1996. "Euro-Megalopolis or Themepark Europe? Scenarios for European Spatial Development." *International Planning Studies* 1 (2): 143-163.

Kunzmann, K.R. and M. Wegener. 1991. "The Pattern of Urbanization in Europe." *Ekistics* 350 (September/October): 282-291.

Lambregts, B. and W. Zonneveld. 2003. *Polynuclear Urban Regions and the Transnational Dimension of Spatial Planning; Proposals for Multi-Scalar Planning in North West Europe, Housing and Urban Policy Studies* 26. Delft: Delft University Press.

Ley, N. 1967. "Die Zukunft der Raumordnung in Nordwesteuropa." *Wegwijzers naar een goed bewoonbaar Nederland* [Signposts to a more liveable Holland], Beschouwingen aangeboden aan Mr. J. Vink bij zijn afscheid als directeur-generaal van de Rijksplanologische Dienst. Alphen aan den Rijn: N. Samsom nv: 145-157.

Lipietz, A. 1995. "Avoiding Megapolization: The Battle of Ile-de-France." *European Planning Studies* 3 (2): 143-154.

Meer, L. van der. 1998. "Red Octopus." *A New Perspective for European Spatial Development Policies*, edited by W. Blaas. Aldershot: Ashgate: 9-26.

Modder, J. 2004. "Europa, zo ver weg ... Over de noodzaak van een geschakelde metropool in Noordwest-Europa." [Europe, so far away ...; About the need for a linked metropolis in northwest Europe] *Stedebouw & Ruimtelijke Ordening* (Supplement 2004/5 "Europa en ruimtelijke ontwikkeling."): 41-44.

MVB, Ministerie van Volkshuisvesting en Bouwnijverheid. 1960. *Nota inzake de ruimtelijke ordening in Nederland* [Report on spatial planning in the Netherlands]. Den Haag: Staatsuitgeverij.

Nadin, V. 2002a. "Visions and Visioning in European Spatial Planning." *European Spatial Planning*, edited by A. Faludi. Cambridge Mass.: Lincoln Institute of Land Policy: 121-137.

Nadin, V. 2002b. "Transnational Spatial Development and Planning. Experience from the Spatial Vision for North West Europe." *Facing ESPON. Nordregio Report 2002 (1)*, edited by C. Bengs. 25-40.

Norvision Spatial Vision Working Group. 2000. *NorVision: A Spatial Perspective for the North Sea Region*. Vision Working Group with representatives from spatial planning offices from the participating countries and regions, prepared by PLANCO Consulting GmbH, Essen.

NSPA, National Spatial Planning Agency. 1991. *Perspectives in Europe*. The Hague: National Spatial Planning Agency.

NWMA Spatial Vision Group. 2000. *A Spatial Vision for North-West Europe: Building Cooperation*. The Hague: Ministry of Housing, Spatial Planning and the Environment of the Netherlands.

NWMA Spatial Vision Group. 2001. *Spatial Vision: Consultation Report on the Vision Document*. Summary of responses prepared by the University of the West of England in consultation with the Lead Partner. The Hague: The Ministry of Housing, Spatial Planning and the Environment of the Netherlands.

Rozenblat, C. and P. Cicille. 2003. *Les Villes Européennes; Analyse Comparative*. Paris: La Documentation Française.

RNP, Rijksdienst voor het National Plan. 1962. *Jaarverslag 1961* [Annual Report 1961]. Den Haag: Staatsuitgeverij.

RV&W, Raad voor Verkeer en Waterstaat. 2005. *Samenwerken in de Eurodelta; Kansen voor de positieversterking van Nederland, België en Duitsland in het economisch kerngebied van continentaal Noordwest Europa* [Cooperation in the Eurodelta, Chances for improving the position of the Netherlands, Belgium and Germany in the economic core area of continental Northwest Europe]. Den Haag: Raad voor Verkeer en Waterstaat.

Shipley, R. and R. Newkirk. 1998. "Visioning: Did Anybody See Where It Came From?" *Journal of Planning Literature* 12 (4): 407-416.

Shipley, R. and R. Newkirk. 1999. "Vision and Visioning in Planning: What Do These Terms Really Mean?" *Environment and Planning B* 26: 573-592.

Stumm, Th. and J. Robert. 2006. *Spatial Visions and Scenarios – Thematic Study of INTERREG and ESPON Activities*. Esch-sur-Alzette/Viborg: ESPON Coordination Unit/INTERACT Point Qualification & Transfer.

Thornaes, F. 2000. "NorVision – A Spatial Perspective for the North Sea Region." *Reviewing Transnational Planning*, edited by F. Schindegger. Vienna: Austrian Institute for Regional Studies and Spatial Planning (ÖIR): 61-71.

Waterhout, B. and A. Faludi. forthcoming. "The Emerging EU Territorial Cohesion Agenda: The Ball in the Court of the Member States." *Sociedade e Território*.

Wiersma, A. 2004. *Het ruimtelijk concept in transnationale planning* [The spatial concept in transnational planning]. Master thesis, Nijmegen School of Management, University of Nijmegen.

Williams, R.H. 1996. *European Union Spatial Policy and Planning*. London: Paul Chapman Publishing.

Zonneveld, W. 2000. "Discursive Aspects of Strategic Planning: A Deconstruction of the 'Balanced Competitiveness' Concept in European Spatial Planning." *The Revival of Strategic Spatial Planning*, edited by W. Salet and A. Faludi. Amsterdam: Royal Netherlands Academy of Arts and Sciences: 267-280.

Zonneveld, W. 2005a. "Multiple Visioning: New Ways of Constructing Transnational Spatial Visions." *Environment & Planning C* 23(1): 41-62.

Zonneveld, W. 2005b. "The Europeanization of Dutch National Spatial Planning: An Uphill Battle." *Disp* 163 (4/2005): 4-15.

Zonneveld, W. 2005c. "Expansive Spatial Planning: The New European Transnational Spatial Visions." *European Planning Studies* 13 (1): 137-155.

r

Heiri Leuthold

Revealing the Social Topography of Mega-City Regions

The two themes around which the current discourse on mega-city regions predominantly revolves are, on the one hand, economic and cultural intertwinement within and between urban regions and, on the other, the relationship between urban regions and the nation-state. This paper focuses on the internal sociospatial differentiation of mega-city regions. Empirical studies conducted in Switzerland are used to show that the formation of polycentric urban clusters is being accompanied by a reconfiguration of the social topographies of mega-city regions as an extensive network of urban quarters.

Under the conditions of globalization, the worldwide process of urbanization has entered a new phase as we move into the 21st century: a phase of metropolization. The knowledge economy is focusing its activities on large urban clusters that are networked with one another but are also competing globally as locations. Large historically developed cities and their agglomerations are fusing to form interconnected mega-city regions, which, both in terms of their population sizes and economies, are taking on the dimensions of world cities like New York, Paris and London. In this context, the differences between urban regions and peripheral rural regions are becoming more pronounced. At the same time, spatial organization within the mega-city regions is changing. The hierarchical system of central places posited by Walter Christaller is increasingly giving way to a topography of specialized places. The system of urban organization sprawls over into former rural areas. It is based on the division of labor, functional specialization, economic intertwinement and the interdependence of different subregions. Medium-sized and smaller towns are being integrated into the mega-city region as subagglomerations or subcenters and are taking on specific functions within the overall framework of the urban region, whether as edge cities, centers of consumption or residential regions.

In the discourse of spatial organization of mega-city regions there are two types to be distinguished. One type is the classic metropolis with a single capital city, its large conurbation and the various smaller towns and cities which were incorporated in the urban system of the main city during the process of city growth and suburbanization in the last decades. They have a clear hierarchical structure with a main center and a functional and social topography which follows this hierarchy. Typical representatives of such mono-centered mega-city regions are the greater areas of Paris, Madrid, Moscow or Milano. The other type, clearly to be distinguished of the first one, is the polycentric urban region also called PUR. The crucial characteristic of such PURs are the specialization but also equivalence of the different centers. PURs are formed by two or more cities that are highly interconnected. There is not

1 / MR Geneva
2 / MR Lausanne
3 / MR Berne
4 / MR Basel
5 / MR Zurich
6 / MR Ticino

Figure 1:
Six "metropolitan regions" in Switzerland.

one main center and the functional specialization groups around and related to this center. Because PURs have various centers their spatial organization develops completely different. Typical metropolized regions with the characteristics of PURs are the Randstad in Holland the "Flemish Diamond" in Belgium or the Rhein-Rhur mega-city region in Germany.

As illustrated here with reference to the "Swiss metropolis," this urbanization is leading not only to a functional-spatial reconfiguration but also to a reordering of social and mental topographies that can be conceived in terms of an extensive network of urban quarters.

Urbanization and Sociospatial Organization

The modern urbanization of Europe began in the early 19th century with the demolition of the city wall structures dating back to the Baroque period. However, this was not a linear process but one marked by breaks and discontinuities. The sequence of the individual phases of primary urbanization, suburbanization, desuburbanization and reurbanization can be clearly discerned in the historical development of European cities. Each of these phases produced a specific form of functional and sociospatial organization. The primary urbanization phase during the 19th and early 20th centuries saw the development of a type of dense urban region with services concentrated in its center. Industrial zones and residential areas occupied by the upper, middle and lower classes formed around this central business district in a circular-sectoral structure. The suburbanization phase in the latter half of the 20th century led a migration of the middle classes into suburban areas, resulting in a difference in socioeconomic status emerging between agglomeration belts and core city areas. The reurbanization phase of the 1980s and 1990s was a consequence of the formation of a new urban middle class and led to a revaluation and gentrification of the core city areas. The current phase of metropolization appears to be reshaping the entire urban region. An extensive framework is forming, characterized by a highly diverse range of localities with specific characters and identities, which are distinguished by their physical locational qualities, spatial relationships to the specialized urban centers and social characteristics.

Quarter Formation – an Urban Principle

Spatial organization in the form of quarters is a characteristic of major cities. Although urban quarters often have populations equal to those of small and medium-sized towns, they are markedly different from them. Villages or small towns, at least in traditional terms, are functionally independent formations. By contrast, urban quarters constitute single elements within a larger functional and social structure and exist only in combination with the other elements of the whole.

On the functional-spatial level, cities are divided into workplace quarters, business quarters, shopping boulevards, residential quarters and industrial quarters, into representative, "front regions" and "back regions" where urban logistical facilities are located. In sociospatial terms, the spatial segregation of populations tends to result in cities being structured according to social, cultural, ethnic or other forms of group affiliation. Quarters are "social habitats," which are shaped by specific mentalities, lifestyles and cultural practices, and which can be recognized and named as upper-class or lower-class quarters, family neighborhoods, "yuppie towns," foreigner neighborhoods, trendy quarters, etc. As a whole, these habitats form a social topography that expresses the social differentiation of the urban population.

Within the quartered structure of cities, the functional-spatial and sociospatial levels overlap to form a texture of specialized spaces that differ in terms of their social profile. A fundamental driving force of a large urban-quarter structure is the everyday mobility of the residents or users. This can lead, for example, to a distinction between the working or recreational population of a quarter and its residential population.

Mega-city regions, whether polycentric or monocentric, are also shaped by mobility like traditional cities. Basic functions such as living, working, consumption and recreation become increasingly decoupled in spatial terms and are based in separate areas of the whole urban sys-

Polycentric Urban System of Switzerland

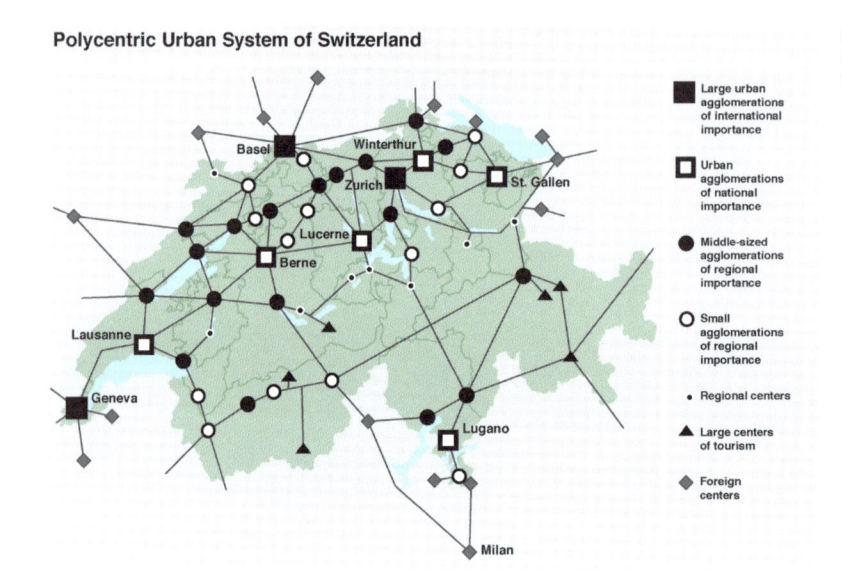

Figure 2:
Switzerland's polycentric urban system.

tem. The result is a spatial reordering of mega-city regions in the same way that quarter or neighborhood formation occurs on the city scale, such that functionally specialized and socially segregated spaces emerge.

Switzerland as a Polycentric Metropolis

Compared to other parts of Europe, the historically developed Swiss urban system has always exhibited a weak hierarchy. The current expansion of urban agglomerations is proceeding from several centers, with the result that the country is assuming the form of a single polycentric urban region. This "Swiss metropolis," with its seven million inhabitants or so, is dominated by the three internationally important economic centers of Geneva, Basel and Zurich and their areas of influence. Between them lie around half a dozen large and many middle-sized and small agglomerations of only regional importance (see Figure 2).

Of late, a range of publications have shared the fundamental assertion that the image of Switzerland as an agricultural alpine state with a decentralized population no longer applies. In constructional, infrastructural and economic terms, Switzerland should now be regarded as a single *Stadtland* or urban country, i.e., as a single, interconnected and closely intertwined urban space.

The urbanization of the country has also had consequences for the sociodemographic and mental topography of Switzerland. As a comparison of the censuses conducted in 1990 and 2000 shows, Switzerland is also undergoing a process of urbanization in sociodemographic terms (see first insert). The social structure of the city is diffusing into agglomeration belts and rural areas. In addition, over the last fifteen years there have also been considerable sociospatial shifts within large urban agglomerations.

Switzerland in Four Dimensions
(Hermann, Heye und Leuthold 2005)

In collaboration with the Swiss Federal Statistical Office, the sotomo research group at the University of Zurich's Department of Geography has developed a system of indicators for describing regional disparities. The system is based on census data and Swiss taxation statistics and can comprehend both large- and small-scale differences in population composition. Four indices are used to describe the basic dimensions of socio-spatial differentiation.

Social status: The status index measures the vertical stratification of the society and is based on income, educational achievement and professional position. Between 1990 and 2000 this index increased throughout Switzerland as a consequence of educational expansion and an increase in high-status professions within the knowledge economy. However, a tendency for the status gradient between urban regions and rural areas to increase is also evident.

Individualization of lifestyles: The individualization index describes horizontal social differentiation in terms of lifestyle. It expresses the degree of social individualization and deviation from the traditional "bourgeois" lifestyle. The index comprises indicators relating to household forms and role models within families. The increase in this index reflects the pluralization of lifestyles and the disintegration of traditional family structures.

Foreign-language use: This index measures the proportion of persons experiencing difficulties with linguistic integration. It comprises several indicators relating language use in everyday professional and family life. A high level of foreign-language use is characteristic of core cities and marginalized suburban areas.

Aging: The age index measures the degree of social aging in a location. Aging has increased in almost all parts of the country. Core cities were the only locations to show a slowing of the aging process in the 1990s. Today the highest age indices are found in areas on the outskirts of cities and in the alpine periphery.

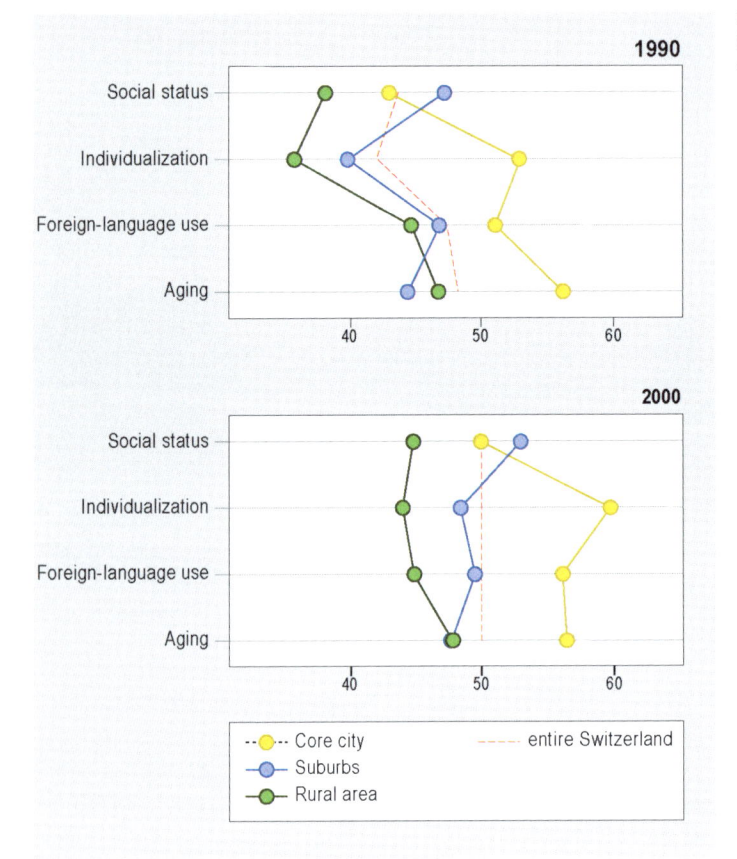

Figure 3:
Switzerland in four dimensions.

Urbanization as Overall Societal Process

A comparison of the four dimensions reveals an overall trend in Switzerland in the direction of higher status, more pronounced individualization, greater foreign-language use and increasing aging. More and more a population profile typical of cities is developing in all regions. Remarkably, the expansion of this "citification" is not leveling differences between the city and the countryside, which are being maintained within the context of urbanization. Not only rural areas and agglomeration belts but also cities are becoming more citified.

The urbanization of the social structure reveals itself in urbanity on both a socioeconomic and a sociocultural level. Both forms of urbanity have a formative significance for the social and mental topography of the Swiss metropolis, although they differ in terms of granularity and the extent of their spatial effects. Both forms of urbanity also shape Switzerland's political landscape and lead to two urban-rural distinctions that are articulated in different political thematic fields.

Socioeconomic Urbanity

On the larger scale, social structure conforms to the economic disparities that arise from the regional division of labor. A key distinction here is that between the economically powerful urbanized regions and the structurally weak rural regions, which is reflected in terms of social topography as a center-periphery gradient on the status axis. It is typical for the economies of conurbation centers to exhibit a concentration of cadre functions, commercial and knowledge-based services distinguished by their high added value. These are paralleled by a growing sector of supporting services with lower qualification requirements of their workforces. The manifold economic possibilities in the country's urban zones lead to a diversified, complex and multilayered social structure characterized by large vertical status differences. The further one moves away from the large cities, the more the economy is shaped by businesses and processing industries oriented to the domestic market, which are now under pressure as a result of economic structural change and stiff competition from low-wage countries. Due to the absence of a broad educated upper- and middle-class stratum, status differences in rural areas tend to be small.

In the political context (see second insert), the difference between center and periphery conditioned by the level of socioeconomic urbanity is manifested as the difference between a liberal and a conservative political mentality. The spatial structure of the economy and associated social structure of the population are reflected in the different political mentalities of metropolitan and rural regions. For "globalization's winners," who live primarily in urban areas, modernization and political openness mean above all new opportunities and perspectives, while in the peripheral regions they are associated with risks and fears. Because status differences in the countryside are small and large parts of the population continue to adhere to more traditional patterns of social life, differentiation along the left-right axis is negligible in rural areas compared to urban regions.

The Political Landscape of Switzerland
(Hermann and Leuthold 2003)

The Political Landscape of Switzerland illustrates the two most important dimensions of political difference within the country: the left-right opposition and the contrast between liberal and conservative. The map is based on a statistical evaluation of 195 Swiss referendums between 1981 and 2002. The closer two places are located to each other on the map, the greater the similarity between their political orientations. The contours show numerical distribution within the system of political coordinates. The back-ground colors indicate the areas of dominance of Switzerland's three large linguistic communities: German (green), French (red), Italian (yellow).

Meaning of Parameters
"Left" indicates a basically social outlook, "right" an orientation to private property and competition. "Liberal" stands for a cosmopolitan, modernization-friendly attitude, conservative for a more self-referential, nationally oriented and protective attitude.

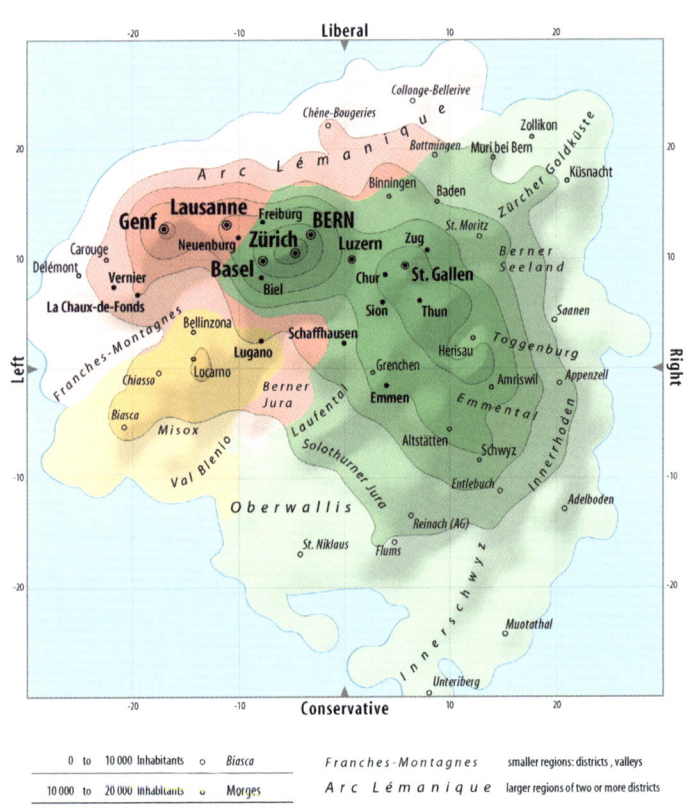

Figure 4:
The political landscape of Switzerland.

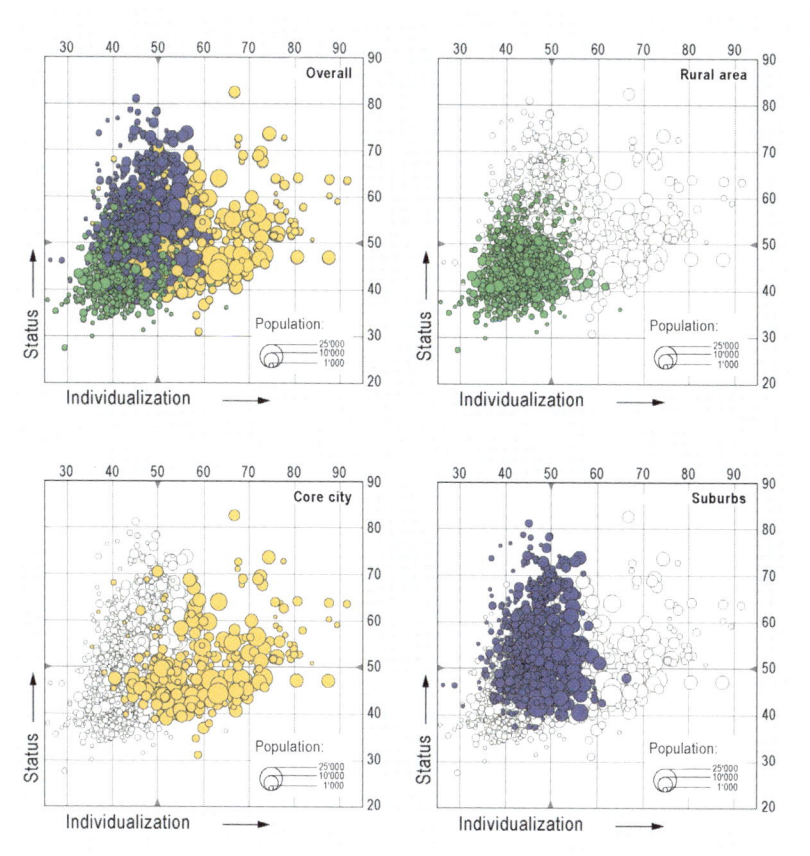

Figure 5:
Sociospatial differentiation according to settlement types.

Sociospatial Structure of Mega-City Regions

For some time now, the urban service economy in Switzerland has no longer been concentrated solely in the core city municipalities but has also been located in medium-sized and small towns. In the suburban environs new service centers have emerged, so-called edge cities, while regions between the centers are developing into residential quarters in which the number of workplaces is declining. As a consequence of this functional specialization and short travel times, the sociospatial structure of mega-city regions is no longer primarily geared to the local availability of jobs but is based rather on residential segregation. This arises through the dynamics of the housing market and is the result of the interplay of a spatially differentiated range of housing on offer, different locational qualities and social differences within the population.

Differences in terms of income, education and other social resources result in preferred residential locations developing into upper-class quarters, while the underclass is forced into less favorable locations. Along with this vertical differentiation according to social status, which stratifies both core cities and suburbs in socio-spatial terms, diverging locational demands lead to a horizontal segregation of the population according to lifestyles and residential ideals. In spatial terms this accords with the contrast between the core-city and suburban life-worlds.

Sociocultural Urbanity

As a living space, the core city is characterized by high spatial density, short routes, an intensive public life, cultural diversity, anonymity and a lack of social surveillance. In the core cities, the traditional bourgeois family unit with a strict division of roles along gender lines has become a minority way of life, and typical urban models now include single-person households, couples living separately, collective households and families with an egalitarian division of roles. By contrast, the suburbs offer space for a lifestyle shaped according to the traditional bourgeois ideal, which is oriented to the classic family model, a home of one's own and privacy.

In contrast to socioeconomical urbanity, sociocultural urbanity is more strongly tied to the actual city in an architectural sense. It is most pronounced where the core city takes its most urban form in the inner cities dating back to the Middle Ages and later to the "promoterism" years (*Gründerjahre*). In the outer quarters, sociocultural urbanity is significantly less pronounced, and in the greater part of the suburbs it is barely more pronounced than in rural areas.

The interplay of socioeconomic and sociocultural urbanity lends the suburbs an interesting character that is halfway between that of city and countryside. In an economic sense they are urbanized and exhibit the strong vertical stratification into upper- and lower-class areas typical of urban regions. In terms of lifestyle and forms of habitation, the majority of inhabitants of the suburbs approximate to the traditional bourgeois ideal that dominates in rural areas.

New Urban Middle Class

The sociological basis of the horizontal polarization of urban spaces is the differentiation of the tertiary knowledge economy into different branches, i.e., commercial (banking, insurance, business consultancies, etc.), social (health care system, education, etc.) and creative services (media, advertising, design, culture, etc.). The so-called "new urban middle classes" of the core cities come above all from the creative and social service branches and have left-liberal values oriented to self-development, emancipation and freedom of thought. Those engaged in the commercial services branch tend to have a political outlook oriented to private property, economic independence and material freedom and tend to live in the suburbs, where the traditional, conservative lifestyle model dominates.

In the political context, the contrast between core cities and agglomeration belts conditioned by sociocultural urbanity is manifested in terms of a contrast on the left-right axis. This contrast is evident above all in relation to social, sociopolitical and ecological issues, with the core city tending to take a more left-wing and the surrounding area a more right-wing position. Due to the pronounced segregation according to social status, the urban regions are also differentiated diagonally between a neo- or right-wing liberal outlook and a left-wing or social conservative attitude that emphasizes the maintenance of the Fordistic welfare state (see Figure 6).

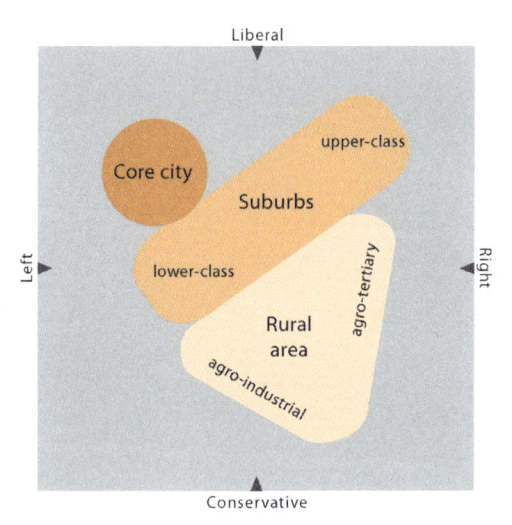

Figure 6:
Political mentality and spatial typology.

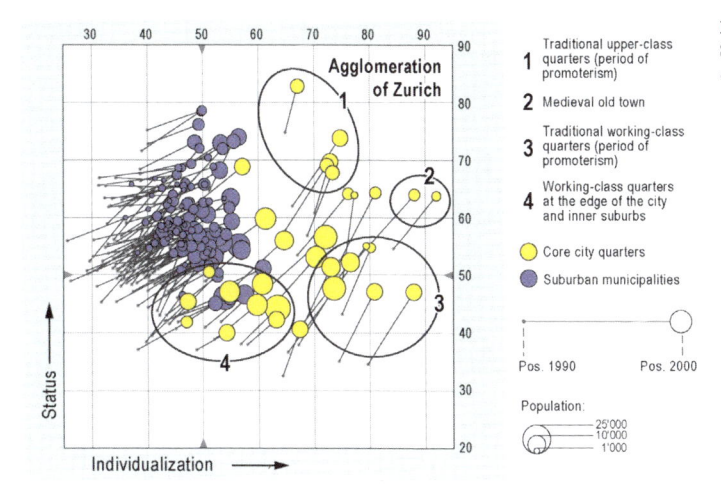

Figure 7:
Sociospatial shifts in Zurich agglomeration 1990 to 2000.

Sociospatial Shifts

The major Swiss agglomerations exhibit two apparently contrary processes relating to population dynamics. On the one hand, growth in the breadth of agglomerations is continuing unabated due to processes of suburbanization and periurbanization. On the other hand, the last fifteen years have seen a renaissance of the urban in Switzerland and the establishment of a new urban middle class in the core cities. As a consequence of this societal change, reurbanization processes are overlaying ongoing suburbanization. This reurbanization is manifested in all major Swiss cities as a social upgrading or gentrification of the inner city areas (see Figure 7).

The spread of the new middle class in the inner cities has led to a displacement of low-status population groups and a relocation of so-called A-city phenomena. This takes the form above all of a concentration of socially disadvantaged groups, including underprivileged foreigners with a migration background, in the working-class quarters on the edge of the city and the inner suburban belt. This at least partial marginalization particularly affects quarters and municipalities with old, low-quality housing in locations burdened with air pollution.

The "Quartered Mega-City Region"

Seen in general terms, Swiss city regions are characterized by a concentric spatial pattern of sociocultural differentiation overlaid by a sectoral pattern of socioeconomic differentiation. The integration of mega-city regions and the above-mentioned sociospatial shifts within this macro-structure point to the formation of a polycentric urban region that is precisely differentiated in functional and sociospatial terms. Extending Peter Marcuse's concept of the "quartered city," one might describe this development in terms of a "quartered mega-city region" within which characteristic quarter types can be identified.

Traditional upper-class municipalities
Habitats of the old-established bourgeoisie. Residential areas with few sites of work, high-status population, dominance of traditional conservative lifestyle, increasingly aging population, right-wing liberal political mentality.

Middle-class suburbia
Residential areas of the middle classes with a traditional conservative lifestyle, primarily right-wing, private property orientation.

Gentrified quarters
Residential areas of the new urban middle classes, former workers' quarters near the inner city. Functional mixture of residential, work and recreation. Dominance of individualized lifestyles, low proportions of the elderly, children and young people, left-wing and left-liberal mentality.

Super-gentrified quarters
Residential areas of the new urban upper classes. Low proportion of young people, children and young adults, high degree of individualization. Habitats of the internationally oriented cadres of the knowledge economy, liberal orientation.

Marginalized suburbs
Residential areas of the underprivileged, high proportion of low-income groups and foreigners with integration difficulties. Located on city edges and in agglomeration belts, social-conservative mentality.

Upgraded suburbia
New habitats of middle and upper classes, in easily accessible and aesthetically attractive locations, right-wing and right-liberal orientation.

Edge cities
Suburban workplace areas, low-status residential population, high proportion of foreign-language use, tendency to social devaluation, social-conservative orientation.

Core cities of the sub-agglomerations
Cells of sociocultural urbanity, mixed population structure, above-average proportion of individualized lifestyles, tending to left-liberal orientation.

Concluding Remarks: the Political Challenge

These observations concerning the internal structure of mega-city regions are based on empirical studies of urbanization and metropolization in Switzerland, and care must be taken when applying them to other European regions. However, there are strong indicators of similar developments both in terms of functional-spatial and sociospatial differentiation and in terms of mental topography in other polycentric urban regions of Europe, although in some cases a lack of data (e.g., in Germany, where censuses are no longer taken) means that it is not possible to obtain the same degree of detail as in Switzerland.

The process of metropolization in Europe is still in full swing. Even if in some EU countries, in particular the countries of the former Eastern Block, there is talk of "shrinking cities" and in some cases deconstruction and renaturization plans are being discussed, the general trend is still towards further economic concentration and the progressive amalgamation of urban spaces to form mega-city regions. It can be expected that this consolidation of urban clusters as a consequence of increased economic and social intertwinement will be accompanied by an increase in the functional specialization of metropolitan spatial elements. This will also lead to a sharpening of the contours of the internal functional-spatial and sociospatial diversification of the urban regions.

The emerging quartered structure of megacity regions has consequences for political institutions and the governance of these regions. Functional specialization and socio-spatial fragmentation place new demands on planning, affect the fiscal equivalence of participation, benefits and financing between spatial sectors, and lead to a spatially unequal distribution of social burdens and tasks. In a conventional urban quartered structure, all functional and sociospatial units are integrated under a common institutional roof, so that collective planning, institutionalized solidarity, financial compensation and fiscal equivalence are guaranteed. However, most mega-city regions are politically fragmented and extend over several municipalities, provinces or even states. This lack of congruence in spatial and political-administrative regionalization gives rise to the challenge of creating institutions for the mega-city regions that, on the one hand, correspond to existing political structures and, on the other, exhibit the flexibility and efficiency as well as democratic legitimacy required to steer and coordinate the development of the entire urban region.

References

Blöchliger, H. 2004. *Baustelle Föderalismus.* Zürich: Verlag Neue Zürcher Zeitung.

Flückiger, H. and M. Koll-Schretzenmayr. 2000. "Das vernetzte Städtesystem der Schweiz. Eine schweizerische Strategie, ein europäisches Modell?" *DISP* 142/2000: 4-9.

Hermann, M., C. Heye and H. Leuthold. 2005. *Soziokulturelle Unterschiede in der Schweiz: Vier Indizes zu räumlichen Disparitäten, 1990-2000.* Neuchâtel: Bundesamt für Statistik.

Hermann, M. and H. Leuthold. 2003. *Atlas der politischen Landschaften. Ein weltanschauliches Porträt der Schweiz.* Zürich: Vdf Hochschulverlag AG ETH Zürich.

Marcuse, P. 1997. "The Enclave, the Citadel, and the Ghetto: What Has Changed in the Post-Fordist US City." *Urban Affairs Review* 33 (2): 228-264.

expe

Ursula Stein
Henrik Schultz

Experiencing Urban Regions

Visualizing through Experiments

"Making Mega-City Regions Visible!" exclaimed the title of the symposium that formed the starting point for this book. The need to comprehend larger spatial contexts in terms of planning and political action is becoming evident in mega-city regions on a world scale just as it is in smaller agglomerations such as the Southern Region of Luxembourg, a prototypical "urban region." But who is supposed to comprehend the urban region in a different way, with a greater degree of awareness and precision? What sorts of approaches are appropriate for the development of images? This paper presents reasons why the technical concept of visualization needs to be supplemented by individual and collective experience and examines this approach with reference to an experimental planning process in the Southern Region of Luxembourg.

What does "making visible" actually imply when applied to regions, whether small or large? Visualization in the sense of a purely technically mediated illustration cannot in itself suffice. It needs to be supplemented and strengthened by perception with other senses. Relevant players in planning processes need to be prompted to experience regional space on a physical level in different ways. This experience can take many forms and may include, for example, guided tours through a region and the "staging" of selected regional locations. Such unmediated experience of the space and the collective reflection it gives arise to allow images to emerge.

The concept of "image" we are employing here is a multifaceted one. It encompasses the perceived appearance and the sensorially experienced (which, a constructivist approach would argue, do not conform to a single reality), the remembered and envisioned, just as it does the concept and the idea. The latter already shapes perception and memory, and as a result these facets or layers of the concept of image cannot be completely separated from one another.

Why do regions need this perceptual and emotional focus? The perception of the metropolitan or urban region is the prerequisite for spatial planning on this scale. The goals are to bundle forces as a means of improving the competitiveness of a region, to use rationalization potentials and to be able to plan on a scale that corresponds to the contexts people actually live in. All this requires new images at the planning level of the urban region. It is not easy to recognize the contextual interrelations of constructed and nonconstructed elements and to form an "image" that transcends these individual parts that does not fall prey to the clichés of "open landscape" and "dense European city." In his 1997 book *Zwischenstadt* (Cities without Cities), Thomas Sieverts argues that images and care are required to deal with a type of area which until then had largely been ignored in Europe on an analytical level and in the development of planning instruments, and for which adequate images or concepts still did not exist (Sieverts 1997).

What shapes the appearance of urban regions? As a consequence of the extension of residentially popular peripheral locations, the "maximization of the periphery" has become just as characteristic as the coalescence of settlement areas and the pressure of certain uses to locate along arterial roads and thoroughfares. The result is an increasing reversal of figure and background in the sense that open space is framed by built structures – in contrast to traditional images of the city embedded in a landscape. Open space in the region is a resource both in terms of land use and in an aesthetic sense (see Hauser, "Vermutungen über die Wunscherfüllung," in Hauser and Kamleithner 2006: 84ff). Since land usage is dominated by the perspective of the individual element and is devoid of an overarching concept, the result is a rudimentarily public space with barely adequate spatial organization (e.g., a lack of footpath links) and featuring random encounters between interest groups in unexpected places (e.g., practitioners of popular sports find themselves in hunting areas or walkers wander into commercial zones).

As long as the perception of this overall picture of the urban region by professionals (planners, environmentalists, policy-makers, etc.) and laypeople (residents, users, voters, etc.) remains obstructed by an ideal construct (namely, the antithesis between "European city" and "European agrarian landscape"), the planning and development of urban landscapes and regions cannot be linked with the experiences and needs of their citizens. According to the "interpretive paradigm" of the social sciences, social reality is not an objective given but rather the product of social constructions based on the interpretations of social actors (Helbrecht et al. 1991: 230). This assertion is based on three premises: "(1) People act vis-à-vis objects on the basis of the meanings these objects have for them. The term object here applies to everything to which people are able to relate their actions... (2) These meanings are generated in the course of social interaction and they are (3) deployed in interaction in the sense that they are constructed in the moment of the respective action situation. Due to this process of situational interpretation, meanings are subject to constant modification" (Meuser 1985: 134; cited in Helbrecht et al. 1991: 230). The development of images for regions by scholars, planners, citizens and policy-makers thus requires attention and perception. Interpretations of phenomena, uses and facts as the basis of individual and institutional action are generated in communicative and learning contexts.

"Experience-based planning" is the term we use for the integrative approach we propose for the development of open space and communicative spatial planning. In what follows we delineate the distinctive spatial type of urban region that we refer to as urban landscapes. We also discuss the SAUL project (Sustainable and Accessible Urban Landscapes) in the Southern Region of Luxembourg as an example of the experience-based planning of urban landscapes and explore a number of relevant methodological approaches. Finally we place the experiments involved in the SAUL project in the context of the future regional planning framework that Luxembourg's Ministry for the Interior and Spatial Planning has been developing in collaboration with the office of Stein+Schultz.

I Urban Landscapes – a Spatial Type Characteristic of Many Urban Regions

City and countryside can no longer be clearly delimited from one another. They now tend to form a new patchwork pattern characterized by interfaces that are both exciting and problematic, weaknesses, but also fascinating places. Rural spaces are increasingly being shaped by urban lifestyles. Intermediate spaces and overarching infrastructures are shaping the phenomenon of the region.

The factual significance of these new elements is supported by statistics. Over 60% of retail turnover in Germany is recorded by businesses on the edge of cities, in commercial areas and at autobahn exits. Many people questioned about their recreational preferences refer to intensively stage-managed experiences with a controlled level of tension but devoid of unpleasant surprises: cinemas, water and wellness parks, indoor tropical environments and indoor skiing. Moreover, 60% of all Germans live in areas that researchers classify as "suburban space."

Urban-landscape residents often describe their living space as practical in the sense that one can quickly get from "here" to "there," for example to the "countryside" or to the nearest big town. However, it is also common for words such as "weird" and "chaotic" to be used in characterizations of these spaces.

Urban landscapes offer space for uses that do not fit in anywhere else, for parking lots that are needed for today's retail and recreational centers, for large infrastructure facilities and commercial sport and recreational facilities. The new urban landscapes are fulfilling the needs of society in the way the "European agrarian landscape" and the "European city" once did. However, they often do not accord with classic organizational and aesthetic criteria and are therefore unpopular with many planners. Compared with the ideally conceived combination of dense city and open landscape, they are perceived as "unplanned" even though their individual elements have been formed by conventional planning processes. The tools of classic town and country planning and landscaping do not function in urban landscapes predominantly determined by self-interest. There is a strong need for local authorities to coordinate their activities, a requirement that makes things even more complicated.

Figure 1:
Experiencing urban landscapes: new partners on new paths through the Southern Region.

Figure 2:
Experiencing urban landscapes: picnic with a special view.

II Example: SAUL in the Southern Region of Luxembourg

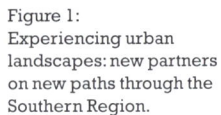

The SAUL project in the Southern Region of Luxembourg, which is sponsored by the EU within the framework of the Interreg IIIB program, represents a response to the problems outlined above. As in the case of partner projects in the UK, the Netherlands and Germany, the SAUL project sponsored by the Luxembourg Ministry for the Interior and Spatial Planning from 2004 to 2006 focused on how impulses for a modern form of regional planning could be generated through research into urban landscapes and collaboration with municipalities, associations and citizens. SAUL looked for answers to the question of how regional identity could be created by means of a new planning culture based on "partnership building." Through a process of networking, discussion initiation, information provision, experimentation and coordination, SAUL explored the potential for experienced-based planning in relation to the urban landscape as a particular type of area (The SAUL Partnership 2006).

Luxembourg's south is a prototypical urban landscape, a multilayered mosaic of settlement areas and open spaces. The region has some 144,000 inhabitants, or 30% of Luxembourg's population, who live on 8% of the country's territory. The structural transformation of the former industrial region into a location for modern services can be clearly recognized in a series of large-scale conversion projects. At the same time, Luxembourg in general is seeing a creeping urbanization of rural areas, and this means that new infrastructure needs are also arising in the peripheral regions.

In the year 2003, the government's "Integrative Transport and Development Concept for Luxembourg" identified the need for further urbanization and aggregation in the Southern Region in order to help the country to cope with the significant increase in Luxembourg's population. This process requires targeted engagement with the development of open spaces and the way in which they are dovetailed with cities and built-up areas.

The Project Group
"Paths and Places in Urban Landscapes"

The idea for the "Paths and Places in Urban Landscapes" project arose from a series of interviews with people knowledgeable of the Southern Region. The resulting project group comprised the Luxembourg Velos Initiativ bicycle advocacy group, the Natur- und Vogelschutzliga (Nature and bird protection league), the Mouvement Ecologique environmental group, the Fond de Gras cultural initiative, the Frenn vun der Haard (Friends of the Haard nature reserve, which is involved in nature conservation as well as cultural issues), Objectif Plein Emploi, a national network that conducts a wide range of community-service and employment-creation projects, and six of the twelve municipalities in the Southern Region.

This group of SAUL-partners was an important element for the understanding of the urban landscape as a particular type of area which needs to be analyzed and planned with a specific approach. These learning points were transmitted into some of the groups which were represented. The integration of different points of view proved to be as helpful as the shared experience of space.

Experiencing:
Journeys through Urban Landscapes

The idea of a "journey in the Southern Region" was developed collectively. The aim was to identify places in the Southern Region that were characterized by a merging of settlement areas and open space, places that exhibited signs of the upheavals and changes of the last years and thus provided clues as to the direction of future development. A selection of stages for the journey was made that ranged from wild to urban. This allowed the urban landscape of the Southern Region to appear in a new light and altered participants' perception of it.

A collective bicycle tour led by the Lëtzebuerger Vëlos-Initiativ provided all participants with greater insight into Luxembourg's Southern Region and enabled them to explore and discuss new perspectives on site. Even aficionados among the cyclists discovered "new" things. This collectively established foundation subsequently contributed decisively to concretely shaping the SAUL process.

Tours with the artist Boris Sieverts in April, May and June 2005 led participants from the southern and neighboring regions along unusual routes to a range of special places in southern Luxembourg. In the program of the planned tour, Boris Sieverts described a section of the urban landscape through which the tour led in the following terms, "On the flat land at the foot of the Doggerstufe, the dense neighborhoods of the Minette dissolve and the elements seem to float arbitrarily in space. The dump, free-standing houses, cement works and shopping center are some of the performative elements of this new urban type, which has the autobahn as its center." The tours, which led through dense and intensively used areas as well as unused ones, produced new perceptual contexts linking old and new elements. Boris Sieverts' way of running his tours had the effect of slowing down the visual experience and dissecting it into its elements. In a very real sense, the tours provided new forms of access to the urban landscapes and enabled participants to discover the hidden beauties of these changing living spaces. New perspectives enabled many of those who took part to form new images – new perceptions, new concepts and new ideas – of their region.

Reflecting: Focusing on Places

The shared memory of the bicycle tour proved very valuable when it came to selecting "typical places within urban landscapes." Project group members were able to recall certain situations and thus share a reference to individual "urban landscape" sites. Initially 83 such places were compiled in a list. Based on a range of criteria, eighteen were then identified as particularly characteristic and thus as suitable fixed points for a "journey through the Southern Region." These places are characterized by dynamism and chaos, particular encounters and sudden breaks, strangeness and beauty. This selection and characterization of the elements of the urban landscape facilitated a more precise image of the region.

For example, one of the selected sites features a steelworks cooling pond adjacent to a road, on the other side of which is a wetland nature reserve. The silhouette of the old steelworks contrasts surprisingly with a vista of pondweed and wooded paths, both forming a place of encounters and breaks. The large, disused site of the former Belval steelworks was selected as a typical site because it represents chaos and dynamism. Huge blast furnaces have been demolished while others are being restored as monuments to industrial culture. The new national rock music center and the headquarters of an international bank have been opened in the immediate vicinity, and they will soon be followed by residential areas and Luxembourg University.

Applied to the context of the Southern Region, the concept of urban landscapes becomes more concrete. Moreover, an engagement with the urban landscape also entails engaging with the concept of beauty. Under what conditions can "strangeness" and "rupture" also be perceived as beautiful?

Documenting: a Map for the Journey

The links between the individual sites were also discussed in detail. Topography, usability for the public and different types of transport and other criteria had to be taken into account when determining the best links. This process of selecting routes and places produced a map entitled "Journeys Through Urban Landscapes." The map represents an interim product and documents ten months of work by the project group. It is hoped that it will convince municipalities, associations and other decision-makers to develop the project further and engage with the diverse phenomena of the urban landscape.

Figure 3:
Reflecting and documenting: map featuring urban landscape locations in the Southern Region.

Networking: the "New Paths in New Landscapes" Symposium

Specialist contributions, consultation with project sponsors and external experts and numerous discussions within the project group have increased the fund of knowledge concerning the emergence and development of urban landscapes. As a result, the spatial effects of social and economic trends have become more transparent, and it is now clearer why dealing with urban landscapes is important for the regional development. In June 2005, within the framework of the SAUL project, the "New Paths in New Landscapes" symposium was held on the site of the former Belval steelworks in Esch-sur-Alzette. The Ministry of the Interior and Spatial Planning, Agora and Fonds Belval, two national institutions involved in the development of large brownfield areas, and the PRO-SUD municipal alliance had invited specialists and interested parties from politics and civil society to attend. Representatives of regional associations and planning offices discussed the challenges of planning in urban landscapes with experts and project developers. How can the development of open spaces contribute to a region's profile and its inhabitants' quality of life? Are new forms of collaboration required for this process? What significance should be attributed to opening up the landscape and creating pathways through it? The discussion of these and other central questions underscored the preparatory function of the SAUL project for regional planning.

Designing: Experiments with a Sense of Place

Finally, experiments in landscape design were used to interpret individual sites within the urban landscapes in a regional context. As a result many observers and users found their perception altered, and thus their reality in the sense of the interpretive paradigm used in the social sciences. Four temporary installations, "Pit Stop," "Network," "Umbrella Meadow" and "Fire Towers," were mounted at sites in the Southern Region to promote reflection among residents, policy-makers and representatives of regional associations regarding their images of urban landscapes. For a short time a former landfill site, a disused inner-city industrial site, a meadow on the outskirts of a town and a site next to an old immigrant neighborhood became focuses of interest. The installations were the result of a competition organized by the Urban Landscapes Studio in the Faculty of Architecture and Landscape at the University of Hanover and supervised by Professor Hille von Seggern and Henrik Schultz. The winning teams worked together with the municipalities of Differdingen, Düdelingen, Esch and Schifflingen to realize their proposals within only one week. These selective interventions represented thematic explorations of boundaries and connections between settlement areas and open spaces as well as the history and future of former industrial locations. They provided a clear, easily comprehensible medium that incited discussion about the individual locations, which had previously been largely ignored and yet are typical of the overall framework of urban landscapes in the Southern Region of Luxembourg. With comparatively few financial and planning resources, the students created new images of these places and of the region as a whole.

Figure 4: Designing urban landscapes: experiment on the Schifflingen landfill site by Lia Deister and Jana Sido, September 2005.

Figure 5:
Designing urban landscapes: experiment on the Esch-sur-Alzette city edge by Marco Motzek and Dennis Ziegert, September 2005.

Summary:
Experience-Based Planning in Luxembourg

Only those who intensively experience the landscapes of their region can change or recreate their images of those landscapes. This form of visualization requires the cultivation of an unprejudiced gaze, and this is why discussions with the residents of these urban landscapes are important. "Striking up" conversations about these new urban landscapes is best done on site. This process can be helped by events such as group "journeys" using different types of transportation, as it can by designs forming anchoring points or connections. The new meanings and interpretations generated by the social interaction and social learning processes that can be sparked by such "perceptual initiatives" can lead to a new image of the region growing out of the existing interpretation of reality, an image that does more justice to the spatial structures of agglomerations than old ideas of "city" and "countryside."

Such perceptual initiatives can themselves also bring about spatial changes. In Luxembourg's Southern Region, the kind of teamwork between municipalities and the relevant ministries envisaged as the basis of future regional planning in Luxembourg is evolving well on the professional level, but remains contradictory on the political one. Nevertheless, discussions between local politicians and the Ministry of the Interior and Spatial Planning have focused more on spatial qualities than ever before. The SAUL project has drawn attention to the fact that open spaces and urban landscapes represent important potentials and challenges for the design of our spatial future and that a spatial vision needs to be developed in parallel to the classic, official regional plan.

III Experience-Based Planning: Situations, Senses, Proximity, Exchange

When it comes to visually representing regions, regional plans that are technically oriented and coded with symbols are really only helpful to planning specialists. Communication about the different ideas of the different groups can result in individual images becoming collective images. Specialist input into this process of exchange between regional actors and spatial experience are major elements of experience-based planning. Such an approach creates situations, works with a range of senses, establishes proximity and distance to places, and maps out phases in the process of collective exchange. In this way, regional actors are able to develop new approaches, criteria and images for their region.

Situations

Experience-based planning attempts to "provoke" regional actors to conceptually appropriate space. To this end, such an approach involves the organization of intensive interaction with spatial situations, as seen in the case of SAUL's approach to urban landscapes. Experience-based planning involves the construction of information and discussion platforms and the design and supervision of projects geared to opening up and networking typical regional locations. "Outsider views" such as found in interpretations by artists allow for new ways of seeing. Experiments can turn a spotlight on particular locations. They can reveal ways of dealing with places and provide impulses for regional development.

Senses

The different journeys undertaken in the context of the SAUL project show that experience-based planning animates people to place themselves physically in the prevailing situation, to focus their attention on the space. Precisely mapped out stages in a journey, an appropriate amount of background information and aspects that appeal to the senses can all be helpful in this respect. The appearance, music, smell and taste of spaces influence the conception of the journeys. In this way access to spaces that would otherwise remain concealed is facilitated. The physical experience of a situation allows people to perceive scales and relationships and understand the way a space is shaped. Reflection on these corporally comprehended situations provides the background against which images of spaces – perceptions, concepts and ideas – are generated (Stein 2005).

Proximity

Experience-based planning compels us to form a direct relationship with space. Whereas in other contexts codification in the form of maps can create a significant distance to the object, the experiential approach is consciously based on a corporeal confrontation with the space. This allows for a productive engagement with the prejudices of participants, which for a short time can be undermined by new perspectives and ways of seeing. Attitudes and potential solutions can subsequently be examined on the basis of the experienced realities.

Exchange

Shared memories and associations serve as references for discussions about the spaces that have been experienced. The process of exchange makes it possible to develop new standards of assessment and generates curiosity concerning other solutions.

Experience-based planning attempts to enter into dialogue with an interested and organized public sphere and links experts, representatives of particular interests and policy-makers. It is not limited to urban contexts and is above all suited to implementation at the level of the urban region, which has until now been abstract and hardly open to experience at all while at the same time constituting the living space of most people.

Figure 6:
Experimental interventions by Jana Sido, Lia Deister, Kirsten Olheide, Johanna Reisch, Christian Kamer, Marco Motzek and Dennis Ziegert, September 2005.

IV The Regional Planning Context: Spatial Vision as the Form of Visualization

Building on the different forms of experience explored in the context of the SAUL project, the next step is to condense the new concepts of Luxembourg's Southern Region into a spatial vision. A communicative process involving regional actors and external experts will aim to combine individual images into a collective image. This image will be developed in association with official regional planning processes and delineate the direction with which the Southern Region is to be developed. Such an image will express less about the organization of settlement and open-space development than about the characteristics of the space.

The office of Stein+Schultz has been working extensively with the Luxembourg Ministry of the Interior and Spatial Planning to develop the instrument of spatial vision as an element of regional planning. The spatial vision helps regional planning to adapt to a specific spatial type and its developmental needs, to elaborate particular characteristics within the overall view and to use images as a means of emphasizing particular elements.

Spatial Vision as Graphic Reference Level

Difficulties with regional planning are usually encountered when conflicts over distribution and jurisdiction prevent the region from being perceived as a whole. Classic regional planning has the character of legally binding systemic planning. Supplementing this process with the graphic element of the spatial vision creates a shared reference level for decisions concerning land use and projects that allows conflicts over distribution to be solved within a framework of shared concepts of development. The instrument of spatial vision enables regional and local actors to experience and discuss the typologies and qualities of the space, and exchange visual concepts of their region and make these visible. In this way an image is generated in the form of a map that emphasizes the particularities of the region and presents integral and atmospheric perspectives relating to the development of different spaces and the region as a whole. The images generated through this process (perceptions, concepts and ideas) are condensed in this map in such a way that previously invisible "talents" of the region are made visible. Every municipality can then answer the questions "What are our particular spatial features?" and "What role do we play in the network of municipalities?" However, rather than forestalling decisions, this image encourages consensus building while making sure that there is still room for interpretation.

The Luxembourg Tri-Level Model

In the future, regional planning for Luxembourg will be organized in three parts: First, the spatial vision; second, the legally binding plan with a graphic and a written element; and third, ideas and concepts for regional development projects. As far as possible, the spatial vision as graphic development concept will be elaborated in parallel and conjunction with the legally binding plan. The spatial vision will profit from the basic groundwork carried out at the level of legally binding planning. Conversely, it will be able to thematically inspire the analysis so that the result does not merely deliver standard information based on interregional comparisons but also information regarding regionally specific themes. Legally binding planning requires a communicable, innovative and convincing graphic tool such as the spatial vision in order to express regional interests independently from municipal concerns.

Anyone aiming to make regions visible should engage key regional actors in a process of exploration and learning (Stein 2006). Experiments with spatial experience, the condensation of experiences and the formation of a spatial vision within the framework of regional planning are key elements of experience-based planning.

References

Hauser, S. and C. Kamleithner. 2006. *Ästhetik der Agglomeration*. Wuppertal: Müller + Busmann.

Helbrecht, I., R. Danielzyk and B. Butzin. 1991. "Wahrnehmungsmuster und Bewusstseinsformen als qualitative Faktoren der Regionalentwicklung: Fallstudie Ruhrgebiet." *Raumforschung und Raumordnung*, 4 (1991): 229-236.

Meuser, M. 1985. "Alltagswissen und gesellschaftliche Wirklichkeit. Sozialwissenschaftliche Alltagsforschung." In *Analyse und Interpretation der Alltagswelt. Lebensweltforschung und ihre Bedeutung für die Geographie*, edited by W. Isenberg. Osnabrücker Studien zur Geographie, vol. 7: 129-158.

Sieverts, T. 1997. *Zwischenstadt. Zwischen Ort und Welt, Raum und Zeit, Stadt und Land*. Bauwelt Fundamente 118. Braunschweig and Wiesbaden: Vieweg. (English: Sieverts, T. 2003. *Cities without Cities. An Interpretation of the Zwischenstadt*. London and New York: Spon Press.)

Stein, U. 2005. "Planning with All Your Senses – Learning to Co-operate on a Regional Scale." *DISP* 162 (September 2005): 62-69.

Stein, U. 2006. *Lernende Stadtregion. Verständigungsprozesse über Zwischenstadt*. Wuppertal: Müller + Busmann.

The SAUL Partnership. 2006. *Vital Urban Landscapes. The Vital Role of Sustainable and Accessible Urban Landscapes in Europe's City Regions. The Final Report of the SAUL Partnership*. London. www.saulproject.net.

stir

Julian Petrin

Stimulating the Second Space

Image Power Space: On Legibility and Stimulation of Space

The power of images over the production of space is indisputable. But what images are we talking about here? Our mental images? Images in the sense of representations, i.e., plans, maps, advertising images, clichés? Are we talking about the space itself and its quality as an image?

This article investigates the complex interdependencies between material structures and conceptions of space as well as the implications of spatial conceptions for the process of spatial production, and sketches a vision of a level of planning that specifically aims to stimulate spatial mental images. It is particularly at the urban regional level, which is often only weakly anchored in perceptual terms, that such "spatial stimulation" could contribute to the process of transforming political-normative spatial constructs into tangible spatial interconnections.

Of Open Books and Buried Treasures.
Some spaces are open books. The entire text of a region lies open before us, only waiting to be read.

These are spaces of fulfilled expectations, clear structures and easily visible landmarks, spaces whose narratives are well known, whose symbols powerfully feed these narratives into the flow of awareness.

They are legible spaces whose representations provide clear reading instructions, whose inner logic is reflected in their external form, whose paths present scenic images and possess a dramatic power. They are places that have been traversed thousands of times in films and books, whose images are permanent features of collective conceptions of space.

There are other spaces. Regions that can barely be deciphered, which lack clear organization in terms of natural features or man-made structures, cities without clear density and typology gradients from the center to the periphery, interim spaces, settlement archipelagos, political spatial constructs without a clear identity. Their text must be laboriously decoded before it becomes legible. Finding one's bearings in such spaces is difficult; the treasures of these regions remain concealed from the fleeting visitor.

Today it seems as if the majority of spaces are difficult to read. No rivers that clearly distinguish a near and far side, no traffic conduits that open the space to experience in the truest sense of the word, no distinctive spatial constellations that are linked with generally recognized images or symbols.

Wouldn't it be helpful if there were a reading guide for such spaces?

Figure 1:
Postcard view of Munich.

What Images?

Making space visible, focusing the image of a region – the concept of image is quite in fashion in planning circles. And yet the process of working with and on spatial images has as many different facets as the concept of image has connotations.

What images are we referring to when we speak of the image of a region? "Depictions" of the space, representations of it, individual or collective mental images of the space or perhaps commercial "images," constructed symbols serving to market a location?

All of these dimensions of meaning inform the following discussion. The point of departure and hub of my reflections are the mental images of a space, commonly referred to as mental maps, although this term is not really adequate, as will later become clear. However, visual "depictions" and narrative "visualizations" of the space, its stories and representations, play an equally important role, as do constructed symbols. And we should not forget the immediate semiotic dimension of the space, its function as spatialized "text," which we reread and reinterpret daily.

My point of departure is a simple thesis: space is generated in the mind, in an interaction between mental maps, representations and the spatial "text" itself. In this process, it is particularly mental maps that determine the assessment, use and thus the "success" of a space. Basing myself on this thesis I would like to present the vision of a process of "spatial stimulation," a bundle of measures that support the synthesis of this "space in the mind" by increasing the legibility of the "text." The idea of "spatial stimulation" applies especially to the urban regional level, a level that is increasingly becoming the decisive level for locational marketing and processes of identity formation.

The idea involves systematizing the different processes that constitute our individual and collective conceptions of space at an urban regional level and searching for possibilities of contributing to the targeted management of these processes, in order to participate in shaping the assessment and utilization of the urban regional space and to increase the visibility of its potentials for different target groups. It is a vision of a type of planning whose task is not so much one of adding new structures but one of "re-framing" (Faludi 1996), of interpreting what is already extant and imbuing it with meaning.[1] It involves making the concealed possibilities of the space visible and using targeted spatial and nonspatial interventions to increase the "legibility" of the possibilities of a space.

It may be that this vision seems to amount to image construction. But it is more than that, it is an integrated process that combines a classic planning material dimension with an immaterial dimension of "building with images." It is not about the application of slogans and decals but the search for clues, empirical evidence, in other words, locating the material and immaterial triggers for mental maps of large-scale spaces and strengthening them. It is a process that takes up ideas formulated by Kevin Lynch (1960), applies these to the level of the region and thus translates his findings into the present-day context, in which immaterial, and in particular "mediatized," triggers for mental images have at least as great a significance as the spatialized triggers that Lynch emphasized (Lynch 1960).

Spatial stimulation adds an independent level to the classic instruments of urban regional management and planning: planned projects and measures are assessed in terms of their perceptual implications and supplemented by additional interventions oriented to the improvement of the "legibility" of a space.

This article can only delineate the vision of such a level of planning – and sketch its theoretical references. Nevertheless, it is hoped that it will contribute to an understanding of image production as a powerful tool for the stimulation of spatial production and as far more than simply a factor of locational marketing. It is time we reread the "heroes of mental mapping" and extended their findings into the present in order to render them useful for current planning practices.

How Is the "Space in the Mind" Generated? An Observation.

The image is familiar to many: behind Munich's Frauenkirche cathedral the mountains seem almost within touching distance; in the foreground, the masts of the Olympic stadium, which even today look futuristic, and the BMW "four-cylinder" tower; the sea of buildings is divided by Leopoldstrasse and Ludwigstrasse and punctuated by the many towers and domes of the city center. There are few photos that capture the essence of Munich so well: the tension between tradition, high tech and nature; IT managers living with mountain views who spend their weekends taking part in the rich cultural and sporting life of the metropolis.

The reality often looks different. Munich in autumn, gray heavy sky, constant rain, crowded trains, not a mountain in sight; instead, the monotony of the Schotterebene (Munich's gravel plain) that reminds one more of the flatlands around Cologne than Upper Bavaria.

Nevertheless, even in such moments of everyday grayness the postcard view of Munich remains present, as a remembered promise, as a collective image that encourages us to persevere in the face of everyday reality. The weekend is surely coming and thus the possibility of at least a small taste of the glamorous metropolis.

The telephoto panorama is an image that can make residents of Munich's bland suburbs proud: "Look! That's where we live." And it is an image that is taken out into the world in a million versions, by the media, by residents and visitors. It is such a powerful and clearly understandable promise that it channels the gaze of both visitors and external observers, a classic reading guide for the entire urban region.

The essential aspects of the image are like an index for the city, like a framework of reference that determines the segment that has been perceived. It is not the everyday grayness, the interchangeable urban aspects that occupy the foreground of perception, but the small reflections and materializations of Munich's essence. The next mountain cannot be that far away; after all, the preferred outfit here consists of an anorak and trekking shoes rather than a suit. And isn't Munich really a closet winter-sports venue, with its signs on walls warning of "roof avalanches"? Surfers in the Eisbach creek, high-tech laboratories next to cowsheds, biotech managers in lederhosen at the Oktoberfest, Andechs beer-brewing monks as corporate consultants – there are echoes of the triad of tradition, globalization and nature everywhere. Traces of Munich's essence can always be found if the gaze is focused and the corresponding expectations have been built up. The fact that the everyday existence of most Munich residents has nothing to do with this image is quickly forgotten.

This initial, associative view of a dominant mental map of Munich shows that the image we form of an urban region and the ideas it evokes in us are generated in the mind; this image is only partially a depiction of real spatial configurations. The individual building blocks of this perception could also be combined to form a different mosaic. However, the "image in the mind" that has already been established has the power to guide perception and action, and to a certain extent it directs our perception into established channels of the collective conception of space. This process involves an interplay between the imprints generated by media and their confirmation, structures and impressions that in turn take our own preconceptions as their reference point, a perceptual spiral that its seems worthwhile investigating.

What Lynch Says about the "Image in the Mind" – and What He Doesn't

How is the "image in the mind" generated? Answering this question from the perspective of city planning inevitably brings us to Kevin Lynch. Even before Lynch produced his oft-cited studies of the "Image of the City," the theme of spatial mental images was already a subject of research. However, it was Lynch who first systematically analyzed mental images of the urban space from a scholarly planning perspective. His empirical data and analyses of spatial structures as perceptual guides continue to provide a sound basis when it comes to understanding processes of spatial perception. However, Lynch does not provide a comprehensive answer to a question that is highly significant to current city and spatial planning, viz., how are conceptions of space generated at the level of the city as a whole or at the urban regional level, particularly under the conditions created by our contemporary media society?

This question has become a pressing one above all because the urban regional context is taking on an ever increasing significance – very obviously since the boom of the new spatial category of the mega-city region. The much disputed criteria for the delimitation of the mega-city region in themselves raise the question of whether these new spaces are in any way based on collective conceptions of space or simply follow the logic of political processes, according to the motto, "the bigger the better" (Knieling and Petrin forthcoming). In order to create genuine spaces of action and perception in the sense of a "perceptual region" (Blotevogel 1996), these new spatial constructs must first be made "legible," both internally and externally.

However, the question of the constitutive mechanisms of large-scale spatial conceptions has also becoming pressing because mediatized processes are obviously having an ever increasing influence on spatial production (Petrin 2006). This is not only illustrated by the clear tendency to imbue urban policy with the character of an event. The staging of urbanity via event architecture and the focusing of city development on symbolic projects also show that political action relating to urban development is increasingly becoming oriented to the level of the image. Put in simple terms, planning is focused on structures that generate images, since this is the only way to ensure visibility within the matrix of locational competition. The media shape the perceptual habits and "consumption patterns" of the city, but the media also represent the hurdle that urban space must successfully negotiate. Today, a media presence is crucial to success when competing with other locations. No image, no significance.

Lynch's work can no longer suffice as a basis for explaining and solving the pressing questions raised by such contemporary phenomena. Lynch focused on the neighborhood and the direct effect of morphology. However, at the level of the city as a whole, which largely eludes the scope of immediate and everyday perception, the mental image of space is constituted in part through the filters and amplifiers created by the media. Lynch does not provide us with explanatory tools in this respect even in his study "Managing the Sense of the Region," in which he applies the results of his research on a more extensive scale and seeks to define the rules of "legible" space (Lynch 1976). He does not consider the interaction of spatial symbols and the media, a phenomenon that is surely more significant in an epoch of the "economy of signs" (Lash and Urry 1994) than it was in Lynch's time.

When considering the question of how the "space in the mind" is generated, and above all the significance of mental images of space for spatial production, we therefore need to look beyond Lynch.

A Tour through the Disciplines

We are thus compelled to go in search of the constitutive mechanisms of conceptions of large-scale spaces. The aim of this search is to use the knowledge gained regarding perceptual triggers in order to increase the "legibility" of large-scale spatial contexts. The many different types of questions informing this search mean that it must necessarily be conducted at an interdisciplinary level. Many disciplines can only supply us with partial answers; we are dealing here with discursive spheres that intersect at only a few points, and we have yet to see a convergence of the range of current research relevant to spatial planning.[2] It is hoped that this article will also provide an impetus in this regard. Researching "images of the space" in the sense of individual and collective spatial conceptions is a substantial and complex endeavor that can only succeed if research is conducted on an interdisciplinary level. The definition of "spatial perception" as a specific research area is long overdue.

The immediate intention here is merely to identify several directions from which answers to our questions might come. The cognitive sciences, for example, provide insights into the selectivity and constructiveness of perception that are essential to any analysis of the genesis of conceptions of space. Neurobiology shows us that we see with our brains and not with our eyes. It is primarily our stored experiences and images that complete and overlay our relatively fragmented perception of our environment and thus generate our "image of the world" (Roth 2003).

These physiological foundations of spatial perception are complemented by findings in the field of psychology concerning the effect of form and color on perceptual processes and the significance of individual developmental processes for spatial understanding (Piaget and Inhelder 1975: 543).

With his theory of symbolic interaction, Herbert Blumer, who studied under the Chicago School's founding figure G.W. Mead, provides us with an insight into how group processes steer the focus and selectiveness of perception. The theory is based on three premises:
1. Humans act towards things on the basis of the meaning they ascribe to those things.
2. The meaning of such things is derived from, or arises out of, the social interaction that one has with others and the society.
3. These meanings are handled in, and modified through, an interpretive process used by the person in dealing with the things he/she encounters.

Blumer sees interaction as constitutive of meaning: "The meaning of a thing for a person grows out of the way in which other persons act toward the person with regard to the thing. Their actions operate to define the thing for the person. Symbolic interactionism sees meanings as social products, as creations that are formed in and through the defining activities of people as they interact" (Blumer 1981).

Even though the theory can be criticized for its lack of an adequate empirical foundation, it draws attention to the significance of the synthetic processes that repeatedly take a central role in sociological debates concerning space and its constitution. Symbolic interactionism provides a clear explanatory model of how the meaning of places, their individually and socially perceived potentiality, is established in a multilayered process of interaction, in a "network of actions" fixed as "lines of action." (Blumer 1981: 99). Although difficult to steer in a targeted way, this process can be potentially "plugged into" in many ways. Blumer and many other psychological and sociological theoreticians describe interaction processes that lead to the elaboration of the meaning of places, and they might well be understood as a possible intervention point for planning programs. Such processes certainly seem worthy of consideration when looking for ways to make regions "legible."

The question of the development of meaning and signification, a question that is central to the understanding of mental images of the urban-regional space, can also be considered within the context of cultural studies, a disciplinary field that offers important theoretical tools for an enquiry into the constitutive mechanisms of the "region in the mind."

Of particular relevance are the ideas and concepts associated with semiotics, which focuses on the interdependence of the "world of things" and meaning formation. However, in the mainstream discourse of the planning sciences (development planning, city planning and geography), semiotics is given only marginal consideration. A "semiotics of the region" that focuses on identifying systems of signification at a regional level and operationalizes these for planning practices has yet to be developed.[3] Such operationalization can hardly be expected from cultural-studies discourse. It is rather a case of the planning sciences needing to make more of the diverse insights offered by related disciplines.

The path from cultural studies leads directly to spatial sociology. While the appropriation and use of space cannot be understood without reference to the cultural context and its influence in terms of meaning, the assessment and perception of space is also conditioned by social situations and frameworks.

This brings us to a lively sociological discourse that is seeking to reposition the study of space as a central theme of sociology – also by referring to older concepts of the constitution of space. In relation to our own search for the constitutive mechanisms of the "space in the mind," this debate has arrived at the very interesting conclusion that in a social scientific sense space cannot be conceived of as an empty "vessel" waiting to be filled. For one area of sociology, space is the result of a complex interaction between material structures, actions, perceptions and evaluations, a social construct in constant flux.

There are many concepts and theoretical models dealing with the connections between evaluation, action and structure, ranging from the work of Foucault, Bourdieu and Giddens, to current contributions to debates by scholars such as Dieter Läpple and Martina Löw (Läpple 1992; Löw 2001). One reference point for the sociological discussion is Lefebvre's model of *production d'espace*, which clearly emphasizes the interdependence of material structures, representations and the experienced space (see Lefebvre 1991; Dünne and Günzel 2006). Lefebvre constructs a spatial model from three mutually overlapping elements: "spatial practice," "spatial representations" and "representational spaces," the "experienced space" mediated by images and symbols. For Lefebvre the experienced space, in particular, is an instrument that can exert influence on spatial production, by providing the possibility of conceiving alternatives to spatial practice (Shields 1999) and thus overcoming the contradiction he describes between (proletarian) spatial practice and spatial concepts shaped by capitalism (Dünne and Günzel 2006: 298). The experienced space thus becomes a type of "secret counterspace" (Shields 1999) that in a certain sense cannot be taken away from one. Even if this idea does not deal with the fact that even the individual "counterspace" is also influenced by the filtering and amplification processes of the media, in a time characterized by market-driven branding processes and economized spatial planning, Lefebvre's view can certainly be interpreted as a call not to leave the "framing" of space to material spatial producers but to use one's own subversive possibilities as a "recipient" of space, a call that cannot be understood without taking into account Lefebvre's situationist and Marxist background.

Läpple's concept of a constantly self-generating "matrix-space," (Läpple 1992: 196f.) which interprets space as an autopoietic system, also points to the interdependence of structures, norms and evaluations and thus indirectly emphasizes the level of synthesis as an independent level of the constitution of space, as does Martina Löw with her distinction between "placing" (the positioning of social goods and people) and "spacing" (the synthesis of space through evaluation) (Löw 2001: 158).

The reflections by spatial sociologists on the constructiveness of space can be seamlessly connected with the conclusions drawn in other disciplines, for example, neurobiological insights into the constructiveness of perception, the findings of developmental psychology regarding the formation of spatial knowledge, the explanation of processes of meaning formation in groups, and the insights provided in the field of semiotics. It is only by taking an overall view across these disciplines that we are able to explain our initial thesis that space first emerges in the mind. Space, in the form in which it "arrives," is a construct of perception and evaluation, of physiology and psychology, of possibilities, experiences and knowledge. Like a "second space," this "perceptual space" overlays the "physical space" and makes the latter's meaning and use visible to us, just as software brings hardware to life.

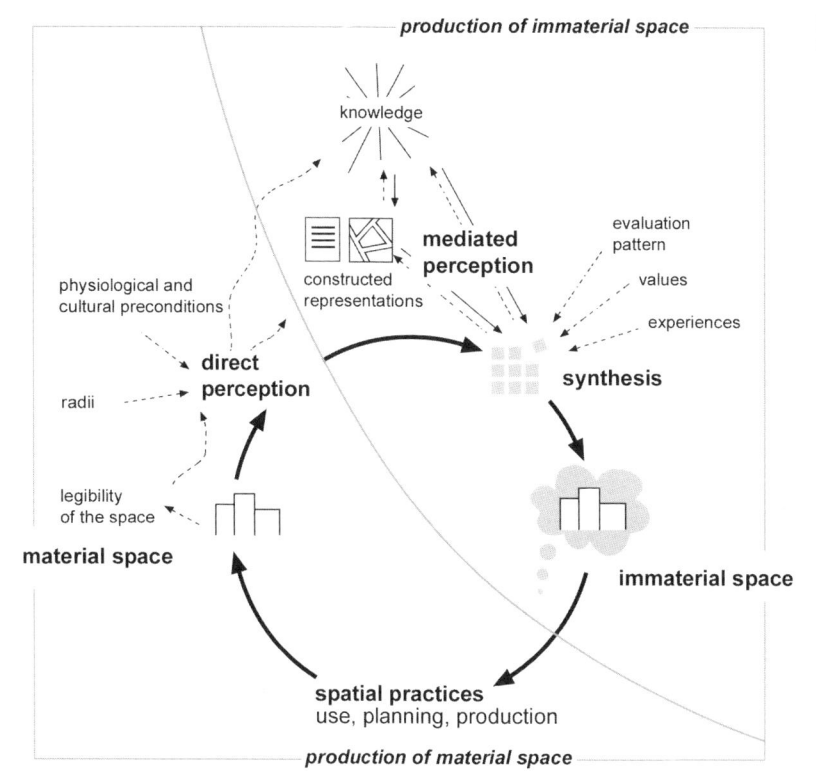

Figure 2:
The perceptual spiral.

The Duality of Space and the Perceptual Spiral

One of my aims here is to compress previous explanatory models of the constitution of the "space in the mind" into a simple model that is manageable for planning practice: the model of the duality of space. This model encompasses many of the ideas referred to above and attempts to provide a synoptic explanation of how the "space in the mind" or, to use the title of this book, the image of the mega-city region is synthesized today.

The goal of this model is to identify the "intervention points" in the synthetic process as the basis of a "toolset" for the "stimulation" of processes of spatial production.

The model of the duality of space is bounded by two poles, a material and an immaterial aspect of space, two "aggregate states" of space that reciprocally reproduce one another in a circular process. Limiting the model to these two aspects of space may seem to be an oversimplification when compared with other (especially sociological) multilevel models of space, and it could be interpreted as a backward step. However, this deliberate simplification serves to strengthen the focus on what, in my view, is the fundamental insight offered by this model, i.e., a focus on the "band wheels" driving the interdependence between the two essential aspects of space.

The first, obvious aspect of the dual spatial model is the "material" side, the measurable space of objects, of pathways, of located things. This contrasts with "immaterial" space, the synthesized image of space that in reality is neither an image nor a "mental map." The immaterial space is more a kind of hologram, an ideational model that is shaped in a constant process of reciprocal feedback between the two aspects of space.

The first band wheel in this process is the direct, sensory perception of "material space," which is restricted in several ways – by the physiologically conditioned constructiveness of perception, collective "perceptual norms" and the socially conditioned limits of our experiential radii.

The second band wheel driving the feedback between material and immaterial space is constituted by a system of filters and amplifiers: the mediated perception of "material space" via published knowledge and representations, e.g., pictures, maps, "spatial narratives" such as travelogues, as well as collective myths of the space and politico-economically motivated framings.

The immediate and the mediated perception of space overlay one another. It is this superimposition that forms the point of departure for the synthesis of individual and group-specific conceptions of space, which together describe the immaterial aspect of space. Interpersonal processes as a genesis of meaning play a role in this context as does an "immaterial background scenery" that comprises culturally conditioned values and evaluation patterns, individual and collective knowledge, and personal experiences.

It is here that the cycle of spatial production is completed: on the basis of individual and collective conceptions of space (the immaterial aspect of space) we select our path through the material aspect of space and reproduce our "immaterial image" of space on the material spatial side.

The model of the duality of space can be described in terms of a circular model that tends to a certain level of stability. We can only indirectly perceive what our perceptual radii permit and what is, so to speak, "extant" for us, a segment of the world that is determined in turn by what we actually allow through the filter of our selective perception. This is seen, for instance, in the confirmation of the previously described, perceptually guiding Munich postcard image in everyday spatial perception. At this point the first "band wheel" comes into play between the material and immaterial aspects of space: the multilayered system of filters and amplifiers that leads to our synthesized spatial image. The postcard picture of the essential Munich is only one part of this system.

As long as the filters and amplifiers only repeat stereotypical segments of reality, the system threatens to embed itself ever more deeply. One only perceives what one's own radius offers; the rest is preformatted by stereotyped images and narratives that stretch through the space like broad channels, common practice in mainstream tourism and locational marketing, which are largely built on stereotypes. As long as alternative or extensive options for framing are lacking, the interplay between "material" and "immaterial" space tends toward a stabilization of conditions, a phenomenon that I characterize as a "perceptual spiral."

Stimulating Spatial Perception

There should be new city maps of the "filled space" and the "hidden possibilities," tours to the "hidden treasures" or the "invisible futures," reading guides for coded spaces – maybe they could help us break through the perceptual spiral that always retracts to the conventional and the easily decipherable.

Such practices already exist in partial form, in the context of architectural tourism and in the tactics of the alternative architecture scene.[4] They bring forth the hidden images of space, which in any case take their own path as an alternative image and narrative cosmos without being able to break through the mainstream stereotype.

Working on the band wheels of spatial perception, particularly in the urban regional context, must amount to more than a cultural add-on to institutionalized planning. As an integrated level of spatial development anchored in the planning process, this process must comprehend the entire system of filters and amplifiers. It must seek coordinated measures on all levels, on the level of morphology, representation, symbol production and narration. The goal of establishing such a perceptually oriented planning layer must be to give equal visibility to what is evident and what is concealed, to improve the "first space" with regard to the synthesis of the "second space" and to offer alternatives to channels of stereotypical spatial images, that is, to promote the legibility of space in all its facets.

This requires research. The filters and amplifiers in the band wheel of the perceptual spiral need to be researched in more detail, as do the constitutive mechanisms of conceptions of large-scale spaces. Practical and experimental action is also required. Planners must embark on a search for the "immaterial space," make it visible and, as critical interventionists, offer alternative framings,[5] which is very much in Lefebvre's sense.

However, it must be clear from the outset that making space legible is not a process that can have a master plan. The complex and capricious processes of synthesis at the level of "immaterial space" constitute a self-steering system that can only be stimulated at specific points, by strategic interventions.

Rather than planning and production, we should speak here of stimulation, image stimulation or, better, spatial stimulation. The mental images that need to be stimulated are, as described, integral parts of the space and are an important key to spatial production. By stimulating mental images, we stimulate the cycle of spatial production and guide the space out of the "perceptual spiral." For this reason, I would like to characterize the work on and with spatial mental images, the improvement of the legibility of space, as spatial stimulation.

One day there may be a strategic planning system for urban regions with a layer dedicated to the improvement of the legibility of the space and its potentialities, a "perception strategy" that supplements the classic planning level and identifies measures and action levels of spatial stimulation.

A wide-ranging analysis of space, its zones, borderlines, gaps and functional networks, as well as spatial and nonspatial triggers, media images, constructed symbols, appellations and stereotypes, can delineate an image of the prevailing situation gained through the comparison of a wide-ranging survey of spatial habits and mental images organized in terms of groups and social situations with morphological and functional spatial analyses.

The result will be an atlas of perceived urban regions.

The knowledge gained will form the basis of the "perception strategy," i.e., media-based interventions that break through perceptual stereotypes, subversive image productions and concrete utopias that open discursive corridors and awaken "urban wishes," spatialized projects and standards for urban-structural measures with which the legibility of the space can be improved – a type of urban-structural guidance system – as well as proposals for the renaming of places, paths and routes through spatial contexts that have previously not been perceived, city maps that are upside down, travel guides for the future, perceptual networks, the irritating and the inspiring. The diversity of the images of space will stimulate the production of space and make the urban region an open book.

Notes

[1] One element of the "Cities Without Cities" discourse is the concept of address formation, the profiling of locational identity (see Sieverts 1997a, 1997b).

[2] A synopsis of research into the constitution of space in a range of disciplines can be found in the anthologies *Die Gesellschaft und ihr Raum* (Krämer-Badoni and Kuhm 2003) and *Raumtheorie* (Dünne and Günzel 2006).

[3] Roland Barthes relates semiotics and planning sciences to one another in his reflections on "semiology and urbanism," albeit at an abstract theoretical level (see Barthes 1985).

[4] The "harbor safari" in Hamburg offers alternative perspectives on the harbor, which is normally largely masked or caught up in stereotypical images (see www.hafensafari.de).

[5] One example of such an alternative framing that subverts Hamburg's mental map is the "Playa Hamburgo" project by urbanista, www.playahamburgo.de.

References

Barthes, R. 1985. "Sémiologie et urbanisme." *L'aventure sémiologique*. Paris: Éd. du Seuil.

Blotevogel, H.H. 1996. "Auf dem Wege zu einer Theorie der Regionalität: Die Region als Forschungsobjekt der Geographie." In *Region und Regionsbildung in Europa. Konzeptionen der Forschung und empirische Befunde*, edited by G. Brunn, vol. 1. Baden-Baden: Institut für Europäische Regionalforschungen: 44-68.

Blumer, H. 1981. "Der methodologische Standort des symbolischen Interaktionismus." In *Alltagswissen, Interaktion und gesellschaftliche Wirklichkeit* (1+2), edited by the Arbeitsgruppe Bielefelder Soziologen. Opladen: Westdeutscher Verlag: 80-146.

Dünne, J. and S. Günzel. 2006. *Raumtheorie. Grundlagentexte aus Philosophie und Kulturwissenschaften*. Frankfurt am Main: Suhrkamp.

Faludi, A. 1996. "Framing with Images." *Environment and Planning B: Planning and Design* 23: 93-108.

Knieling, J. and J. Petrin. forthcoming. "Das Bildversprechen der Metropolregion – Potenziale und Risiken einer bildmächtigen Raumkategorie." Article worked out in the context of "Arbeitskreis Metropolregionen der Akademie für Raumforschung und Landesplanung."

Krämer-Badoni, T. and K. Kuhm (eds.). 2003. *Die Gesellschaft und ihr Raum. Raum als Gegenstand der Soziologie. Stadt, Raum und Gesellschaft* vol. 21. Opladen: Leske + Budrich.

Läpple, D. 1992. "Essay über den Raum: Für ein gesellschafts-wissenschaftliches Raumkonzept (Diskussionsbeitrag 12)." In *Stadt und Raum: Soziologische Analysen. Stadt, Raum und Gesellschaft* vol.1, edited by H. Häußermann et al., 2nd ed. Pfaffenweiler: Centaurus-Verlag: 157-207.

Lash, S. and J. Urry. 1994. *Economies of Sign and Space*. London: Sage Publications.

Lefebvre, H. 1991. *The Production of Space*. Oxford: Blackwells.

Löw, M. 2001. *Raumsoziologie*, Suhrkamp Taschenbuch Wissenschaft 1506. Frankfurt am Main: Suhrkamp Verlag.

Lynch, K. 1960. *The Image of the City*. Cambridge, Massachusetts, and London, England: The M.I.T. Press.

Lynch, K. 1976. *Managing the Sense of a Region*. Cambridge, Massachusetts, and London, England: The M.I.T. Press.

Petrin, J. 2006. "Die gemachte Metropole – Hamburgs medialisierte Planungs- und Baukultur schafft sich ihre Realität." In *Architektur in Hamburg Jahrbuch*, edited by Hamburgische Architektenkammer. Hamburg: Junius Verlag.

Piaget, J. and B. Inhelder. 1975. *Die Entwicklung des räumlichen Denkens beim Kinde*. Stuttgart: Klett-Cotta.

Roth, G. 2003. "Ich – Körper – Raum. Die Konstruktion der Erlebniswelt durch das Gehirn." In *Die Gesellschaft und ihr Raum. Raum als Gegenstand der Soziologie. Stadt, Raum und Gesellschaft* vol. 21, edited by T. Krämer-Badoni and K. Kuhm. Opladen: Leske + Budrich: 35-52.

Shields, R. 1999. *Lefèbvre, Love & Struggle, Spatial Dialectics*. London and New York: Routledge.

Sieverts, T. 1997a. "Wiedergelesen. Kevin Lynch und Christopher Alexander. Das Aufbrechen und Wiedererfinden der Konvention – auf der Spur des Geheimnisses lebendiger Räume und Städte," *DISP* 129 (2/1997): 52-59.

Sieverts, T. 1997b. "Zur Lesbarkeit und inneren Verfügbarkeit der Stadtregion Berlin als Lebensraum." *Raum und Identität. Potentiale und Konflikte in der Stadt- und Regionalentwicklung*. Graue Reihe 15. Erkner bei Berlin: IRS: 53-69.

vis

Remo Burkhard

Visualizing Desires, not Cities

How can we visualize the multifaceted qualities of a mega-city region? By using complementary visualizations. We have extensive experience visualizing explicit information, such as statistical and geographical data (e.g., population, borders, climate, commuters, distances, transportation networks, municipalities), and along with that using visual formats that support cognitive functions. However, we have neglected to exploit the emotional and social functions of visualizations and to visualize desires. Here we can learn from writers, travelers, architects, filmmakers. This article examines how we can visualize the different spatial dimensions of a mega-city region and lays out existing visualization approaches with the overall goal of improving planning, understanding, and communication of mega-city regions – especially when different stakeholders are involved, such as in participatory planning processes. Finally, the article introduces the knowledge visualization framework with four perspectives that are relevant to the development of customized visualizations. Its application is then discussed in a case study where the goal was to visualize nonphysical concepts of the Science City campus planning project.

I   Introduction

Visualizing knowledge so that it can be better understood, discussed, planned, or communicated is an old objective in different fields – also in the planning disciplines.

When we think of visualizations and mega-city regions we might first think of regional marketing campaigns with photographs of lakes, recreation spots, shopping streets, local events, monuments, and museums. While such images work well for physical objects (e.g., Eiffel Tower, a lake), they are often too generic and exchangable when they address nonphysical contents, such as "quality of living," "business networks," or a "knowledge city." On the other hand, we might think of maps or statistical charts from geographers, economists or statisticians. Their formats allow one to master high degrees of complexity. However, this level of detail is often too complex or too technical for communication with a broader audience or different stakeholders, such as local authorities, politicians, industry, and others. Finally, what is missing are formats that exploit the social and emotional functions of visualizations. This becomes important as soon as different stakeholders are involved, which is the general situation in the context of mega-city regions.

Why visualize a mega-city region?

First, we have difficulties perceiving and communicating mega-city regions. While referring to a traditional understanding, cities are made up of clear opposites like center and periphery; mega-city regions are more like a network that bridges different scales, such as local, regional, and global scales. Furthermore, mega-city regions consist of different not necessarily corresponding spatial dimensions, such as morphological and functional, material and immaterial. Due to these multidimensional attributes of a mega-city region and its network character, we have trouble perceiving it. Both researchers and the public cannot answer simple questions such as, Where does the mega-city region start and end?

Second, we do not have enough experience to use visualizations in participatory planning processes, for example, to establish a mutual vision, or to map the desires of the involved participants, as was done in the project "Quartier 21" in Lausanne (see www.quartier21.ch). Here a diagrammatic visualization of the 37 projects improved the participatory planning process and served as a mirror reflecting the desires of the different stakeholders. In such projects where different stakeholders are involved novel visualization formats appear promising.

Third, we have not yet mastered the challenge of visualizing nonphysical contents. How can we map functional relationships and interdependencies of subparts in mega-city regions? Which methods allow us to visualize long-term planning processes? How do we map clusters of knowledge in mega-city regions?

Additionally, we also have to keep in mind that spatial planning involves two main processes similar to the design of a product that are also applicable in the context of mega-city regions: First, the process of engineering the product or spatial intervention in the mega-city region and, second, the process of communicating the added value of the product or spatial intervention in the mega-city region to the user. This second process is challenging because it involves the user, who has to create his own mental image of the product or mega-city region. Here, visualizing desires plays an important role. Just think of Aston Martin, Apple's iPod, or Jamie Oliver and the emotions that are evoked. The claim of this article is that if we want to visualize mega-city regions we should also address social and emotional factors and visualize desires.

To answer the above questions and in support of the analysis, planning, and communication of mega cities, new visual formats need to be developed. A first step in this direction is the use of visualizations that complement each other.

II The Use of Complementary Visualizations

Most of our brain's activity deals with processing and analyzing visual images. To understand perception, we have to know that our brain does not differ greatly from that of our ancestors, the troglodytes. At that time, perception helped for basic functions, for example, hunting (motion detection), seeking food (color detection), or applying tools (object-shape perception). Since then, visual representations have served a variety of functions, such as addressing emotions, illustrating relations, discovering trends, patterns, exceptions, getting and keeping the attention of recipients, supporting remembrance and recall, presenting both an overview and details, facilitating learning, coordinating individuals, establishing a mutual story, or energizing and motivating people. Before we come back to this functional perspective, seven main visualization types are distinguished. They are derived from the practice of planners, cartographers, architects, marketing experts, writers and filmmakers.

The visualization types can be structured into seven groups: Sketches, Diagrams, Images, Maps, Objects, Interactive Visualizations and Stories (Burkhard 2005a).

Sketches are atmospheric and help quickly visualize a concept. They present key features, support reasoning and arguing, and allow room for one's own interpretation. Sketches are heavily used by architects and urban planners for analytical and design tasks and to communicate ideas or visions. Another type is instant napkin sketches, for example, to explain the way to a specific place, which is heavily used in Tokyo.

Diagrams are abstract, schematic representations used to explore structural relationships among different parts by denoting functional relationship. Diagrams explain causal relationships, reduce complexity to key issues, structure and display relationships. Quantitative diagrams are used to visualize statistical information or economic indicators, such as climate curves, population, growth, etc. Diagrams are used by architects and urban planners to visualize elements of cities, such as functional zones or flows of persons. Diagrams are also used to visualize the phases of urban or regional planning projects.

Images are representations that can visualize impression, expression or realism. An image can be a photograph, a computer rendering, a painting, or another format. Images catch the attention, inspire, address emotions, improve recall and initiate discussions. Images are instant and rapid, instructive, and they facilitate learning. In the context of mega-city regions we can benefit from satellite images of mega cities. Alternatively, mega-city regions can be communicated by means of visual metaphors. Such visual metaphors support recall, lead to aha effects, and buttress reasoning and communication. In the marketing of a city or region, images are often used to visualize highlights, e.g., urban places, monuments, cosy restaurants, shopping streets, business centers, museum districts, recreation sites, local events. This works well. However, images could also be used to explain abstract concepts, such as value propositions or synergies for companies. An example is the strong image of an elderly man in a traditional costume in a beer garden working with a high-tech laptop. This image illustrates that Munich is both a site with traditional roots and a high-tech industry.

Maps represent individual elements (e.g., roads) in a global context (e.g., a city). Maps illustrate both overview and details; they show relationships among items, they structure information through spatial alignment and they allow close-ups and easy access to information. Maps generally have a scale that determines the size of an object represented on the map in relation to its actual size. Some maps are not scaled, for example, the subway train map that uses a visual system that distorts the real distances to obtain a more readable map. The features on a map depend on its purpose: a road map displays roads, a subway map shows the underground train system, and thematic maps represent thematic entities such as the thematic similarities in the top right window in Figure 1. Further examples of maps are interactive satellite maps (Global Positioning System, GPS), combined with superimposed layers of location-based information (e.g., restaurants, shops, history of a building), for car drivers or users of mobile devices. Such interactive and location-based information systems could in the near future serve as a compass for users of cities and regions.

Objects exploit the third dimension and are haptic. They help attract recipients (e.g., a physical dinosaur in a science museum), support learning through constant presence and allow the integration of digital interfaces. Many cities have a wooden three-dimensional model of themselves, but often only of their core cities. An impressive model is Shanghai's. The creation of such models is expensive and time consuming. Despite all the wonderful possibilities of virtual reality applications, the qualities of a physical model still attract us more and are more suitable for gaining an overview and understanding spatial relationships. While such models are helpful and attractive, they also face a problem when it comes to mega-city regions. Here the very large territory leads to a problematic relationship between the heights and lengths – models of mega-city regions more closely resemble a landscape model than a city model. As soon as we need to filter or work with the model and switch on or off different layers of information, a virtual model can become more powerful. Such a virtual three-dimensional model annotated with additional information (e.g., Google Earth) could be used to simulate all kinds of information (weather, history, people, cars, etc.) or to simulate temporal data, such as potential future development scenarios.

Interactive visualizations are computer-based visualizations that allow users to access, control, combine and manipulate different types of information or media. Interactive visualizations help catch people's attention, enable interactive collaboration across time and space, and make it possible to represent and explore complex data or create new insights. Interactive geographic information systems are appreciated by the general user and have lately been used by companies or portals as an orientation layer to map additional information, such as hotels, cafés or instant mapping of the amount of rain that is falling, be it integrated into websites or the onboard computers of cars. Figure 1 shows a tool to explore and compare cities according to roughly twenty criteria, such as average salary, average price for a bus ticket, or population size (Brodbeck and Girardin 2003). Each line in this "parallel coordinates" view connects the values of the individual attributes of one city. Comparing two lines (and thus two cities) shows similarities and differences with regard to all attributes. In the thematic similarity view each city is visualized with a dot. The closer two dots are, the more similar the two cities are with regard to the criteria and vice versa. Sliders can be used to interactively filter the dataset. This kind of visualization allows users to explore a larger amount of structured data. It is good for analytical purposes, but too complex for communication with the general public or different stakeholders.

Another subgroup of this type is interactive animations, fly-throughs, or movies that need a storyboard. Thanks to the film industry, we are familiar with many cities, even if we have not been there. However, when we watch a movie of the city we live in, we often realize that it is a distorted reality. One reason why many guests from India visit Switzerland is that "honeymoon in Switzerland" is a key element in the Indian film industry. That's why a lot of them come to visit the original sites. A similar sector that will become more important in the future is virtual cities and the gaming industry. Another example of interactive visualization is augmented reality, which means superimposing relevant information in real time on windshields of cars or special eyeglasses.

Stories and mental images are imaginary and nonphysical visualizations. When we think of a city we automatically remember stories associated with it. Stories are a very effective method to share different impressions and experiences. One format that captures personal experiences is a diary. A new form of a public diary is weblogs. They exist for cities and could also be applied to the new spatial scale of mega-city regions. Another

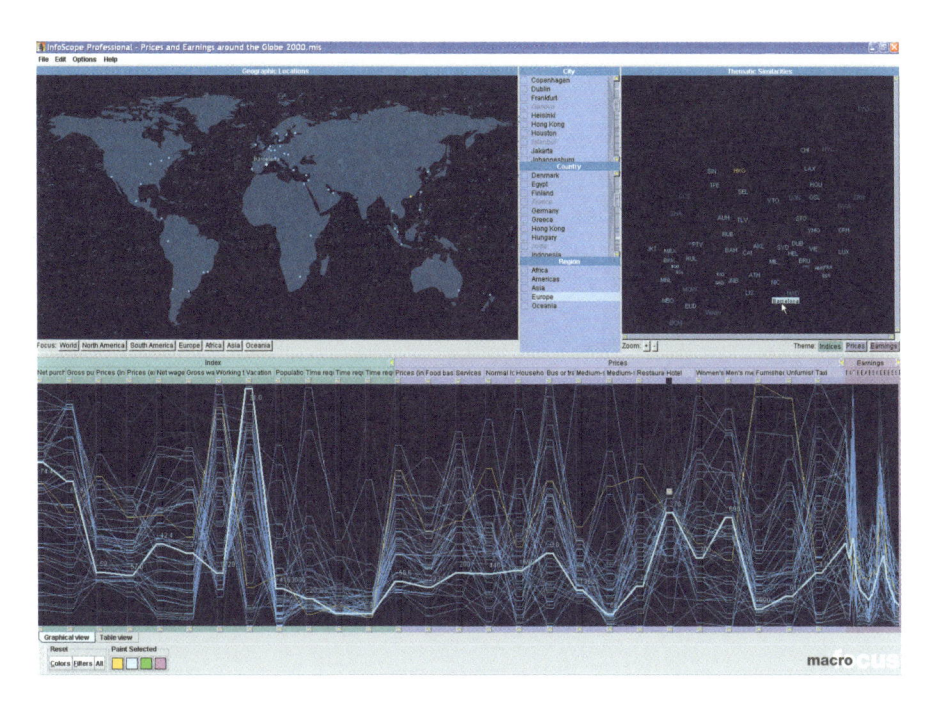

Figure 1:
An interactive visualization allows one to visually analyze a high-dimensional dataset.

Above, Barcelona and Hong Kong are selected and the slider "Hotel" is filtering the dataset.

type is mental images of a city. Kevin Lynch (1960) pointed to the spatial perception of city users and the associated mental maps, which consist of five elements: (1) *paths* on which people travel, such as streets and trails; (2) *edges* and perceived boundaries, such as walls, buildings and shorelines; (3) *districts*, such as sections of the city with a specific identity or character; (4) *nodes*, such as focal points, intersections or loci; (5) *landmarks*, readily identifiable objects that serve as reference points (Lynch 1960). Architects often envision and discuss scenarios. In order to explicate these ideas, architects might rediscover the power of narrative texts to explain their concepts to the general public. Here we can learn from novelists. One example is Italo Calvino's novel where Khan is too busy governing his empire to travel, so he asks Marco Polo to describe the cities he has seen (Calvino 1974). The short descriptions of the 55 cities combine facts and tales Marco Polo has heard about the city regions and cities. Some of them only exist in our imagination, such as an underground city of the dead.

Storytelling is of course also used to explain how to get from one place to another. In some situations such narrative descriptions can be more suitable than a map, for example, to navigate the narrow and mazelike streets of a North African medina. The key to orientation here is to remember the different souks.

This section introduced seven visualization types and thus presented a *visualization type perspective*. However, before we are able to pick one or more visualization types we need to answer the questions why, what, and for whom a visualization is necessary.

III   Knowledge Visualization Framework

The research field *Knowledge Visualization* concentrates on the use of complementary visualizations in knowledge-intense processes, where knowledge has to be created or reconstructed by each individual (Eppler and Burkhard 2005; Chen 2003; Burkhard 2005b; Burkhard 2005a). Knowledge Visualization research (1) identifies the related fields that investigate visual methods for the transfer and creation of knowledge; (2) integrates their insights into theoretical frameworks and models; (3) serves in this way as a mediator among isolated fields; (4) relates these insights to predominant problems in different domains, such as business and science; and finally (5) invents novel visual approaches where no suitable visualization technique could have been identified.

One of these theoretical frameworks is the Knowledge Visualization Framework (KVF) that describes four perspectives that should be considered when using visualizations in knowledge-intense processes. This general model can be applied to the context of mega-city regions and can also serve practitioners. The perspectives are based on four questions: (1) What is the purpose of using a visualization method? (2) What type of knowledge needs to be visualized? (3) Who is being addressed? (4) What is the most appropriate visualization type? Answers to these questions lead to the Knowledge Visualization Framework that is illustrated in Figure 2 (Burkhard 2005b; Eppler and Burkhard 2005).

The *Function Type Perspective* distinguishes different functions of visual representation for processing information based on research in perception and neuroscience (Farah 2000; Ware 2000; Koffka 1935). Six functions with social, emotional and cognitive functions are summarized in the CARMEN Acronym (Eppler and Burkhard 2005): *C*oordination: Visual representations help coordinate individuals in the communication process. *A*ttention: They catch people's attention by addressing emotions, hold their attention and allow one to identify patterns, exceptions, and trends. *R*ecall: They improve memorability and recall. *M*otivation: They inspire, motivate, energize and activate viewers. *E*laboration: They foster the elaboration of knowledge in teams. *N*ew In-sights: They support the creation of new insights by embedding details within context, by showing relationships between objects, or by leading to aha effects.

The *Knowledge Type Perspective* aims to identify the type of knowledge that needs to be transferred. Five types of knowledge that are grounded in the knowledge management literature (Alavi and Leidner 2001) are distinguished: Know-what (declarative knowledge, as facts); Know-how (procedural knowledge, as knowing how things are done); Know-why (experimental knowledge, as knowing why things occur which captures underlying cause-and-effect relationships and takes account of exceptions, adaptations, and unforeseen events); Know-where (orientational knowledge as knowing where information can be found); Know-who (individual knowledge, as knowing experts).

The *Recipient Type Perspective* aims to identify the target group, the context, and the background of the recipients. The recipient can be an individual, a team, an organization (one culture), or a network of subjects (different cultures). Knowing the context and the educational, emotional, and cultural background of the recipient/audience is essential to finding the most promising visualization type.

Only if we know why, what, and for whom we have to develop a visual format can we decide which visualization types need to be chosen or combined. But how can we visualize a higher degree of complexity – the "in-between complexity," that is, a complexity that lies between "too complex" and "too simple"? The next section shows how the in-between complexity has been visualized in an actual case.

Function Type	Knowledge Type	Recipient Type	Visualization Type
Coordination	Know-what	Individual	Sketch
Attention	Know-how	Group	Diagram
Recall	Know-why	Organization	Image
Motivation	Know-where	Network	Map
Elaboration	Know-who		Object
New Insight			Interactive Visualization
			Story

Figure 2:
The Knowledge Visualization Framework presents four perspectives and key elements.

IV Case: Visualizing Science City

Science City is the vision and project for a sustainable campus of ETH Zurich that consists of new buildings and programs. From the very beginning it was easy to communicate the idea of the new buildings. But the challenge was to illustrate nonphysical concepts, such as student exchange programs, public events, systematic development of international relations, integrated sustainability concepts, wireless access from everywhere for everyone, or a new alumni program. To explain such nonphysical projects, which are the key to improving the quality of living, researching, and working, complementary visualizations were used.

Three concepts needed to be visualized: First, a shared vision. Second, interlinked programs. Third, an integrated sustainability concept.

The first challenge was to use visualizations to co-create *a shared vision*. To do so, key visuals were used to inspire different target groups. The different ideas, dreams, needs were then collected in a participatory planning process, where the group sketches were used to collect and externalize imaginations. The resulting stories, metaphors and sketches of different participants helped everybody better understand the desires and needs, be it from a professor, a student, a local inhabitant, a donor, or a politician. The process made it possible to sharpen the original vision and to motivate various persons to contribute their own resources to support the process and the vision. In these "design labs" and "future labs," Science City emerged as an idea that could find broad support while inspiring the individual. However, the question was how to visualize these different ideas and dreams. The first step was to use the power of storytelling to describe the different scenarios in which the participants had imagined what the finished project could look like in 2011. Ten short stories, fictitious portraits, illustrate the individual benefits for each specific stakeholder from different points of view. The stories integrate facts and desires. These stories are easy to understand and tell to friends. The stories are the starting point for the development of a frame for these stories (Figure 3). This poster integrates the stories at the bottom and links them to either Science City, Zurich, or the world map through lines.

The Science City Map is a poster that conveys the programs and associative information. It combines different graphic elements, such as geographic maps, building plans, statistical information, text, arrows, hotspots, or fictitious stories. The map consists of three parts, viz., a world map, a map of the new Science City campus and a map of Zurich. Interrelations of the programs with the world or the city of Zurich are illustrated with pink lines that are tagged with short sentences (e.g., "*a professor from MIT moves to Science City and*

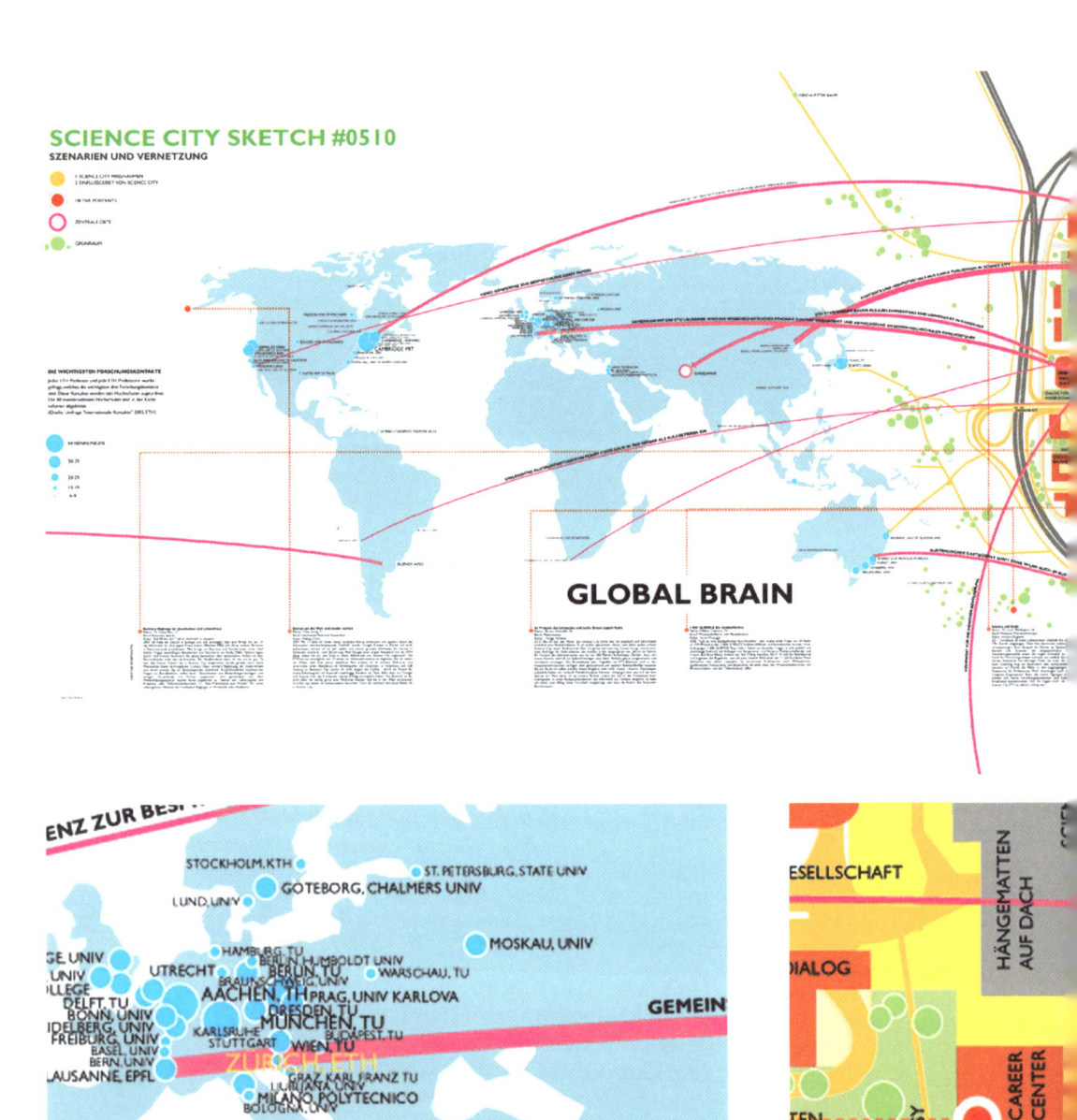

Figure 3:
The 2 x 5 m Science City Poster combines stories, geographic maps, statistical information and other visual elements.

SCIENCE CITY **ZURICH**

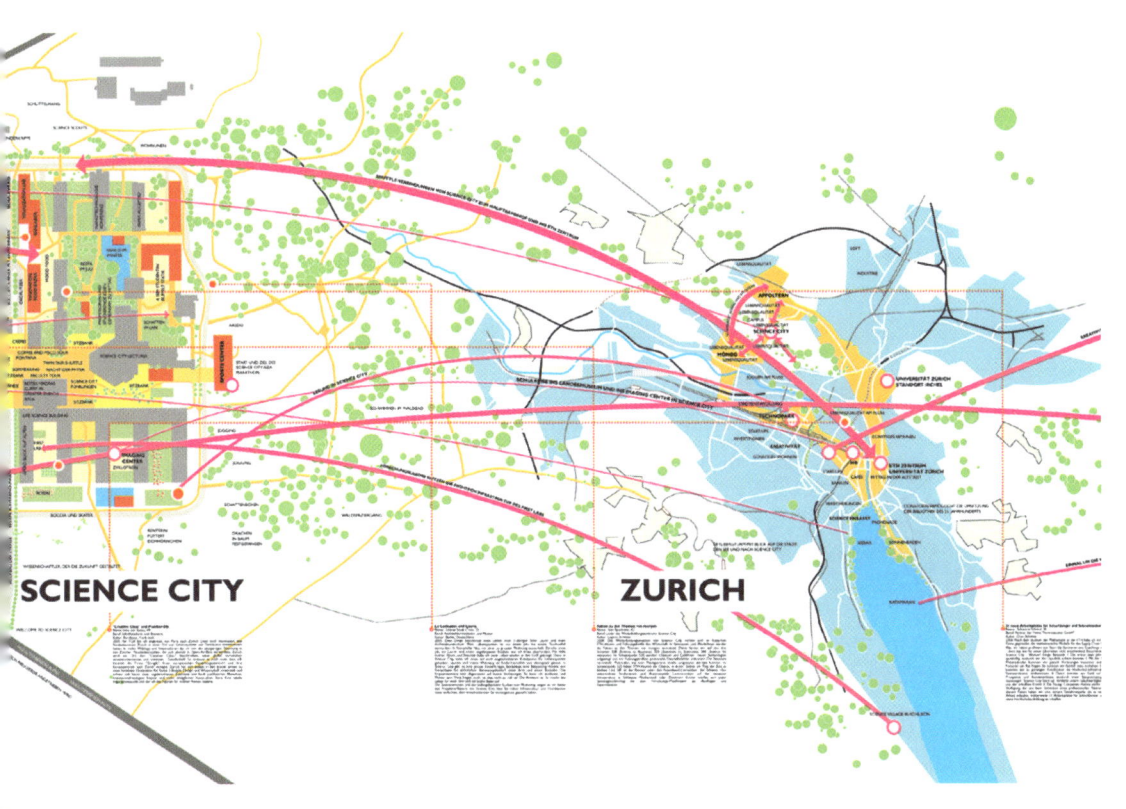

Fakten zu den Themen von morgen
Name: Ivan Spielmann, 42
Beruf: Leiter des Weiterbildungszentrums Science City
Kultur: Lugano, Schweiz
2008: Das Weiterbildungsangebot von Science City richtet sich an Experten, ETH-Alumni und Führungskräfte der Wirtschaft. In Seminaren und Workshops werden die Fakten zu den Themen von morgen vermittelt. Dabei fahren wir auf den drei Schienen S2B (Science to Business), S2S (Scientists to Scientists), S4E (Science for everyone). Im Schwerpunkt S2B werden Chancen und Gefahren neuer Technologien aufgezeigt und mit Führungskräften potentielle Geschäftsfelder diskutiert. Die Seminare vermitteln Methoden, die vom Management direkt umgesetzt werden können. Im Schwerpunkt S2S haben ETH-Alumni die Chance, in ihrem Gebiet am Puls der Zeit zu bleiben. Und S4E ist der Renner unter den Feierabend-Lernenden der Schweiz. Hier

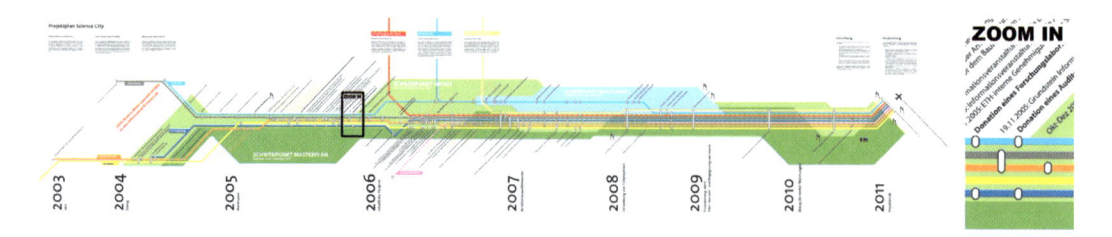

Figure 4:
The Project Subway Map uses an underground train map system.

establishes a new institute"). The map was used as a physical poster in exhibitions and integrated into the website as a digital map, where visitors were able to click on individual elements. Interviews and observations of persons examining the map during the exhibitions showed that the average reader studied the map between five and ten minutes. The individual short texts in the plan or the labeled lines were easy to read and gave viewers a deep understanding of the project on the whole. The spatial localization of the different ideas and concepts helped people imagine what living in Science City could be like. Readers could see how different programmatic elements interrelate, which led to aha effects. It can be argued that the map is a clever way to sell the idea and has more to do with marketing than with the visualization of different dimensions of the project. This is partly true. However, the reason for this visualization was to capture and visualize desires of the different stakeholders. It is therefore more like a mirror of desires and a mutual vision than a top-down marketing campaign. This first example is relevant for all participatory planning processes.

A second challenge in the design of Science City was the communication of complementary programs that support campus life. In 2005, more than 60 programs and projects were suggested that aimed to bring life into Science City. Finally, the collected ideas were consolidated into 30 projects, grouped in the areas of Research, Teaching and Campus Life. But how could it be made possible to communicate both an overview and the individual status of the 30 projects? The power of visual metaphors was used. Instead of a project Gantt chart, a "Project Subway Map" was created. Figure 4 shows the project and milestones of the project. Each line represents a target group, each station a collective or individual milestone. The 5 m long poster gives detailed information and illustrates who is collaborating with whom at different milestones. This visualization was presented in the *Infospot*, a physical project information space. An evaluation of another Project Subway Map can be found in Burkhard and Meier (Burkhard and Meier 2005). This second example is relevant for all participatory planning processes.

Currently, we are tackling a third challenge: To visualize the integrated sustainability concept that involves alternative and sustainable methods for financing and long-term-oriented sustainability concepts, ranging from the city scale to the energy concept and the materials of an individual building. The question is how to address the concept in a way that is less technical and more emotional. Only if we also reach the hearts of the users for this integrated sustainability will it be possible to go beyond technical standards and benchmarks.

In conclusion, to visualize the three important nonphysical concepts of Science City, the approach visualizing the in-between complexity was chosen. Not replacing but complementing traditional formats, such as images, diagrams and interactive visualizations. The large-scale maps further tried not only to map facts, but address emotions and visualize desires. Feedback from diverse groups has shown that our initial fears that people might get confused or become disoriented were unfounded. Negative aspects were that some people were confused by a few sentences in the fictitious portraits. From a resource perspective, writing the fictitious portraits took two working days, the design of each map around six.

V Summary: Use Complementary Visualizations and Visualize Desires

This article proposed that one successful way to visualize a mega-city region is to use complementary visualizations. That means we should combine different functional benefits of visual representations, such as cognitive, social, and emotional functions, to illustrate a mega-city region from different points of view. The approach was applied to a topic that has been neglected: the aspect of evoking emotions and visualizing desires.

References

Alavi, M., and D. Leidner. 2001. "Knowledge Management and Knowledge Management Systems: Conceptual Foundations and Research Issues." *MIS Quarterly* 25 (1): 107-136.

Brodbeck, D., and L. Girardin. 2003. "Design Study: Using Multiple Coordinated Views to Analyze Georeferenced High-dimensional Datasets." Paper read at CMV 2003, at London.

Burkhard, R. 2005a. *Knowledge Visualization – The Use of Complementary Visual Representations for the Transfer of Knowledge. A Model, a Framework, and Four New Approaches*. PhD Thesis, ETH Zurich, Zurich.

Burkhard, R. 2005b. "Towards a Framework and a Model for Knowledge Visualization: Synergies between Information and Knowledge Visualization." In *Knowledge and Information Visualization: Searching for Synergies. LNCS 3426*, edited by S.-O. Tergan and T. Keller. Heidelberg: Springer-Verlag.

Burkhard, R., and M. Meier. 2005. "Tube Map Visualization: Evaluation of a Novel Knowledge Visualization Application for the Transfer of Knowledge in Long-Term Projects." *Journal of Universal Computer Science* 11 (4): 473-494.

Calvino, I. 1974. *Invisible Cities*. Orlando: Harcourt.

Chen, C. 2003. *Mapping Scientific Frontiers: The Quest for Knowledge Visualization*. London: Springer.

Eppler, M., and R. Burkhard. 2005. "Knowledge Visualization." In *Encyclopedia of Knowledge Management*, edited by D. Schwartz. New York: Idea Press.

Farah, M.J. 2000. *The Cognitive Neuroscience of Vision, Fundamentals of Cognitive Neuroscience*. Oxford: Blackwell Publishers.

Koffka, K. 1935. *The Principles of Gestalt Psychology*. London: Lund Humphries.

Lynch, K. 1960. *The Image of the City*. Cambridge, Massachusetts, and London, England: The M.I.T. Press.

Ware, C. 2000. *Information Visualization: Perception for Design*. San Francisco (CA): Morgan Kaufmann.

pe

Eckart Lange

Perceiving and Visualizing Changing Environments

Images are powerful means of communication. This article addresses issues of how we perceive images as physical representations of our environment, i.e., how we see our environment, how mental images, that exist in our minds, influence the perception of our environment and how we represent the existing "reality" and alternative future scenarios in the planning context through visualization techniques. While the future is always characterized through a high degree of uncertainty, visualization techniques offer options for making the future look as if it were real. This raises some questions regarding modes of representation.

Perceptions of Mega-City Regions

When taking a closer look at the title of the symposium, "The Image and the Region – Making Mega-City Regions Visible!" several questions immediately come to mind. For example, on the one hand we can ask *how* one makes mega-city regions visible but we can also ask *why*? Of course, next to showing the actual extent of a mega-city region, from a planner's point of view the challenge is how to make the future of the mega-city regions visible. Also, as planners and designers we should be concerned about how we communicate with the public and the clients and even how we communicate as planners and designers among ourselves.

One valid question to be asked is also, *What is a mega-city region*? Undoubtedly such a label can be attached to a number of places on our planet, such as the Tokyo metropolitan area. The same applies to New York, Mexico City, etc. But does this label also apply to cities such as Berlin, Munich, Copenhagen, Brussels or Amsterdam? Perhaps. How about cities such as Torino, Stockholm or Zurich? Perhaps not. It is certainly a matter of scale and placing it in context. Someone visiting from sparsely settled Sweden might perceive Stockholm as a mega-city region, whereas a visitor from Tokyo might be thinking of Stockholm as a lovely little town.

Also, it is extremely difficult to define the extent of a mega-city or a metropolitan area. Typically, the center is relatively easy to mark, but where does the city end? For example, traveling out of Tokyo by car or by high-speed train it is quite tricky to judge the city's limits because to the north and south for a long distance it is all built-up area. Only in aerial/satellite view the actual outline of the mega-city region is revealed – so to speak, the Google Earth view.

Natural borders created through terrain or water bodies, such as in the case of Tokyo with the Japanese Alps to the west and the Pacific Ocean to the east, typically influence the borders of mega-city regions. Such natural borders are often visually highly prominent. Together with artificial, superimposed, invisible administrative borders they play a key role in influencing and shaping the visual outline of such regions and how we perceive them.

In addition to the physically perceivable features of such mega-city regions it is the mental image, i.e., the image that already exists in our minds and is influenced by past experiences and knowledge, that shapes our perception of mega-city regions. For example, the mental image that one might have of a city like Sheffield, the fourth largest city in England, is to expect industrial landscapes. Once the largest place for steel production in the UK, the "mega-city region" extending to the north, east and south ends very abruptly to the west. Within just a few miles of the city center there is a highly visible and distinct border between built-up and rural landscape defined by the invisible administrative border of the Peak district national park, permitting easy access to large open spaces of the park.

While the perceptions or the mental images of mega-city regions might differ considerably on an individual level, or are perhaps even contradictory to the apparent "reality" as outlined earlier, a similar phenomenon might apply to images that we create as representations of the physical reality to illustrate contents of existing environments or designed and planned futures as in scenario studies. We generally assume that images speak for themselves and increasingly images play a crucial role when discussing options for making mega-city regions visible. However, even potentially highly realistic images of the future can be characterized through a high degree of uncertainty, not knowing what the future holds. Furthermore, visual representations potentially possess considerable leeway for individual interpretation as a result of existing knowledge about a subject and related issues of communication and perception.

Images, Representation of Reality

Some decades ago, the psychologist and communication scientist Paul Watzlawick (1976) asked "how real is real" and questioned the objective perception of reality (Watzlawick 1976). He claims that so-called reality is a result of communication, and that there exists not just one reality but instead numerous perceptions of reality, connected to individual differences in communication and perception. Reality is always somehow and in some way perceived and interpreted by the individual.

A common type of representation of reality is images and visualizations. They are increasingly used in the scientific world but also in our everyday environment. In fact, the media provide us with massive numbers of visual stimuli, and we can certainly say that we are living in a visual era (see e.g., Gombrich 1984). An extreme example is the recent BBC documentary "Planet Earth," the most expensive nature documentary series ever produced. It is distinguished by highly artistic sequences of nature scenes that are presented as short and, in geographic terms, mostly disconnected clips as on MTV, and are hardly supported by explanatory comments, intentionally neglecting the fact that images never just stand on their own and that words accompanying the images, either written or spoken, potentially have a very high influence on the way the visual information is perceived (Lange 2005).

In recent times we have been continuously exposed to visual stimuli through television, commercials, etc. Virilio (1994) points out that more and more we are faced with the problem of visual pollution and compares it with the well-known problem of noise pollution (Virilio 1994).

We used to believe that what we saw represented in an image was reality, the truth. Increasingly, but only since a little more than a decade, we have been confronted with imagery in which it is sometimes difficult to judge whether the images are representations of real scenes or objects (i.e., landscapes, products, etc.), or are entirely digitally synthesized through 3D-modeling and rendering, 2D-image manipulation, or image compositing, or by using techniques that combine different approaches. Questions regarding the perception of such virtual representations have only been asked recently (Lange 2001). Not long ago a critical observer of such virtual representations of physically nonexistent scenes was able to identify whether he was looking at something that was in essence "real" or generated artificially. These borders have now shifted dramatically towards a situation where we are nowadays looking at visual representations that perhaps do not even puzzle us anymore in terms of their realism because they look as if they were real. Even our natural environment, which has always been particularly difficult to represent because of the high level of complexity of vegetated scenes (that is, compared with the level of complexity encountered in the built environment), can be rendered in a highly realistic fashion (see Figure 1).

Sensing Our Environment

We perceive our environment through a system of senses. Commonly these are distinguished as an auditive system (hearing), a tactile system (touching), a kinaesthetic system (sensing and coordinating movement), a vestibular system (balance), an olfactory system (smelling), a gustatory system (tasting) and a visual system (seeing). By far the most dominant component is visual perception (e.g., Albertz 2000). According to Bruce et al. (1996) around 80 % of man's perception is based on sight (Bruce et al. 1996).

The dominance of the visual sense is also underscored by terms used in everyday language such as "seeing is believing," "what you see is what you get," or the well-known phrase "a picture is worth a thousand words."

Figure 1:
Photorealistic visualization of a natural vegetated scene, Biosphere reserve Entlebuch, the Canton of Lucerne, Switzerland.

How the Planning Disciplines Represent the Environment

In contrast, the planning disciplines, encompassing in a wider sense architecture, landscape architecture as well as landscape and urban planning, used to express the contents of proposed planning action often in a relatively abstract fashion, i.e., by writing reports illustrated by diagrams and tables, but also by communicating with 2D plans and sections.

Consequently, several years ago it had already been pointed out that planning needs more images. While photographs, maps or even image sequences such as films or video provide us with a somewhat static slice of a certain period in time (despite perhaps a movie sequence) and certainly help to illustrate the past or an existing condition, representations of this kind fail to provide a look into the future.

Only recently, virtual landscape models, encompassing both urban and "natural" nonexistent (at least not yet) landscapes are gaining increasing importance and more widespread recognition (see Bishop and Lange 2005).

Predicting Future Change: Scenario-Approach, Alternative Futures

By nature of their disciplines all planners (in the broadest sense), whether they are dealing with mega-city regions, rural landscapes (Figures 2 to 4) or more natural landscapes, are interested in predicting the future. Forecasting change would be very easy if there was a linear relationship between the past, the present and the future. Unfortunately, this is not the case and therefore studying past changes only helps to a certain degree in dealing with the future.

Throughout history people have tried to make decisions today by studying the possible changes of tomorrow. There can be a clear distinction made between prognoses and forecasts, on the one hand, and scenario-techniques on the other. Prognoses and forecasts aim to predict a specific state of the future (e.g., Stiens 1993). In contrast to this, scenarios provide an array of possible or even unlikely or extreme future changes in the sense of "what would happen if ..." (see Figures 2 to 4).

Figure 2: Seewis, Prättigau, Graubünden: 360° panoramic visualization, situation 1971, before improvement.

Figure 3: Seewis, Prättigau, Graubünden: 360° panoramic visualization, "what if scenario," without improvement.

Figure 4: Seewis, Prättigau, Graubünden: 360° panoramic visualization, situation today, after improvement.

The formalization of scenario studies dates back to the Manhattan Project around 1942 when nuclear physicists used computer simulations to tackle uncertainties of the impact of a nuclear explosion (Schoemaker 1993). Nowadays, scenario techniques are a widely used approach in the environmental sciences to support strategic planning (see Alcamo 2001, Lange and Schmid 2000). Steinitz et al. (2003) fashioned the term "alternative futures studies," enabling scientists, planners and stakeholders to address a variety of issues across different geographies and at different scales (Steinitz et al. 2003).

Ringland points out that the contents of scenarios are difficult to communicate: "Scenarios are about ideas, and ideas are notoriously difficult to communicate" (Ringland 1998: 111). Metaphorically, scenarios can be seen as images describing an uncertain future in verbal form. Xiang and Clarke expand this idea and even speak of "synthesized images" (Xiang and Clarke 2003: 886). Consequently, translating scenarios into visual representations has become increasingly popular in recent years. Examples include hand-drawn sketches used by Heißenhuber et al. (2000) or digital photomontages as used by Nassauer and Corry (2004) (Heißenhuber et al. 2000; Nassauer and Corry 2004). More sophisticated techniques for the virtual representation of scenarios offer increased control of the visualizations and are by far superior in terms of showing alternative landscapes from any desired viewpoint.

In the example from Seewis, Prättigau in the Canton of Graubünden in the Swiss Alps we investigated the effects of agricultural improvement measures on the landscape scenery in the sense of a postproject evaluation.

By interviewing the farmers in the community we tried to find out which areas of alpine pastures would have been given up, if agricultural amelioration measures, i.e., mainly improving access, had not been taken. In combination with observed vegetation succession patterns in the area we predicted a landscape that would have been much more wooded, displaying a "wilder" character because of no or low-intensity land use.

While in this example scenarios for a rural landscape are shown, similar representations can be performed of course for urban settings ranging from small to large scale. Depending on the actual extent of the study site one will have to aim for adequate representations in terms of their level of detail as highly detailed representations that cover a large area might not be feasible.

Words of Caution for Using Visual Representations

Using imagery can help to illustrate complex cases and improve communication. By exploring different scenarios an understanding for a range of possible futures is fostered, helping to assist in decision-making. Interpreted in terms of their underlying scientific and philosophical premise, forecasting methods such as prognoses follow Leibniz to the extent that they seek a single truth and representation of reality, whereas scenario methods court contradiction, thereby following Hegel (Schoemaker 1993).

Photorealistic visual representations of possible future situations characterized by uncertainty, as in planning for example, are in essence a visual equivalent of a prognosis, i.e., seeking a single truth. Consequently, the degree of realism in such a prediction can and should be questioned: on which hard data it is based, what are the assumptions taken, what kind of methodology is used, etc. Nowadays visualizations can be produced that appear as realistic as the real world. Ethically this can be problematic if the same technology is used for predictive visualizations, e.g., in the case of scenarios of future landscapes. That is, the observer might look at them as if they were real because no visual indication is present providing a hint that the depicted scene is entirely virtual and the underlying base data may be highly speculative. These include visual cues, such as a high level of detail (e.g., the material of a facade, or the vegetation groundcover), or a deceivingly realistic representation of artificial or natural lighting at a stage in the planning and design process when decisions about details to such a degree have not been taken (e.g., zoning, land-use plans). Translated in terms of making mega-city regions visible, the degree of realism in a visualization should appropriately reflect the underlying base data. Particularly, in the case of data with an uncertain or predictive character, as they are used in scenario studies, a lower degree of realism resulting in a more abstract representation would be more "honest," i.e., less deterministic in terms of the visual appearance, and should be aimed at.

References

Albertz, J. 2000. "Sich von der Welt ein Bild machen – Gedanken zur Wahrnehmung unserer Umwelt." In *Naturschutz und Landschaftsplanung – Moderne Technologien, Methoden und Verfahrensweisen*, edited by D. Gruehn, A. Herberg and C. Roesrath. Berlin: Mensch & Buch Verlag.

Alcamo, J. 2001. "Scenarios as Tools for International Environmental Assessments." *Environmental Issue Report*, Vol. 24. European Environment Agency. Luxembourg: Office for Official Publications of the European Communities.

Bishop, I. and E. Lange (eds.). 2005. *Visualization in Landscape and Environmental Planning. Technology and Applications*. London, New York: Taylor & Francis.

Bruce, V., P.R. Green and M.A. Georgeson. 1996. *Visual Perception, Physiology, Psychology and Ecology*. East Sussex: Psychology Press.

Gombrich, E.H. 1984. *Bild und Auge. Neue Studien zur Psychologie der bildlichen Darstellung*. Stuttgart: Klett-Cotta.

Heißenhuber, A., J. Kantelhardt and E. Osinski. 2000. "Ökonomische Aspekte einer ressourcenschonenden Landnutzung." *Agrarspectrum* 31: 20-30.

Lange, E. 2001. "The Limits of Realism: Perceptions of Virtual Landscapes." *Landscape and Urban Planning* 54: 163-182.

Lange, E. 2005. "Issues and Questions for Research in Communicating with the Public through Visualizations." In *Trends in Real-Time Landscape Visualization and Participation*, edited by E. Buhmann, P. Paar, I. Bishop and E. Lange. Heidelberg: Wichmann: 16-26.

Lange, E. and W.A. Schmid. 2000. "Ecological Planning with Virtual Landscapes." *Landscape Journal* 19 (1-2): 156-165.

Lange, E., U. Wissen and O. Schroth. 2005. "Sich die Landschaft ausmalen. 3D-Visualisierungen als Instrument für partizipative Planungen." *tec21* (45): 10-14.

Nassauer, J.I. and R. Corry. 2004. "Using Normative Scenarios in Landscape Ecology." *Landscape Ecology* 19: 343-356.

Ringland, G. 1998. *Scenario Planning. Managing for the Future*. Chichester: John Wiley.

Schoemaker, P.J.H. 1993. "Multiple Scenario Development: Its Conceptual and Behavioral Foundation." *Strategic Management Journal* 14: 193-213.

Steinitz, C., H.M.A. Rojo, S. Bassett, M. Flaxman, T. Goode, T. Maddock III, D. Mouat, R. Peiser and A. Shearer. 2003. *Alternative Futures for Changing Landscapes. The Upper San Pedro River Basin in Arizona and Sonora*. Washington: Island Press.

Stiens, G. 1993. "Prognostische Geographie." *Geographische Rundschau* 4: 224-231.

Virilio, P. 1994. "Das Privileg des Auges". In *Bildstörung. Gedanken zu einer Ethik der Wahrnehmung*, edited by J.P. Dubost. Leipzig: Reclam: 55-71.

Watzlawick, P. 1976. *Wie wirklich ist die Wirklichkeit? Wahn, Täuschung, Verstehen*. München: Piper.

Xiang, W.-N. and K.C. Clarke 2003. "The Use of Scenarios in Land-Use Planning." *Environment and Planning B Planning and Design* 30: 885-909.

going

Urs Primas

Going Beyond Identity

As illusions about our ability to control the global dynamics of urbanization wane, urbanism is experiencing a renaissance of mapping. While the current discourse on identity and the application of branding strategies to urban regions boils down to a new edition of top-down planning ideologies, mapping seems to represent a more promising approach. Maps are drawn first of all out of curiosity and the need to unravel a complex reality, but they can simultaneously ask questions, promote views or challenge assumptions. They are essential tools to discuss the future of our cities.

beyond

Figure 1:
Coloring the map.
The alliance of architects known as "De 8" preparing the 1934 CIAM exhibition at the Stedelijk Museum, Amsterdam.

Pluto is no longer a planet. Recently, the International Astronomical Union has deprived the small orb of the status of a full-fledged member of our solar system. Even though it is nearly round and it orbits the sun, Pluto fails to meet a third, new criterion for planethood, i.e., it hasn't sufficiently cleared its surroundings of debris. Without this steeping up of criteria, at least three other objects would have needed to be granted planet status, possibly diluting the notion of planets altogether.

In the case of cities, such definitional strictness turned impractical long ago. Since the industrial revolution and the razing of city walls, the system of confined entities with not too much debris floating around in between has exploded to form an ever mutating galaxy of urban material. Drawing boundaries, assigning names or defining clusters within this sprawling nebula becomes increasingly cumbersome. While Paris, Venice or Munich are cities beyond dispute, this is less obvious for Castrop-Rauxel or the Dutch "Randstad" and becomes debatable indeed in the case of "edge cities" emerging at highway intersections or around airports.

Planners and politicians have long struggled with this evaporation of urban identity. As early as 1915 Patrick Geddes observed in his seminal work on regional planning, "Cities in Evolution," that neither the names nor the administrative boundaries of cities such as Birmingham, Manchester or Liverpool were any longer suitable given the emerging reality of industrial conurbations (Geddes 1915). Anybody who bothered to study the population density maps provided by standard atlases, Geddes complained with characteristic zeal, would quickly understand that the new phenomenon of city-regions demanded a different political organization, along with new and more befitting designations. Several waves of urbanization after Geddes, we still speak of Birmingham, Manchester and Liverpool and not of "Midlanton" or "Lancaston" as he proposed. A considerable tenacity of established labels and identities seems to hamper their adaptation to changing realities.

Since Geddes' discussion of the population maps he had taken from the Royal Geographic Society's "Atlas of England and Wales," maps have become the instrument of choice to promote new urban identities. Like other forms of visual communication – images or logos – they are a core ingredient of city branding strategies. I believe, however, that the main potential of mapping in urbanism lies elsewhere. It might be useful to start the discussion by questioning the relevance of concepts like identity and branding as applied to cities and urban regions.

Identity or Fitness?

While cities have long provided self-evident brands for products or even whole lifestyles – the Frankfurt sausage, Eau de Cologne, the Vienna Schmäh – contemporary urban regions claim to be in need of "branding" themselves. From an urbanistic point of view, the concept of "city branding" raises a couple of questions. To start, there are problems of delimitation. Cities are no longer like fixed stars, clearly identified points of reference in the landscape. A continuous field of urbanity in various densities has emerged, dotted by smaller and larger remnants of unsettled countryside. This figure-ground reversal is paralleled by a problem of perception. Historical cities still draw from the power of their well-established identities. But how to achieve visibility for urban entities that have been defined mostly along the lines of demographic or economic indicators? How to create a brand for something that has neither a clear boundary nor significant history, has been defined mainly on grounds of statistical evidence, consists largely of exchangeable, generic components, and undergoes constant change?

Furthermore, the quest for clear-cut identities seems to be incompatible with the heterogeneity of contemporary urban landscapes. Consisting of many distinctive fragments and layers, their potential draws from an unpredictable and unstable coexistence of diverse and often contradictory urbanities. A branding strategy, which seeks to establish a clear identity beyond the scale of a distinct fragment or layer of urbanity risks producing little more than vague statements that might apply anywhere – while failing to express the qualities arising from the very complexity and unpredictability it is struggling to avoid.

Finally, it is important to stress that the "city as product" is but one aspect of a vastly more complex reality. Branding creates visibility for products, services or the companies providing them. It works, because the quality of the products or services themselves and the way in which they are advertised, presented and sold can be controlled to a great extent. In the case of a city, such an amount of top-down control would, if it were possible at all, lead to the suffocation of conflicts and contradictions, of the essential instability that forms the core of urbanity.

In an essay titled "Individualization without Identity," the American architectural theorist Michael Speaks challenges the assumption that globalization simply transforms difference into sameness (Speaks 2002). He argues that the concept of "identity," understood as the difference between "same" and "other," is losing relevance in the context of the contemporary city. The opposition between universal "sameness" and national, regional and local difference is displaced by a multitude of differential networks – such as multinational corporations, NGOs, criminal organizations or museum consortia – competing for dominance in an interconnected global marketplace. New forms of self-organization emerge also on the consumer side. So-called lifestyle clusters, for instance, are increasingly independent of geographical location, class, race or gender and indicate "forms of individuation no longer dependent on even temporarily fixed identity." Cities and urban regions might be described as nodes where networks and lifestyle clusters overlap.

Network theorists have introduced the notion of "fitness" to describe the ability of a particular node to compete for links at the expense of other nodes (Barabàsi 2003). As networks become more important, competition between cities will no longer only be for market share, but increasingly for links that add value through the introduction of difference. The "fitness" of cities or urban regions seems to depend on the wealth of opportunities they offer, but also on their adaptability in a constantly changing environment. For nodes in a network, dynamic equilibrium – constantly changing while remaining the same – is more viable than static equilibrium that can only change by becoming another identity altogether.

As opposed to top-down branding strategies aiming at communicating an identity or representing a community, Speaks consequently proposes "strategies of active destabilization" to enhance the performance and adaptability of nodes by constantly introducing external information and encouraging a proliferation of difference. Drawing on the example of Rem Koolhaas' proposal to renew the Prada brand by "counteracting and destabilizing any received notion of what Prada is, does or will become"(Koolhaas 2001), Speaks develops the concept of "individualization without identity": a flexible and fundamentally unstable actualization of potential differences.

Rather than representations of clear-cut brands or identities, we seem to need tools for exploring – and thereby eventually influencing – this constant evolution of urban potentials. In the following, I would like to discuss a couple of historical examples to sketch a range of interactions between the evolution of urban areas and their cartographic representations. I will focus on some operational aspects of mapping that go beyond the mere representation of identities, i.e., on the virulent, challenging and sometimes dangerous roles that maps have played in the gray zones between analysis, representation and politics.

Country Branding

"The Alps appear incredibly flat, as if compressed from above, and fail to impress at all"[1] (Heim, Mauerer and Spelterini 1899: 58; author's translation). In 1898 the geologist Albert Heim crossed the Swiss Alps in Eduard Spelterini's balloon. At first, he was excited by the possibility of viewing the subject of his lifelong study and passion from above. However, his initial enthusiasm quickly gave way to disappointment. When compared to the dramatic plasticity of the relief in General Dufour's new map of Switzerland, the view from the balloon failed to live up to his expectations.

The 25 sheets of the Dufour Map had been completed and exhibited at the occasion of the 1883 Swiss National Fair in Zurich, assembled on a panel measuring 3.5 x 2.5 m. The emerging nation state was visualized in its entirety in a cartographic representation that didn't fail to amaze visitors. Against much resistance, Dufour had started to work on the cartographic unification of Switzerland in 1832, sixteen years before the political unification became a fact in 1848. The cartographic historians David Gugerli and Daniel Speich have interpreted this act of mapping the entire country based on standardized procedures and uniform cartographic language as a cornerstone of the demanding project of constructing a national identity for a heterogeneous federation of cantons lacking an obvious common denominator such as language or religion (Gugerli and Speich 1999).

Firstly, and most obviously, the Dufour map was a cartographic *analysis* of the country, a compilation of its topography, its rivers, lakes, forests, roads, railways and buildings in unprecedented accuracy. As such, it would soon become an indispensable tool for travelers, scientists and the army. But the map was also a *design* for Switzerland: Dufour managed to unify the previous patchwork of independent surveys by creating and applying national standards for coordinates, triangulation and leveling as well as for the graphic language of the map. He also went to great lengths to assure a homogeneous density of information all over the country lest any part of it would appear underrepresented. The patchwork of differ-

Figures 2 and 3:
A mixture of wild nature with human industry: The Lötschental on the black-and-white Dufour map with hatching representing the slopes, and on a recent map using contour lines and relief shading.

Going Beyond Identity

ent objects, landscapes and places was generalized to form a coherent national space. Differences were systematically suppressed, similarities emphasized. Dufour created an idealized view of the country, unified and homogenized by the pervasive gaze of the cartographer.

Last but not least Dufour had produced a powerful *image* of Switzerland. The map was a perfect medium for promoting Swiss virtues such as precision, thoroughness and craftsmanship. By representing the mountains in no less detail than the urbanized parts of the country, it perfectly visualized the peculiar "mix of wild nature with human industry"[2] that Jean-Jacques Rousseau had identified already in 1762 as Switzerland's unique quality (Rousseau 1776-1778). A key role in this masterpiece of graphical nation-building was to be played by the representation of the topographic relief – which, as Albert Heim attested, turned out even better than the original.

Although the necessary data would have been available, Dufour did not use contour lines for his map. He relied on hatching the slopes because that technique rendered the image of the topography more vivid. The subsequent editions by General Siegfried included contour lines, sacrificing dramatic effect for the sake of precision. In the 1920s, when a fundamental revision of the Siegfried atlas became inevitable, a year-long struggle about the scale of the new maps ensued. The young Eduard Imhof, newly appointed professor of cartography at ETH Zurich, finally managed to convince the authorities to produce the new maps in a series of scales starting at the exceptionally detailed level of 1:25,000, not only for the urban areas but for the country as a whole (Imhof 1981). The new maps combined contour lines with elaborate relief shading, finally providing an image that was both precise and dramatic. When the Swiss National Fair in 1939 attempted to redefine and reinforce Swiss identity in the shadow of World War II, Imhof, a gifted artist and passionate mountaineer, was put in charge of the cartographic exhibition. The first sheets of the new map edition were presented next to amazing scale models of mountains produced by Imhof himself.

The construction of identity involved in the mapping of Switzerland could be summarized as a strategy of *homogenization*. All the maps, whether they showed urban, rural or alpine areas, had a characteristic similar look. A vast array of objects was presented against the backdrop of topography. Houses, factories, trees, rock boulders, glacier crevasses – everything was drawn at the same unique level of detail, suggesting ubiquitous knowledge and control and absorbing differences – not only between competing cantons, but also between almost incompatible layers of the country. Urban hubs, rural hinterland and alpine wilderness were merged into a single, national landscape. This idea of a unity of differences guided the construction of the nation-state and played an important role during the World War II and well into the postwar period. More recently however, the corresponding myth of an isotropic national space seems to have turned into something of a mental straitjacket, blocking flexible approaches to future challenges (see for example Diener et al. 2006).

Identity through Shape

In 1924 the urbanist Th. K. Van Lohuizen presented a map of the western Netherlands where he had compiled the population growth per municipality between 1869 and 1920 (Lohuizen 1925; Rossem 1993). On this map, a horseshoe shape emerged, highlighting a zone around the cities of Utrecht, Amsterdam, Leiden, The Hague, Delft, Rotterdam and Dordrecht, where growth had been significantly higher than in other areas. Van Lohuizen's map was an *analytical drawing*, localizing census data in space and thereby facilitating interpretations and speculations.

In 1958 a similar map showed up in a government report about the development of the western Netherlands (Werkcommissie 1957; see also Bosma and Hellinga 1997). This report summarized years of studies about strategies of spatial planning. Although the map looked very similar to the one presented by Van Lohuizen more than 30 years ago, it had been assigned a completely different role. The demographic analysis had been turned into a *design sketch*. The horseshoe-shaped "Randstad" was to be condensed while the rural "green heart" in its center should remain empty. The suggestive labels invented by the planners to turn Van Lohuizens discovery into a strategy proved their worth. Books were written in praise of the "Greenheart Metropolis" (Burke 1966). The idea of a unique Dutch urbanity that organized itself around a void became popular with politicians and the general public. A myth was born (Rossem 1994).

Governmental planning subsequently focused its energies on reinforcing the Randstad-Greenheart dualism and constricting developments that ran against it. Despite these efforts, contemporary satellite images and population maps fail to show a ring-shaped green-heart metropolis. What we see is rather a metropolitan region stretching from Brussels to Frankfurt and further, urbanized in remarkably continuous densities and punctuated by smaller and larger towns and rural areas. The image of an urban ring surrounding a green heart may have the compelling clarity of a Renaissance ideal city plan, but it is inadequate given the condition of such a large urbanized field. That said, a Randstad *logo* published in 1998 by OMA suggests that the myth of the green heart has not yet lost its power entirely and might still be exploited, if only as a communication strategy. As part of a project promoting the dislocation of Schiphol airport onto an island in the North Sea, OMA proposed the development of a new city on the terrain of the present airport (Koolhaas et al. 2000). Perfectly served by the existing infrastructure, this new hub of density could absorb the growing pressure to urbanize the green heart and thereby save the Greenheart Metropolis.

Locating the landscape, rather than the city itself, at the heart of an urbanistic strategy offers flexibility. While the city remains free to evolve in many ways, the landscape can be protected to provide "identity." Such a model seems to work well, for example, in the Capetown metropolitan region where the Table Mountain serves as self-evident landmark, recreational landscape and nature reserve for the urban sprawl surrounding it. The Greenheart, on the other hand, never lived up to the expectations raised by its label. Dedicated mainly to large-scale agriculture, it is rarely visited for its own sake. It is slowly filling up with all kinds of urban programs and infrastructures because, apart from a vague notion of open landscape and greenness, it is not clear what exactly should be protected. The Randstad-Greenheart concept relays upon *shape* to provide identity. While its history proves the persuasive power of such a strategy, it equally highlights its fundamental weakness.

Figure 4:
1924: The "Randstad" discovered. Analytical drawing highlighting areas with exceptional population growth.

Figure 5:
1958: The "Randstad" conceptualized. Charcoal sketch for the future development of the western Netherlands.

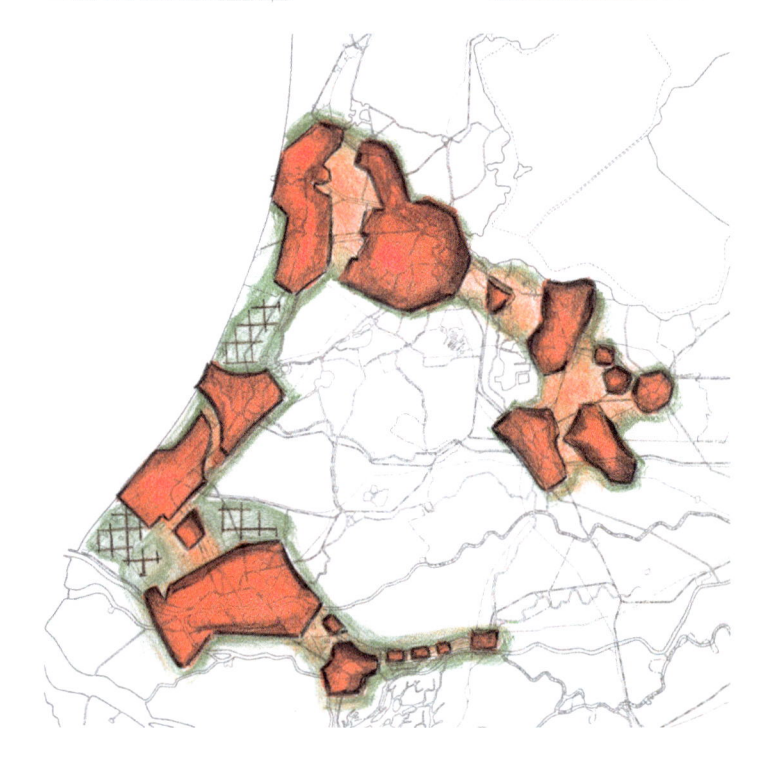

Figure 6:
1998: The "Randstad" idealized. Logo from OMA's Schiphol project.

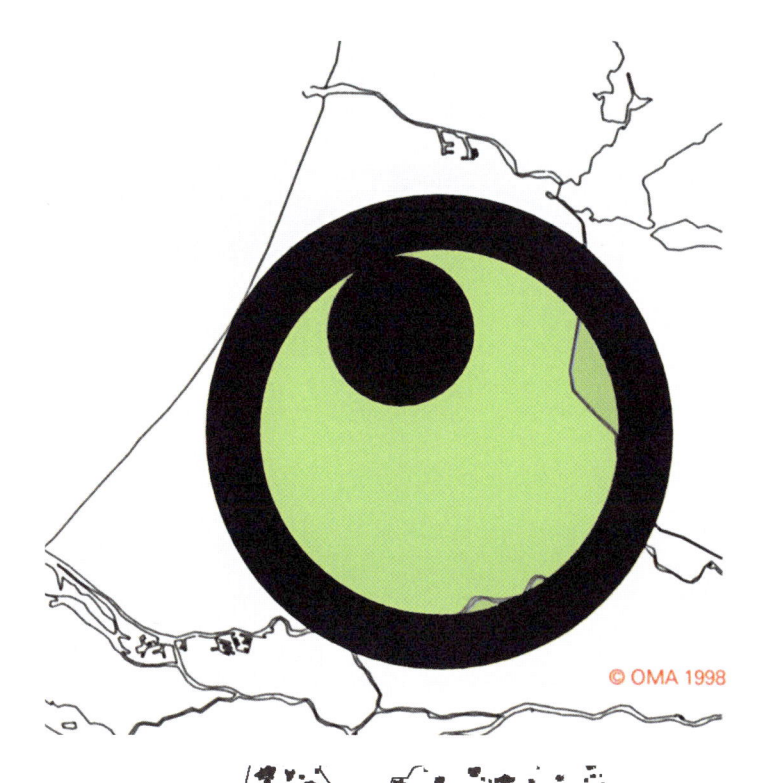

Figure 7:
Where is the Randstad? Map of Northwestern Europe on which areas with a population density of more than 200 inhabitants per square kilometer have been colored black.

Self-Fulfilling Prophecies

The rapid growth of cities during the second half of the 19th century brought about new types of mapping. Sociological maps such as the 1889 London Poverty Map by the businessman and sociologist Charles Booth were no longer representations of the city as viewed from far above. Rather than compiling physical features of the cityscape, such maps focused on the inhabitants and on hardly visible phenomena like income, religion, housing, working conditions or crime. Sociological mapping could no longer rely on the gaze of the cartographer and his instruments. Charles Booth's pioneering notebooks are noteworthy examples of new types of survey that were invented to visualize hidden social realities. Booth conducted countless interviews and inspected the city street by street in the company of police officers and School Board visitors. His methodical framework allowed him to quantify and localize the misery of the poor in the industrial city, an elusive phenomenon, which had, until then, been grasped mainly in terms of loose, general impressions (Hall 1996).

If maps in general are hybrid tools at the intersection of separate domains, their role at the borderline of science and politics becomes particularly delicate where they represent social geographies. Even when intended to play a merely analytical, descriptive role, such maps may quickly turn into programs for measures to be taken.

In "Crabgrass Frontier," his account of the history of American suburbanization, Kenneth Jackson links color-coded real estate risk level maps of US cities that have been produced from 1935 onward by the Home Owners Loan Corporation (HOLC) and other institutions to the practice of mortgage and insurance "redlining" (Jackson 1985). The term "redlining," coined by Chicago community groups, refers to the designation of areas that have been excluded from the services of lenders and insurance providers. Redlining has been identified as one of the causes for the wave of disinvestment and neglect that led to the decline of American downtowns. It was prohibited following the 1968 Fair Housing Act.

The City Survey program of the Home Owners Loan Corporation conducted surveys of 239 American cities and produced a series of maps that assigned residential areas a grade from one to four. Poor areas, areas with many old houses and areas with a lot of African Americans were consistently given a fourth grade or "hazardous" rating. They were colored red and often matched the areas "redlined" by lenders and insurance providers. There is an ongoing discussion about the role of these maps – which are not publicly accessible –

Figure 8:
"Walk with Police Constable Robert Turner on July 12, 1898." A page from one of the 450 notebooks filled by Charles Booth during his "Inquiry into the Life and Labour of the People in London," undertaken between 1886 and 1903.

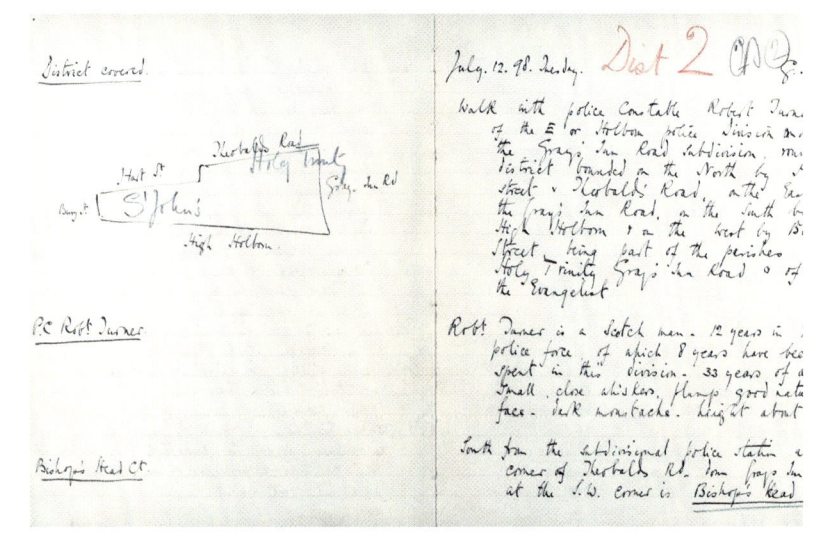

Figure 9:
A section of Charles Booth's "London Poverty Map" with color codes ranging from black ("Lowest class. Vicious, semi-criminal") to yellow ("Upper-middle and Upper classes. Wealthy").

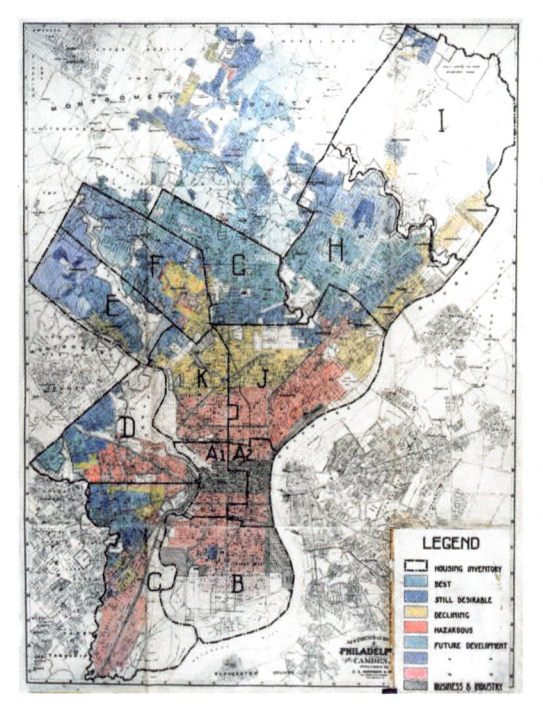

Figure 10:
Color-coded real estate map of Philadelphia, compiled in 1936 by the Home Owner's Loan Corporation (HOLC) as part of the "City Survey Program."
The "best" locations are shown in light blue, "hazardous" areas in red.

in the history of suburbanization and segregation, and about the links between the maps and the practice of redlining (Hillier 2003).

The history of redlining reveals a feedback loop of self-fulfilling prophecies peculiar to real estate analysis: Once an area has been judged "risky" by a surveyor, investment flows away from it, causing further neglect which results in further exclusion from investment. The survey triggers a downward spiral and, intentionally or not, turns into a program, a design. Redlining in the crude and overtly discriminating way it has been practiced in postwar America might no longer be considered good practice. Still, the mechanism persists in a softer but hardly less debatable way. The annual reports of real estate monitoring agencies present their observations and forecasts in matter-of-fact ways using the familiar graphical language of histograms and thematic mapping. If most investors base their policies on the same report, they are quite likely to draw the same conclusions. Consequently, a critical approach in real estate development – and in urbanism – should start out with a different analysis, drawing a different map.

The color-coded real estate maps suddenly fixed evasive and fluid identities through spatial *demarcation*. They assigned precise locations to ambiguous and constantly shifting phenomena like poverty, neglect and danger. While every street and every block was assigned a grade, subjective impressions of poverty or decay were converted into precise delineations of "bad neighborhoods." To a large extent, the violence of these maps lies in their unambiguity.

Figure 11:
The existing as inspiration: Continuous ground floor plan of the city of Zurich within the limits of the baroque fortifications, compiled by students of Aldo Rossi in 1973.

Raising the Inventory

In 1973 a group of architecture students compiled building permit and fire insurance archive plans to assemble a ground floor map of the historical core of Zurich within the boundaries of the baroque fortifications (Rossi et al. 1974). Their map did not only show the streets and squares as city maps usually do, but included the ground floor plans of all buildings. Applying the graphic language of an architectural floor plan to an entire city district, the map revealed the relationship between the typology of the buildings and the structure of the city. It visualized the architecture of the city.

The map was part of an effort to overcome the lack of understanding of the city in the architectural practice of the time. Similar maps of Italian cities had been drawn up from 1952 on by the Roman architect Saverio Muratori and his pupils in an attempt to render the history of the city operative in the design process. When Aldo Rossi became teacher at ETH in Zurich in 1972, he introduced design strategies involving an appropriation of the urban fabric through analysis. Rejecting both the "tabula rasa" attitude of late modernism and preservationist attempts to conserve the historical city as an open-air museum, Rossi focused on studying the existing as a source of inspiration for the architectural project[3] (Rossi 1972).

The Zurich map was exhibited at the 1973 Triennale in Milano and was to become a point of reference for an entire generation of Swiss architects. As Marcel Meili recalls in his 1985 "Letter from Zurich," the Zurich "Rilievo" had been most important as an "analytical and subversive instrument for urban knowledge in confrontation with the banal visions of urbanism of the 1960s" (Meili 1988). He suggests that the intentions of the plan had been betrayed as tourism and shopping have gradually conquered the structures of the old city center later on, turning it into an "image of itself" and pushing contemporary dynamics away into underground oblivion.

The black-and-white graphics of the "Rilievo" reduce the city to its bare bones. The map draws its power from a process of *reduction*. Excluding other layers such as program, traffic or greenery, it focuses exclusively on the architectural structure of urban space. Like an X-ray image, it unveils properties of the urban fabric that are invisible to the naked eye. As opposed to studies of individual historical buildings, their representation as a continuous map allows one to read and appreciate the structural qualities of the urban fabric as a whole. On the one hand, the map was a manifesto for the existing city as a source of inspiration for the city of the future. On the other hand, it effectively avoided nostalgic obsessions with historical imagery that might lead to musealization and the suffocation of contemporary development. The map appeared at a time when the identity of the city center was negotiated anew between technocratic visions and rising concerns for the preservation of the historical image. The attempt to focus on the potentials of the urban fabric, rather than on a discussion on progress versus imagery, was an important – if ultimately unsuccessful – contribution to the urbanistic debates of the 1970s.

Agents of Change

Mapping renders invisible data into tangible and beautiful illustrations. It is embedded in the visual culture of scientific rationalism and generally associated with accuracy and veracity. Rather than telling a linear story or forcing a single perspective upon the viewer, a map can organize many layers of information in a planar matrix. It allows for the representation of complex and even contradictory phenomena, and for many parallel ways of reading.

Urbanists like to present their maps as "research" or "analysis." However, as the cartographic historian John Brian Harley has emphasized, "The steps in making a map – selection, omission, simplification, classification, the creation of hierarchies, and 'symbolization' – are all inherently rhetorical"(Harley 2001: 163). According to Harley, the rhetorical dimension in maps is neither limited to propaganda maps or advertising cartography, nor can it be confined to an "artistic" or esthetic element as opposed to the scientific core of maps. By creating a spatial panopticon, cartographers manufacture power – a power embedded in the map text.

As we have seen, the process of mapping includes a wide range of interpretative strategies such as homogenization, the identification of shapes, demarcation or reduction that might be rendered productive in urbanism. The task of analyzing and visualizing contemporary mega-city regions and their interconnections adds challenges that might require the development of new cartographic tools. For instance, the rising importance of global networks of communication, travel or trade calls for simultaneous representations of interconnected local and global scales – a task to which conventional scaled maps are ill suited.

Likewise, the dynamism of developments and the rising pace of change add renewed importance to the representation of time in maps.

The recent renaissance of mapping in urbanism indicates, first and foremost, a renewed need to understand what is going on. Maps are drawn to unravel layers of urbanity, to identify forces that are shaping the cityscape, to scan the urban field for potentials. But mapping is also an attempt to influence this condition. Urbanism is rapidly abandoning illusions about its ability to guide and steer the global dynamics of urbanization. Instead, it sets out to discover, and maybe realize, potentials that emerge within these dynamics. For such an urbanism, maps are more than just tools for identification and branding. They are pivotal as undercover agents of change, i.e., hybrid tools, not belonging to either one of two separate worlds, crossing borders between research and design (see for example Latour 1991). Maps can visualize hidden relationships, cast light on opportunities that would otherwise go unnoticed, challenge established interpretations, fuel public discussions: they can help to bridge the gap between the scientific and the political.

Notes

[1] "Die Berge erscheinen unglaublich flach, wie von oben herab zusammengequetscht und imponieren gar nicht mehr. Selbst die beste Beleuchtung giebt bei weitem nicht die vielen Abstufungen in der Schattierung wie wir sie in Landkarten anwenden, um das Relief herausspringen zu lassen" (Heim, Mauerer and Spelterini 1899: 58).

[2] "Mais en effet qui jamais eût dû s'attendre à trouver une manufacture dans un précipice. Il n'y a que la Suisse au monde qui présente ce mélange de la nature sauvage et de l'industrie humaine. La Suisse entière n'est pour ainsi dire qu'une grande ville dont les rues larges et longues plus que celle de St Antoine, sont semées de forêts, coupées de montagnes, et dont les maisons éparses et isolées ne communiquent entre elles que par des jardins anglois" (Rousseau 1776-1778:1070-1072).

[3] "Das geschichtliche Erbe scheint nur dann verteidigt zu werden, wenn es touristisch interessant wird. In Wirklichkeit stellt es die Struktur eines Territoriums dar" (Rossi 1972: 690f.).

References

Barabàsi, A.-L. 2003. *Linked. How Everything is Connected to Everything Else and What it Means for Business, Scicnce, and Everyday Life*. New York: Plume.

Bosma, K. and H. Hellinga. 1997. *De regie van de stad II. Noord-Europese Stedebouw 1900 – 2000*. Rotter-dam: NAI Publishers.

Burke, G.L. 1966. *Greenheart Metropolis. Planning the Western Netherlands*. London: Macmillan.

Diener, R., J. Herzog, M. Meili, P. de Meuron and C. Schmid. 2006. *Die Schweiz – ein städtebauliches Portrait*. Basel: Birkhäuser.

Geddes, P. 1915. *Cities in Evolution. An Introduction to the Town Planning Movement and to the Study of Civics*. London: Williams and Norgate Press.

Gugerli, D. and D. Speich. 1999. "Der Hirtenknabe, der General und die Karte. Nationale Repräsentationsräume in der Schweiz des 19. Jahrhunderts." *Werkstatt Geschichte* 23: 53-73.

Hall, P. 1996. *Cities of Tomorrow. An Intellectual History of Urban Planning and Design in the Twentieth Century*. Malden, Mass.: Blackwell Publishers.

Harley, J.B. 2001. "Deconstructing the Map." In *The New Nature of Maps. Essays in the History of Cartography*, edited by P. Laxton. Baltimore: Johns Hopkins University Press.

Heim, A., J. Mauerer and E. Spelterini. 1899. *Die Fahrt der "Wega" über Alpen und Jura am 3. Oktober 1898. Mit Profilen, Karten und zahlreichen Lichtdruckbildern*. Basel: B. Schwabe.

Hillier, A.E. 2003. "Redlining and the Home Owners' Loan Corporation." *Journal of Urban History* 29 (4, May): 394 - 420.

Imhof, E. 1981. "Rendez-vous am Mittag." Interview with Prof. Dr. h.c. Eduard Imhof. Swiss Radio DRS 1, 14.12.1981. Available from: http://www.karto.ethz.ch/archive/ika_radio.

Jackson, K.T. 1985. *Crabgrass Frontier. The Suburbanization of the United States*. New York: Oxford University Press.

Koolhaas, R. 2001. *Rem Koolhaas: Projects for Prada Part 1*, edited by R. Koolhaas, J. Hommert and M. Kubo. Milano: Fondazione Prada.

Koolhaas, R., R. de Graaf, J. Hommert, M. Poli, A. Kurdahl, A. Little, and B.K. Deuten. 2000. "SchipholS." *Architecture and Urbanism* May 2000 special issue: 176f.

Latour, B. 1991. *Nous n'avons jamais été modernes – essai d'anthropologie symétrique*. Paris: La Découverte.

Lohuizen, Th.K. van. 1925. "Concentratie en decentralisatie. De bevolkingsbeweging in de stedelijke invloedssfeer Holland – Utrecht." *Tijdschrift voor Economische Geografie* 16: 341-350.

Meili, M. 1988. "Letter from Zurich." *Quaderns d'arquitectura i urbanisme* 177. Barcelona.

Rossem, V. van. 1993. *Het Algemeen Uitbreidingsplan van Amsterdam. Geschiedenis en ontwerp*. Rotterdam: NAI Publishers.

Rossem, V. van. 1994. *Randstad Holland, Variaties op het thema Stad*. Rotterdam: NAI Publishers.

Rossi, A. 1972. "Architektur und Stadt, Vergangenheit und Gegenwart." *Werk* 12: 690f.

Rossi, A., S. Cantoni, B. Keller, L. Martini, O. Pampuri, A. Pisoni and L. Serena. 1974. "Zürich. Grundrissplan Erdgeschoss." Zurich: gta Archiv, ETH Zürich.

Rousseau, J.-J. 1776-1778. *Les Rêveries du promeneur solitaire*, published posthumously in 1782. *Œuvres complètes I*, edited by B. Gagnebin and M. Raymond. Paris: Gallimard (1959 – 1995).

Speaks, M. 2002. "Individualization without Identity." In *Urban Affairs: City Branding. Image Building & Building Images*, edited by Urban Affairs and V. Patteeuw. Rotterdam: NAI Publishers: 48-65.

Werkcommissie voor her onderzoek naar de ontwikkeling van het Westen des Lands. 1957. *Rapport over de ontwikkeling van het Westen des Lands*. Den Haag.

se

Meret Wandeler

Setting up a Perception Instrument

Documentary photography confronts abstract, conceptual reflection with images of a concrete place. Based on residents' everyday perception, it shows what the living spaces of the mega-city region look like. Photographic images can provide a bridge between theoretical concepts of spatial development and the everyday perception and experience of space. The use of photography for the observation and analysis of spatial processes is illustrated here with the example of the Zurich University of the Arts project "Long-Term Photographic Observation of Schlieren 2005–2020."

The "Image of the Region" as Interplay of Different Visualization Strategies

Mega-city regions are made up of different heterogeneous spaces. This polymorphism cannot be represented with a single visualization strategy, and it is therefore necessary to develop a framework of perception that incorporates a range of perspectives. The "image of the region" is not constituted by a single photograph, computer-generated rendering, diagram or map, but can only be generated by a combination of these visualization techniques.

Pictorial representations have different functions according to the context in which the theme of the mega-city region is being discussed. In the scientific context, forms of visualization are themselves deployed as tools in the research process. They provide a graphic representation of complex circumstances and relationships, and serve as a means of communicating research results both to specialists and the general public (Heintz and Huber 2001). In marketing and advertising, on the other hand, visual communication is oriented predominantly to addressing the public on an emotional level. All images have an emotional effect. However, in the scientific context forms of visualization serve foremost as a source of information, and their emotional and aesthetic potential is barely registered at a conscious level. This potential only comes to the fore when scientific images are transferred to other implementation contexts. Marketing and advertising purposefully employ the specific aesthetic of scientific visualization forms. Scientific images are also used in the artistic sphere.

The choice of visualization strategies that are utilized depends on the content and media in question. In the scholarly discourse on mega-city regions, visualization needs to be deployed differently to the way it is used in marketing and public relations. Aesthetic questions are equally important to both contexts: factual images that primarily appeal to the intellect also require a specific formal and aesthetic design.

Documentary Photography

Contemporary photography employs a range of photographic strategies. Documentary photography is motivated by different intentions to those informing reportage or commercial photography. This difference is also expressed in the formulation of specific aesthetic and formal concepts that define the role of the author, the position of the observer, the reference to reality, etc. However, in a time of crossover cultural practices[1] documentary strategies are finding their way into advertising and fashion; conversely, the use of "staging" is being seen in the documentary field. Photographs can only represent certain aspects of an abstract concept such as the "mega-city region." Staged photography, commercial photography, reportage, architectural, art and documentary photography all illuminate the phenomenon of the mega-city region from different perspectives. Deciding on which photographic vernacular is to be deployed depends on the question being posed, the context and the target audience.

Documentary photography is distinguished by its specific reference to reality. Its goal is a precise visual analysis and description of working and living situations, specific places, urban contexts, landscapes, etc. The photographer must be able to capture the particular character and atmosphere of a situation. It is equally important to maintain an appropriate distance from the object. It is only in this way that precise observation becomes possible.

Every photograph, documentary or otherwise, is an image that is manufactured by means of an apparatus. The photograph always presents a particular view of what it is representing. Considering this constructed aspect of the photographic image is decisive for documentary photography. Photographers must make visible the position from which they have developed their view of the world. The conditions of observation must be comprehensibly formulated in the work itself. Seriality as a design principle therefore plays a central role in documentary photography. The standardization of certain photographic parameters makes a visual analysis of the pictorial object and the way it is perceived possible. Such established parameters include object distance, picture angle, perspective, lighting conditions and photographic technique (film format, camera type, etc.). On a formal level, a series is based on continuous compositional principles. In this context, the number of established parameters can vary. Strategies based on conceptual art operate according to a consistently strict set of rules that minimize aesthetic and emotional aspects of pictorial composition. Documentary photography oriented to the pictorial essay works with more open pictorial compositions that are intended to render both the singularity of the specific place and the individual view of the photographer visible. Documentary photography based on the traditional use of the panel in Western painting operates with a series of "tableaus." It attempts to formulate both a valid perspective in each individual picture and a photographic synthesis of a situation.

The aesthetic of documentary photography is not an artistic end in itself but is intended to facilitate a perception of the represented situation that is as precise as possible. Documentary photography argues in factual and analytic terms: the emotional and aesthetic effect of its images is the result of this analytic modus operandi.

The photographic image is an image that stands still. At first glance this may appear to be a disadvantage in comparison to other visualization techniques, but in terms of sharpening perception it is an advantage. In the case of photography, in contrast to video for example, the viewing time is not prescribed. The observer is free to determine the rhythm at which he or she views certain sections and to return to them repeatedly. The photographic series constructs a pictorial space in which different objects can be brought into relation with one another. This makes visible contextual relationships between places and objects that are not linked in the context of everyday perception.

The specific correspondence between the documentary photograph and reality is not founded in the medium itself but in its position within the semiotic system. The photograph is distinguished from other (visual) signs through its indexical relation to the pictured object (see for example Barthes 1980; Dubois 1983). Nevertheless, a documentary photograph can only be read as "documentary" when it is positioned within a defined system of reference. The history of photography has produced a specific aesthetic canon for documentary photography, as it has for other photographic approaches.[2] Within the field of visual culture, documentary photography has the function of producing images that have a direct relationship with reality. Documentary photographs are read as "authentic" or as referring to reality because their language is culturally coded in this way.

The power of this reality reference becomes particularly evident when documentary photographs are specifically contrasted with other visualization strategies, e.g., computer-generated renderings, animations, illustrations, staged photographs, etc. Different scales of perception can be represented in the combination of photographs with maps and diagrams. However, the interplay of visualization techniques must be structured in such a way that they do not abrogate one another. The aim should be to generate a multiperspectival view that shows the different spaces of a megacity region with their specific qualities and deficits. It is essential that the aesthetic tools deployed be attuned to one another. All pictorial representations must be considered in relation to each other and the context and target public must be appropriately defined. It is thus important that complex visualizations are developed in collaboration with visual communication specialists.

Photography and Spatial Development

Maps and plans represent space from a bird's eye view. Computer-generated renderings present ideal versions of landscapes and urban situations. Diagrams represent data and relations in abstract form. Documentary photography confronts abstract, conceptual reflection with images of a concrete place. It shows what real living spaces in the mega-city region look like. The point of departure for photographic analysis is inhabitants' everyday perception. Photography provides a means by which the abstract concept of the "mega-city region" can be related to a municipality, a city or an agglomeration.[3]

Photographs depict the elements that constitute the use, design, characteristic atmosphere and identity of a place. They illustrate the qualities and deficits of spatial situations. Spaces that are only perceived in isolation on the everyday level are brought into relation with one another. The photographic visualization of spatial contexts makes the interdependence of conflicting developments within a mega-city region perceptible on a sensory level. For example, it can be shown how the dynamics of "spatial development on the quiet" (Thierstein et al. 2006) affect the urban development of a specific location within a mega-city region.

In the context of planning and development processes, documentary photographs provide concrete pictorial examples of both desirable and undesirable developments. They can play a role in discussions with relevant actors and affected parties to determine how those involved in the planning process assess possible developmental scenarios. Images evoke a more emotional and direct reaction than maps or plans. However, the visual language of documentary photography avoids evaluating the pictured places and objects. By arguing in factual, sober terms, it opens up a space for the observer's own assessment of the situation. The images particularly facilitate the discussion of those aspects that are significant for the aesthetic and emotional quality of spaces. These aspects cannot be communicated in the maps, plans, diagrams and texts with which spatial development usually operates. Hopes and fears that are difficult to thematically integrate in decision-making processes can be more effectively put into words with reference to photographic images.

The Zurich University of the Arts Research Project "Long-Term Photographic Observation of Schlieren 2005–2020"

The project "Long-Term Photographic Observation of Schlieren 2005–2020" serves here as an example of transdisciplinary collaboration in the fields of spatial development and documentary photography. The project was conceived by Professor Ulrich Görlich and Meret Wandeler in the Department of Photography/Institute for Contemporary Arts Research at the Zurich University of the Arts (ZHdK). Project partners in the field of spatial development are Metron Raumentwicklung AG and the City of Schlieren's Office of Building and Planning. The project's supporters include the Swiss National Fund and Documenta Natura.[4]

This project represents Switzerland's first long-term photographic observation of an entire settlement area. The example of Schlieren, an agglomeration municipality in the Zurich city region, is being used to develop exemplary photographic methods for the visualization of developmental processes in suburban space. This long-term observation represents a new visual form of monitoring settlement development in the agglomeration. As a pilot project, the case study in Schlieren is developing an observation model that can be used for other long-term documentations.

The research project is designed to cover a period of fifteen years. The starting point of the photographic observation is the new urban development concept formulated by Metron Raumentwicklung AG for Schlieren. In 2005–06 the ZHdK developed a photographic observation concept in collaboration with its project partners and carried out an initial photographic survey. The first evaluation from a spatial planning and photographic perspective is scheduled for 2010, with a further evaluation planned for 2015 and a final evaluation in 2020. The present paper introduces the observation concept and images from the initial photographic survey.

The project is documented on the Internet at www.beobachtung-schlieren.ch.

Schlieren as Case Study of an Agglomeration Space

Schlieren is an agglomeration municipality in Zurich-Limmattal. The town has over 13,000 inhabitants and is located in a working and business center within the Zurich city region.[5] Over the last 150 years Schlieren has developed from a farming village into a modern service center. The development of the village into an urban space, from industrial zone into a service and technology location is a representative example of the processes of change currently affecting many agglomeration areas in Switzerland. Within a relatively small, politically unified space, the town encompasses all the elements typical of Swiss agglomerations. It therefore represents an ideal case study for the observation of spatial development in agglomerations.

The structural development of the city of Schlieren has until now chiefly been shaped by economic dynamics and the development of transport routes. The town accordingly exhibits the qualities and deficits typical of agglomerations. In 2003 Metron Raumentwicklung AG was commissioned to develop an urban development concept for the area.[6] The application of this concept from 2005 onwards has instigated a comprehensive process of improving Schlieren as a residential and working center. The central tasks of urban development are the reinvigoration of the city center, improved linkage of the districts, the development of large agricultural reserves and disused areas, the improvement of public spaces, the tailoring of transport to the urban space, and the improvement of the perception and use of the spatial qualities of the landscape. The urban development concept is designed to serve as a conceptual basis for development projects by public authorities and private investors.

The goals of the urban development concept are similar to those being formulated by spatial development concepts for agglomeration areas across Switzerland. For this reason, the photographic observation of the effects of the Metron AG urban development concept should provide a basis for inferring the efficacy of urban development concepts in agglomerations in general.

Photographic Observation Concept

The observation concept defines photographic strategies for making the process of settlement development visible. The photograph's specific reference to reality is central to this process. The photographic observation asks how the goals and measures formulated in the urban development concept affect the concrete location. The images should make visible how the urban space is changing as a consequence of different interventions by the various actors using and shaping the space. In particular, the photographic observation makes it possible to observe those aspects of urban development that are decisive in terms of aesthetic and emotional qualities. The point of departure for the development of the observation concept is the question as to which processes of spatial change are consciously perceived and which processes occur beneath the perceptual threshold. The long-term photographic observation contrasts succinct changes and massive inventions (e.g., large-scale building) with discrete changes that occur slowly and continuously. The project will make the different speeds of parallel processes of change visible and show how extensively smaller interventions also change the character, atmosphere and quality of living spaces.

The photographic observation concept forms the basis of the ongoing documentation process over the period 2005–2020. It identifies the places and objects to be photographed and defines the rhythm of observation. Metron Raumentwicklung AG and the city of Schlieren have identified particular, exemplary areas and districts in which the themes and issues of urban development are being observed. These are: city-center development, streets and squares, open-space development, development of restructured areas, development of residential areas, development of settlement peripheries. In contrast to the representation of space in plans, the explanatory power of a photographic observation is not based on a comprehensive depiction of the entire urban space but on the distinctiveness of selected situations. The photographic visualization of space operates in terms of examples.

The ZHdK observation concept combines two types of spatial perception: overall and detailed views. The overviews show spatial interconnections while detail photographs focus on individual objects that are typical for the atmosphere and utilization of an area. The overviews will be rephotographed from the same point of view every two years. The details will be rephotographed every five years within a thematic framework. Overviews and detail photographs together form a flexible pictorial system, which allows for different types of assessment from a spatial planning or photographic viewpoint. Series of images can be combined in relation to particular areas, themes and processes of change and provide visual examples of the central aspects of urban development.

The contrast between mobile and static elements is fundamental to the everyday perception of urban space. The space itself is perceived as static; people and vehicles are moving within it. For this reason, people are not featured in the photographs. When comparing images, the observer's attention should focus on the spatial changes mapped by the photographs from the same point of view and not be distracted by the different positions of people in the images. The users are present in the traces that they leave behind.

Overviews

The overviews present spatial contexts and interconnections. The quality and singularity of the urban space are generated by the confluence of different elements in a spatial situation. The overviews track how interventions in the interplay of streets, buildings and open spaces alter a spatial situation. In contrast to architectural photography, the focus is not on an individual object; instead, streets, squares, potential building sites, green spaces and their adjacent buildings are photographed in such a way that all elements constructing the respective space are accorded equal value. The series of overviews photographed from the same position show change as a slow, continuous process. A comparison of the images reveals both massive interventions and discrete, barely perceptible changes.

The overviews are conceived as individual images based on a selected location. They make visible the particularities of the selected areas and districts. However, the standardization of selected photographic parameters means that at the same time the overviews form a conceptually designed series of images. The flexible combinability of the images is a precondition for being able to compare different spaces and situations in the entire urban space with one another. Expected and unpredicted processes of change, which differ in terms of perceptibility, speed, progress and controllability, can be examined in particular areas or across the entire urban space.

The following photographic parameters have been prescribed for all overviews:
- The location from which the photograph is taken is based on inhabitants' everyday perception. The view is directed straight ahead to correspond with everyday perception. The height of the camera is 170 cm.
- The location from which the photograph is taken is evident in the image. The camera is always positioned on public ground.
- The focal length lies within the wide angle range so that spatial depth can be shown.
- Lighting is even so that all details are clearly visible.
- Photographs are taken between July and Sep-

tember. Vegetation should be visible without dominating the atmosphere of the location (e.g., by creating a pronounced spring or autumn mood).
- Elements that are expected to change (e.g., demolition, renovation and remodeling of buildings, changes to road layout) are always shown in combination with elements that remain unaltered.

The plan defined by Metron and Schlieren, which assigns certain thematic programs of urban development to specific areas, forms the basis of the selection of the viewpoints. In the key areas of restructuring and development and in the city center, series of up to thirteen points of view have been established. Other themes are being observed via a system of individual photographic locations that are spread across the urban space. The 63 locations chosen in 2005 are to be maintained during the entire observation period. In the case of unforeseen new projects that have an overall significance for urban development new points of observation can be added.

Details

Detail photographs show selected objects and situations that are characteristic for different areas and districts. The series do not constitute an "inventory" but make clear which uses and designs are typical for a certain area. Series of detail photographs are being taken in the city center and the areas most important for the program of urban development. A thematically defined series of detail photographs shows ground floor use (residential and small business) over the entire urban area. The series relating to the individual areas each comprise twelve to fourteen photos. This allows the individual image to remain perceptible and emphasizes the exemplary significance of the represented object. As in the case of a pictorial essay, the combination of individual detail photographs forms an "image" of the area concerned. The initial photographic survey made in 2005 contains a total of 84 detail photographs.

The developments observed via the detail photographs are not tied to a specific photographic point of view. The design and use of an area form a reaction to measures that are being set in train on a larger scale by the urban development concept. Where and how new forms of design and use develop cannot be foreseen. Therefore the detail photographs are repeated within a thematic framework. Based on the initial photographic survey in 2005, the question of whether the character, use, design and atmosphere of an area have changed will be examined every five years. Contrasting this pictorial series makes for a more acute perception of changes. The detail photographs accentuate the point at which an area "tips" and its character changes (e.g., when interim uses of a former industrial area disappear).

Internet Presence

Specialists and interested members of the public can follow the development of the city of Schlieren via the website www.beobachtung-schlieren.ch. The pictorial archive is accessed via a map of Schlieren that shows themes and questions informing the urban development project. The map indicates all locations from which the overviews have been photographed and the direction of view. The detail photographs are linked with the individual areas as series. The descriptions of areas that can be accessed via the map summarize the goals of urban development for the individual areas. Detailed descriptions of each overview present the initial situation, discuss the planned development and identify the relevant actors influencing changes to the location. New photographs are successively integrated into the archive and presented on the website. In the course of observation an archive of 800 images will be generated. This material will be used for regular presentations, exhibitions and other events related to the theme of urban development throughout the observation period.

Evaluation

The first interim evaluation from a spatial planning perspective will take place in 2010. A key focus will be the qualitative evaluation of processes of spatial change. As a planning instrument, the urban development concept will not only be assessed in terms of its efficacy at the planning level but, on the basis of the photographic observation, will be examined in terms of its effects on concrete locations. The point of departure for the evaluation is based, among other things, on the following questions:

- Have the expected/desired changes taken place in the individual areas?
- Which actors have been involved in the changes?
- Have authorities been able to exercise control over developments?
- What has been gained through development, and where have qualities been lost?
- How can the authorities use the urban development concept as a planning instrument, and does it provide support for planning on a day-to-day basis?
- To what extent are unforeseen/undesirable developments affecting the design of the urban development concept?

The Schlieren Project as a Model for Further Photographic Spatial Observation Projects

It is intended that the "Long-Term Photographic Observation of Schlieren 2005–2020" project will also illustrate the general potential of long-term photographic observation. The observation model for Schlieren has been conceived in such a way that it can be applied to other municipalities and locations. A series of long-term observations could show the overall changes mega-city regions and their divers parts are subject to. Urban development in Schlieren provides an example of the attempt to influence the development of a space within the Zurich city region from the local level. However, the urban development concept only formulates guidelines; the large building and development projects are financed and carried out by private investors. The city of Schlieren can only partially influence concrete developments. The long-term photographic observation will therefore also make visible how the functional logic powering the development of mega-city regions affects a concrete location within the Zurich city region.

In everyday experience, space is perceived as an immobile, stable background. Ideas of urban space and landscapes as immobile and fixed are reproduced not least by the conventions of spatial representation in the (photographic) image. The photographic gaze fixes the space in the image. The method of re-photography (repetition of a photograph under the same conditions at the same location) renders the relationship between space and gaze dynamic. The landscape itself begins to "organize" the image, and this effect increases with the number of repetitions and the length of time involved. Comparable long-term projects in Europe show that significant changes already become visible within the relatively short observation period of five years (Mollie-Stefulsecu 1997, 2000).[7] However, presenting a comparison of the different speeds of parallel processes of change requires a longer observation period. Cities and landscapes have their own tempo. Observation points "throw a net into the space" in which planned as well as unplanned changes can be captured. The question of which locations will provide fruitful pictorial series can be answered in advance to only a limited extent. For this reason, the observation period and the regularity of re-photography constitute decisive factors in determining the success of a long-term observation project. The greater the duration of a project, the more fruitful its results will be. Long-term observations require stamina from all participants. They should be linked to institutions that can guarantee the continuity of observation over the entire period, irrespective of the personnel involved.

Photographic spatial observation provides scholars and planners with a tool for visual analysis and perception. In the political context, photographic series can help sharpen public awareness of the constantly increasing tempo of spatial change and the urgency of sustainable spatial development. However, this can only take place if the images are integrated into political and scholarly discourse. Despite their apparent readability, photographs are complex visual events. The process of mediation is of decisive importance: in the context of exhibitions, symposiums, publications, etc., photographs must be read and interpreted with specific reference to themes and questions of spatial development. Long-term photographic observations should therefore always be carried out as transdisciplinary projects involving experts in both photography and urban planning.

Notes

[1] "Crossover" is understood here as referring to hybrid forms drawing on different genres within a discipline, e.g., music and photography, but also to hybridization between different cultural practices, e.g., between art and pop culture.

[2] Walker Evans, one of the 20th century's most influential documentary photographers, refers in this regard to a "documentary style."

[3] An overview of photographic projects in the context of spatial development can be found in Giertsberg 1998.

[4] The Swiss foundation Documenta Natura produces photographic documentations of building, transport and tourism projects and reportages in the field of landscape and environment. www.documenta-natura.ch.

[5] Further information on Schlieren can be found at www.schlieren.ch.

[6] The complete urban development concept can be found at www.beobachtung-schlieren.ch/pages/konzept/02.php.

[7] For example, "Observatoire photographique du paysage," France. Since 1991, this project run by the Ministry of the Environment has conducted a series of continuous long-term observations in selected landscapes, villages and agglomerations throughout France (Mollie-Stefulescu 1997, 2000).

References

Barthes, R. 1980. *La Chambre claire. Note sur la photographie*. Paris: Gallimard.

Dubois, P. 1983. *L'Acte photographique*. Paris, Brussels: Nathan, Labor.

Giertsberg, F. (ed.). 1998. *SubUrban Options. Photography Commissions and the Urbanization of the Landscape*, Rotterdam: Nederlands Foto Instituut.

Heintz, B. and J. Huber (eds.). 2001. *Mit dem Auge denken. Strategien der Sichtbarmachung in wissenschaftlichen und virtuellen Welten*. Zurich, Wien, New York: Voldemeer, Springer.

Mollie-Stefulescu, C. (ed.). 1997. *Séquences paysages. Revue de l'observatoire photographique du paysage*. Ministère de l'Aménagement du Territoire et de l'Environnement. Paris: Hazan.

Mollie-Stefulescu, C. (ed.). 2000. *Séquences paysages. Revue de l'observatoire photographique du paysage-2000*. Ministère de l'Aménagement du Territoire et de l'Environnement. Paris: Arp Editions.

Thierstein, A., C. Kruse, L. Glanzmann, S. Gabi and N. Grillon. 2006. *Raumentwicklung im Verborgenen. Untersuchungen und Handlungsfelder für die Entwicklung der Metropolregion Nordschweiz*. Zürich: NZZ Buchverlag.

Map of Schlieren
Development areas in which the themes
and issues of urban development are
being observed:

- ■ City-center development
- ▢ Streets and squares
- ■ Open-space development
- ▢ Development of restructured areas
- ■ Development of residential areas
- ■ Development of settlement peripheries

Rietbach

Schlieren West

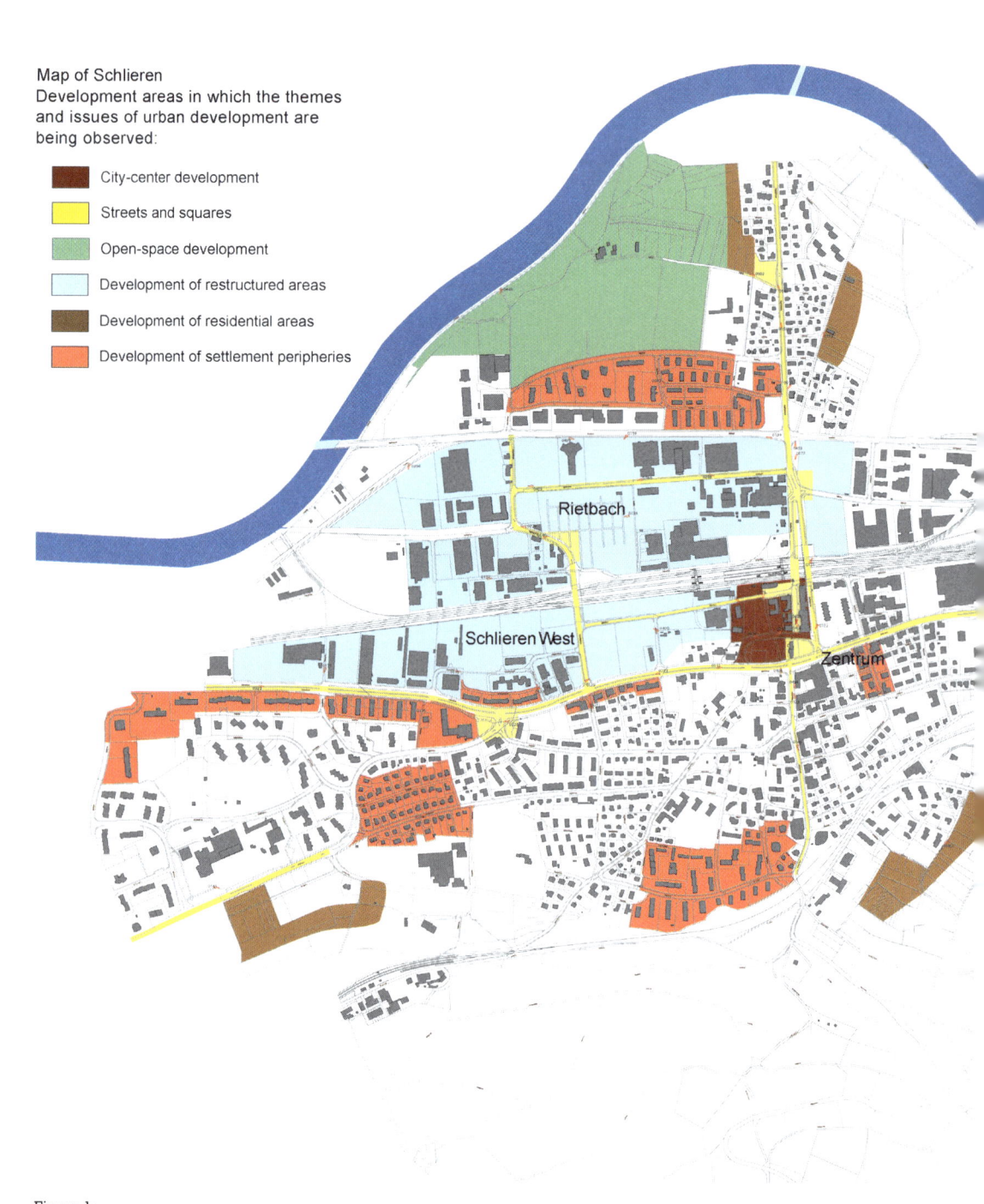

Zentrum

Figure 1:
General view on the concept
of photographic observation.

Long-Term Photographic Observation of Schlieren 2005 – 2020: Examples of the First Phase of Photographic Observation in 2005

The overviews are photographed from the same position every two years. Details are photographed every five years within a thematic framework. Detailed descriptions of all overviews can be downloaded at www.beobachtung-schlieren.ch. Area descriptions explain the initial situation and the goals relating to each development area. The area and picture descriptions are provided here in summarized form.

Schlieren West Development Area

Due to the main artery road running along its boundary, the Schlieren West development area is isolated from the surrounding urban space. The level of noise exposure is high. The interior of the area is poorly served by public roadways, and large parts of it are taken up by disused industrial sites, storage facilities and interim-use enterprises (car dealerships). Isolated residential and commercial buildings can be found on the eastern and southern edges. Large areas along the railway line are completely undeveloped and are currently being used for farming.

The most important development goals are opening up of the area, establishing better links with the overall city structure and integrating public spaces. The city of Schlieren is aiming to expand its residential function, and Schlieren West offers a large area for potential development within the residential zone. Plans include compact residential and mixed uses of sections close to the city center, mixed use along the east-west traffic axis and residential buildings in the interior of the area. Construction is expected to begin around 2008 on the agricultural land along the railway line, and further development will take place in stages until 2030.

Figure 2:
Overview from the Schlieren West development area:
Züblin area, Storchenstrasse, view to the east.

Projected development:
Short term – until approx. 2008:
construction of a turning facility as per the plan for
the quarter.
Medium term – until approx. 2015:
construction of predominantly residential buildings
with an integrated park while retaining existing
residential buildings (right in picture).
Long term – from 2015 onwards:
demolition of existing buildings and construction
involving new lot divisions and a direct connection to
the public space behind the residential buildings on
the right-hand edge of the picture (currently not visible).

Figure 3:
Overview from Schlieren West development area:
Badenerstrasse, view to the west.

Projected development:
Residential buildings in the left of the picture:
renovation and, where required, demolition and
new development. Periodic assessment of the
residential environment with the aim of maintaining
or increasing residential quality.
Badenerstrasse: unchanged until approx. 2015;
where appropriate, integration of bus lane
or light rail link and bicycle path.
From approx. 2015: remediation.
Agricultural area in the right of the picture:
residential and commercial buildings of at least
four stories; construction expected by approx. 2010.

Center

The center of Schlieren is currently divided in two. The main commercial center is located to the south of the east-west road axis, while the northern area between this busy four-lane road and the railway station has a less pronounced commercial function. Connections beyond the east-west axis function poorly, and the northern and southern parts of the center do not form a unified whole. The old village center and its park are separated from the east-west axis by a noise barrier. The main pedestrian connection between the railway station and the existing commercial center leads though an underpass rather than the Bahnhofstrasse (historical north-south axis). Extensive undeveloped or under-used plots can be found 100 m from the railway station. The island in the middle of the center features extensive green areas and a single old residential and commercial building.

The center around the historical north-south axis is in urgent need of development and constitutes the link between the existing commercial center south of the east-west axis and the railway station. The major focuses of development are the future city square to be located on the island in the middle and the north-south axis (Bahnhofstrasse). The emphasis of planning is on additional retail areas, new cultural and recreational uses and public facilities. It is also envisaged that the city square will contain a central intersection point for public transport.

Figure 4:
Overview relating to the theme of center:
intersection of Engstringerstrasse and Ringstrasse,
view toward the southwest and the center.

Projected development:
Remodeling and remediation of the street areas;
new city square with bus stops and light rail stops
on current green areas. Development expected
to continue until 2010. Shopping center
(left in picture) and the residential and commercial
building (right in picture) are to be retained.
Increased visual and functional access to the
shopping center is to be established.

Setting up a Perception Instrument

Residential Development
The majority of housing in Schlieren is regarded as of a high quality and secure. Planned measures to improve the quality of the residential environment include protection from traffic noise, the improvement and development of the footpath network and access to the surrounding landscape. However, particularly in the case of residential buildings constructed in the postwar period, ongoing renovation and modernization are required. In relation to traffic, the introduction of traffic-noise protection measures and a speed limit of 30 km/h are required in the short term. Urgent action is required in the case of residential buildings along the major road arteries, and priority needs to be given to solving the noise problem and improving the quality of buildings and facilities.

The most important developmental goals are strengthening Schlieren's residential function through the construction of high-quality housing in areas along public transport axes (internal densification and increase of the utilization coefficient in accordance with the zone plan), a general improvement of housing and the creation of new mixed zones as urban residential neighborhoods. Improving the design of the main traffic arteries and integrating them into the urban environment are necessary to the overall improvement of residential quality. In the case of residential buildings dating back to the 1950s and 1960s, comprehensive renovation and, in some cases, demolition and rebuilding are required. Buildings constructed in the 1970s along the east-west traffic axis also require ongoing modernization and maintenance.

Figure 5:
Overview relating the theme
of residential development:
Zelgli quarter, Gewobag housing estate
Feldstrasse 33–27, view to the east.

Projected development:
Demolition of the cooperative housing estate
built in the 1950s, construction of new
multifamily dwellings of between two and
five stories. Street to be retained as private
internal access road.

Figures 6, 7 and 8:
Detail photographs relating to the theme
of ground floor use.

Figures 9 and 10:
Detail photographs from the Schlieren
West development area.

Beatrix Bencseky

Creating Identity
Scale Design for Mega-City Regions

This essay deals with the question of how mega-city regions can be comprehended from a design perspective as a means of lending them a distinctive character and identity. The theses elaborated below have been generated in the process of exploring this theme.

Design is understood here as a phenomenon that can be comprehended in sensory terms, that has the capacity to emotionally move the observer and that facilitates communication between loci within a space. It is also argued that one necessary aspect of design is that it adds value for the user. These considerations lead to the conclusion that the increasing importance of a core area of design that draws on a range of fields and disciplines requires the delineation of a new area of expertise that can be termed scale design.

Figure 1:
Appenzell idyll in no man's land. The highly romanticized scene portrayed on the poster referring to a particular rural region contrasts starkly with its nameless surroundings.

Mega-city regions are economically and structurally coalescent cities, agglomerations, urban cultural landscapes, regions and subregions. One of the motors driving the agglomeration of urban centers and the increasing formation of mega-city regions is globalization. This process of the national and international integration of economic activity, education, advanced technologies, environmental management, politics, culture and communications is not new. However, the speed at which it is now progressing and the evidence of its spatial reach are giving it a new level of readability. Electronic communications media that span the globe and rapid means of transportation are integrating economies, knowledge transfer and service provision across space to a previously unknown extent and in a highly visible way. This process of integration affects us all, and one of its results is the formation of conurbations. Nevertheless, the coalescence and formation of mega-city regions still often proceed unconsciously, unintentionally, stealthily and unnoticed.

This lack of awareness leads to the emergence of undefinable, shapeless regions devoid of identity. In such no man's landscapes we repeatedly find visual excrescences that underscore the forlornness of a location.

Take the example of a poster designed to advertise a typical Swiss cheese featuring three men in traditional costume sitting on a bench. The rural surroundings pictured on the poster contrast starkly with the environment in which the poster has been hung, i.e., the concrete pillar of a railway bridge in a faceless location. All that can be made out are general nondefining elements such as a street, a field and an apartment block: a geographical blank, an anonymous place that is difficult to identify. There is a radical divergence here between idea and reality.

Identity as Central Existential Concept

This brings us to the central question of identity, which forms the basis of my first thesis: A megacity region must be circumscribed in relation to other regions by means of a clearly recognizable character. As in the case of individuals, mega-city regions need to develop a personality that entails the evolution of distinctive features. The time axis, deliberate planning and design and repetition play a key role in this context. Identity is the decisive quality with which mega-city regions can profile themselves both internally and externally. Identity encompasses inhabitants' identification with their domestic space, their neighborhood and their regional network. Generating such an identity requires the definition of living and action spaces. A mega-city region needs to develop an awareness of its specificity, its particular qualities, and form, radiate and communicate this identity as a distinctive image.

Thesis I: A mega-city region must, like an individual, develop an identity and a personality.

The formation of a mega-city regional identity entails working on a larger and more complex spatial scale than we are accustomed to when dealing with urban spaces. The task is a complex one, and the question of how it can be solved brings me to my second thesis. The answer is design, for design creates superordinate structures while also working on a scale that is comprehensible in human terms. Design is able to react to predetermined situations, generate structure and personality, and integrate people into their environment in a meaningful way. Design functions visually, in a physically objective way, moves us emotionally and can be perceived in its totality. Design is a consciously formative process and encompasses everything we see around us, comprehend and experience in tactile terms. Design penetrates both the private and the public sphere because it corresponds to the fundamental human need to characterize, define and communicate both the smaller and larger elements of existence by naming them and rendering them recognizable, more "beautiful" and more useful.

Thesis II: Giving mega-city regions an identity requires design.

The creation of any design object, from the smallest to the largest, requires a specific creative and conceptual input. This conceptual work enables us to shape our environment, create new interrelationships and make them visible, modify that which already exists and delimit things from one another.

Design is still a young discipline, but its career has burgeoned since the Industrial Revolution. It has now well and truly emancipated itself from the role of being a mere provider of accessories. Its permeation of our living and work spaces has seen the significance of design become increasingly anchored in the public consciousness.

The interdisciplinary character of design links architecture, engineering technology, art, urban planning and landscape architecture; it also generates identity. Design is in permanent flux and can react flexibly, restructure, organize and optimize. The philosophy of design encompasses not only aesthetically convincing solutions, the satisfaction of demands and needs, and functionality, but also, importantly, the generation of added value for the user.

The following discussion employs a number of examples to illustrate how design on both small and large scales contribute to identity formation.

The Ubiquity of Design

It is not only external space but also the interior life of a space that is largely shaped by design and indeed defined by it, whether in the case of private space, workroom, studio, office, factory, gallery, bakery, kiosk, service center, government authority, museum, swimming pool or fitness center. The designed objects communicate nonverbally and are universally comprehensible. The following examples illustrate the significance of design as an aspect of identity formation in the context of enclosed spaces such as workrooms and auditoriums. Exhibition spaces also belong to this category, and the example here evokes an intimate, private character.

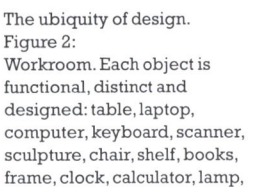

The ubiquity of design.
Figure 2:
Workroom. Each object is functional, distinct and designed: table, laptop, computer, keyboard, scanner, sculpture, chair, shelf, books, frame, clock, calculator, lamp, mobile phone, wooden box, computer mouse, street-map, headphones and microphone, ruler, speakers, picture frame, paper clips.

Figure 3:
Exhibition space (installation) in the Migros Museum, Zurich. The colorful dots painted over the ceiling, floor, walls, organic shapes and passageway generate a specific atmosphere, a cheerful, surprising, but also bewildering spatial impression.

The ubiquity of design.
Figure 4:
Remodeling of a veterinary clinic in Zurich. The design is tailored to the scientific function of the space; the limited range of colors produces a harmonious, calming effect. The light brown squares on the wall draw the observer's gaze. They emphasize internal circulation within the space and provide spatial closure. The light brown takes up the color of the wood of the elongated shelf. The shelf is thus spatially absorbed and more consistently integrated into the library space. The lighting is neutral without being impersonal. It is designed to be concealed in some places and visible in others. In this way the color and lighting concept supports the existing architecture and strongly emphasizes the interior-architectural statement.

Figure 5:
Remodeling of a veterinary clinic in Zurich. The proportions of the materials, particularly in the acoustic deck, which I designed as part of the process of interior fitting, had not only to be visually pleasing but above all to accord with acoustic requirements. The distribution and orientation of the different materials that absorb, reflect and disperse sound respectively were calculated extremely carefully. This applied to the blue felt back wall, the aluminum panels forming the acoustic ceiling and the perforated metal masking of the table, as well as the materials used in the cloakroom area.

Intensifying Awareness of a Location
with Design

The following example relates to the public sphere. In July 2006 the "Weltoffenes Zürich" (Cosmopolitan Zurich) committee mounted a widespread and well-designed poster campaign to draw attention to the importance of an international airport for ensuring the competitiveness of Zurich as a location.

Nobel Prize winners also like Chicago…

… which doesn't exactly please Zurich students.

We need an airport that links us to the world.   www.weltoffenes-zuerich.ch

---

Japanese also enjoy shopping in Munich …

… which doesn't exactly please Zurich traders.

We need an airport that links us to the world.   www.weltoffenes-zuerich.ch

---

Figures 6 and 7:
Succinct, catchy phrases communicate a clear message that the Swiss economy is closely linked with global development and that the Zurich airport must have an international status if Switzerland is to remain economically viable and continue to develop.

Creating Identity

Name Design and Identification, or How Real-Estate Branding Functions

The personal name is a fundamental element of identity. The explosive rate of spatial development, plethora of new structural projects and range of purchasing preferences in the urban sphere we are seeing today are resulting in an increasing demand for real-estate companies and design offices to create name designs for specific buildings and subregions. In Zurich, newly developed regions and residential estates attract attention with names like Limmat-West, Neu-Oerlikon, Zürich-West, Riverside, N-Joy, City Bernina, Sihlcity and Wohnhaus Heinrich. The following example illustrates how name design can generate identification and visually condense related elements.

A property developer wanted to create a shared image for four office buildings located in Zurich-West, a former industrial district now emerging as one of the city's trendier business and residential quarters. However, the developer did not want the process of creating this image to entail any alteration to the facades of the four buildings. Each of the buildings was also to be given its own name and all four names were to be integrated into a logo that would visually express the link between them.

The coherent and externally recognizable solution that was developed involved linking the "first names" Atlas, Netzwerk, Bienenkorb and Orion with the shared "surname," or logo, A&O. This plays on the idea of "from Alpha to Omega" (from A to Z), which in this case is translated into "Atlas to Orion."

Design as Conceptual and Interdisciplinary

It is not only the design of names but also the design of objects that contributes fundamentally to identification. Developing a coherent design solution that gives visual expression to the relationship between buildings and imbues them with an identity involves a close analysis of topography, existing and historically developed structures and their context. Design always needs to involve the conceptualization of overall appearance and the development of different formative scales that accord with different perceptual perspectives. The design for the A&O project drew on the concepts _FAR, _CLOSE and _IN. The design interventions _FAR and _CLOSE have a public character, whereas _IN relates to the interior of the office buildings, which fulfills the promise projected by their external appearance. This is an essential requirement if the effect of corporate identity is to be sustained.

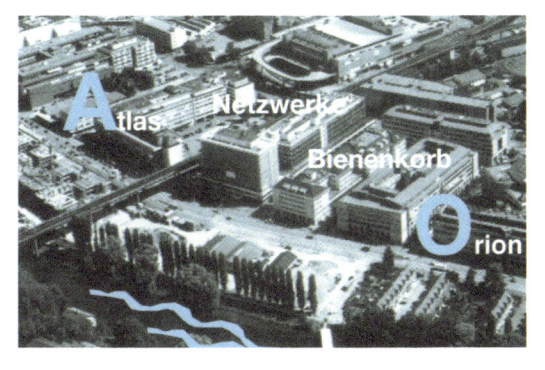

Figure 8:
Name design for complex of buildings in Zurich-West: the bird's eye perspective provides an overview of the complex of buildings and its integration into the district. It also shows how the four buildings have acquired a shared identity while also retaining their individuality.

Figure 9:
Name design logo. The partial overlaps in the design clearly express the fact that the buildings are linked with one another yet also independent.

Figure 10:
_FAR. The first design application, _FAR, was developed in relation to the pre-existing architecture. It entailed the strategic positioning of colored panels, which are represented in the photo by the blue surfaces. The colored panels mark and delineate the buildings as an integrated unit in relation to their surroundings. They are also back lit, which increases their aesthetic appeal by night and provides a source of orientation.

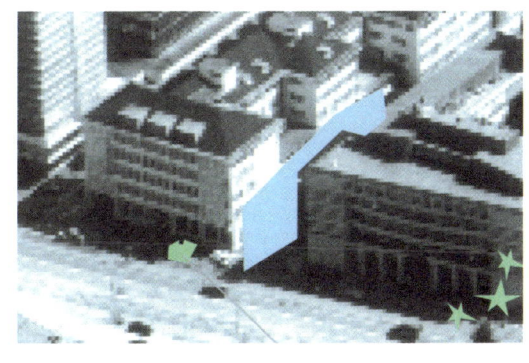

Figure 11:
_CLOSE. The second design application, _CLOSE, relates to the access area to the office buildings, which is represented in the photo by green stars. This area is to be emphasized by means of a sculpture with a tactile character that also plays on the names of the buildings. In addition, the access area is lent emphasis by the lettering. The work of design draws on disciplines such as architecture, interior architecture, art and graphic design.

Design and Communication

A bird's eye view makes the smaller and larger contexts of the A&O buildings apparent. Side streets provide access to the different buildings, a network of streets leads into the surrounding neighborhood, and cantonal highways and an autobahn connect the area with the city. Transport systems are prime examples of linkage. They form networks composed of a variety of threads and can only function on the basis of understanding, communication and agreement, which rely on the tool of design. Design delivers the information we need to find out where we are; it pilots us through regions, cities and neighborhoods.

Figures 12, 13 and 14: Traffic flow, linkage, communication. Whether traffic is human or penguin, nothing functions without precise rules and communication.

Street and public transport networks have long formed the arteries of extensive, indeed cross-border, regions, and thus also of mega-city regions. Means of transport are an integral aspect of the cityscape and represent an important medium of communication. Shaping and reshaping their design provides a very rewarding opportunity to lend a mega-city region a specific character.

Means of transport.
Figure 15:
London bus. Its particular character is what distinguishes it and makes it memorable. It is only in London that red, double-decker buses are used as regularly scheduled public transport vehicles.

Figure 16:
Low-floor tram in Zurich. Apart from its blue stripes, the tram does not exhibit any prominent design features. Its effect is every-day and inconspicuous, hardly a good example of identification promotion.

Means of transport
Figure 17:
Cabs in New York. Always the same yellow car! The yellow color, constant repetition and large number of vehicles have made New York cabs an indispensable part of the urban landscape.

Figure 18:
Old-fashioned vehicle (featuring rounded forms). In this case, color plays a subordinate role, whereas the character of the car is decisive.

Traditional and New Sources of Identity

The most important mediums of identification for a region or a city are its topographical features, prominent buildings and specific interrelations (in the sense of ensembles) in the built environment. These elements characterize a region or a city, giving it an image and a clear profile.

Until relatively recently, it was above all architecture that was central to the design of living space. For millennia, architecture and engineering have focused on housing, statics and structures.

Today, technical developments mean that topographical factors are playing an ever decreasing role in the expansion and aggregation of regions. Rapid spatial development is now creating a need for processes of characterization and profiling that traditional elements of identity formation are no longer capable of generating. Spatial development is simply too rapid, comprehensive, complex and invisible. Uncovering interrelationships within this flux of spatial development involves meticulous detective work.

However, it is essential that the developmental potential and associated dangers to the environment and nature of a region be subject to research and deliberate planning at an early stage. The extensiveness of mega-city regions means that they require a specific planning concept and appropriate implementation of it. In this context, design can play a connective and guiding role, one that entails shaping the interconnectedness of a mega-city region, giving it a visual aspect and contributing to the formation of a shared identity.

Topography and landmarks. Figures 19 to 24: Topographic and structural landmarks facilitate an immediate and explicit classification that is anchored in the public consciousness (above and below, left; clockwise from above): Matterhorn in Zermatt, Switzerland; Rhine falls in Schaffhausen, Switzerland; Eiffel Tower in Paris, France; Pyramids in Cairo, Giza; Sydney Opera House, Australia; Guggenheim Museum, Bilbao, Spain.

Swissair-Swiss.
Figures 25 and 26:
The fact that the difference between Swiss and Swissair is not immediately obvious is intentional. This clever move allowed a link to be forged with an already established identity. The differences are in the details: the red color on the fins of the new company's planes does not completely extend to the edges, while the new lettering is positioned differently and supplemented by a new logo.

Identity through Design

The role of design as a comprehensive formative tool even in a situation where loss of identity seems imminent is illustrated in the Swiss context by the grounding of Swissair in October 2001. The fact that the Swiss national air carrier was forced into liquidation at the end of 2001 after 70 years in operation had a profound effect on national identity and national pride. The sense of national identity associated with the carrier resulted in the subsequent auction of objects associated with Swissair bringing extremely high prices. The sense of national tension only relaxed with the founding of "Swiss," a subsidiary of Deutsche Lufthansa. The visual and symbolic statement launched with the new airline was a gamble that paid big dividends. The idea behind the design was to give the new airline its own visual profile while also building on that of its predecessor, altering it as much but also as little as necessary. This approach has proved very successful. The image of the airline as a positive symbol of Switzerland for the outside world has remained intact as has the Swiss population's identification with the carrier.

Design Provides an Overview and Orientation

As already discussed, perception and perspective play a crucial role in identity formation. The sheer scale of urban space exceeds our capacity to form a general view. Perception becomes limited to the perspective of the observer, who orients himself according to complexly arranged spatial details. While traversing the urban space, the observer uses these details, which usually incorporate several branches of design, to assemble different aspects like parts of a puzzle and compress them into an image. If the observer experiences the relevant design signals in a positive way, then over time a sense of linkage, of identification, develops. On the other hand, if the observer is not provided with adequate guidance through this space, he will find it difficult to orient himself. He will not be able to discern a profile and identification will be impossible. And anyone who finds that ongoing development renders them unable to recognize their neighborhood or region will suffer from a loss of identity. However, design is also able to make a profile visible in urban space and in a mega-city region and thus generate identity retrospectively. Public spaces have a significant role in every society in that they represent that society's values. And it is for this reason that design is becoming ever more important as a formative tool and medium of identification.

Design Creates a Profile
London is a good example of the degree to which design shapes the identity of an urban space. Red telephone booths, double-decker buses and black taxis are distinct codes for London and are read as such throughout the world.

The design products belong to the category of urban furniture. This category also encompasses ticket machines, waste bins, mailboxes and bicycle stands as well signage lettering, artificial lighting, seating and transport stops, the significance of which is briefly discussed below in relation to concrete examples.

Design products in public space illustrate how design shapes our perception and the collective consciousness and the emotional and functional significance it has assumed.

London codes.
Figure 27:
Even the design of road signs and their typography awaken different memories and associations specifically related to London.

Figure 28:
The design of the typical telephone booth embodies a trace of London's bygone culture of conversation and has long been an identifying feature of the city. A noise-reduced urban space is also an advantage for today's mobile-phone users.

London codes.
Figure 29:
When a design object decorates thousands of homes in the form of a toy that recollects a holiday in London, then this design piece can be seen as having a dream career.

Figure 30:
The typical underground station logos have also embedded themselves in the cityscape and the public consciousness.

Lettering and Design

Lettering is the only design discipline that established itself at an early stage in the urban space, and for this reason its biography already reveals a long and rich process of development. It serves as a means of orientation, is an attention-getter and can be deployed to create a distinctive focus. Lettering is a recognized design tool and today is deployed intensively in architecture and advertising. Lettering and images are extremely effective in our society. The significance of lettering is illustrated by the fact that it is not only used as a means of orientation but also as a tool in the design of buildings and urban locations.

Figure 31:
Here, on Broadway in New York, billboards and signage dominate the architecture of the building.

Figure 32:
Evocative lettering on a jewelry store in Vienna. The lettering forms a unit together with the entrance to the store.

Figure 34 (left):
Conservative, businesslike fluorescent lettering in Zurich Central. The script has an indecisive effect, relating neither to its environment nor the architecture. The building serves merely as a fastening surface, and the sense of a real metropolis is not really projected.

Figure 33 (above):
London's Piccadilly Circus by night: the context and relationship to the surroundings is unambiguous and the sense of metropolitan groove is clearly comprehensible.

Design and Artificial Lighting

Artificial lighting as a design tool in urban space is interesting in a dual sense. By night it replaces natural light, facilitates spatial orientation and generates a particular atmosphere; by day the lighting fixtures themselves function as design elements.

Figure 36:
The Angel of Peace monument in Berlin, a historical location with an appropriately ornate lighting column.

Artificial lighting fixtures.
Figure 35 (above):
Reichstag in Berlin: modern, functional lighting fixtures coupled with a pleasingly generous spatial design.

Figure 37 (right):
Design is a formal vernacular. This lighting fixture resembles a shovel and, while not pretty, is full of character.

Figure 38:
Römerhof, Zurich: lighting fixtures from the 1980s combined with a historic building dating back to the turn of the century. This detail could come from anywhere in Europe if it were not for the parking sign identifying the location as Zurich.

Design and Seating

Along with lighting, seating design is increasingly being used to create a particular atmosphere in public spaces. The older our society becomes, the more seating we need. Demographic research indicates that today's designers should already be developing and realizing ideas relating to the needs of older people in order to ensure that we are better prepared for the future. Here, too, design must react to specific functional requirements and environments. The result is a range of seating possibilities exhibiting quite different forms and color designs, which appeal to the potential user in different ways.

Seating.
Figure 39:
Bahnhofstrasse Zurich:
A classic bench that is designed exclusively for sitting and is quite comfortable.

Seating.
Figure 40:
Museum Quarter Vienna: Visitors are invited to relax on specially designed U-formed benches, which can be combined in different ways and thus take on a private character. The seating offers a variety of uses. Visitors can lie comfortably next to one another on them, enjoy the sun, talk, read a book or eat food they have brought with them.

Figure 41:
Raiffeisenplatz in St. Gallen by Pipilotti Rist and Carlos Martinez exhibits a cheerful and creative, albeit less practical approach.
All the benches and a small drinking fountain are covered with a red rubber "rug." Should one sit on the rug or is sitting even permitted? It is this ambiguity that lends the area its light-hearted, nonchalant atmosphere. The rubber surface has the effect of a large carpet laid between the buildings to create the impression of a living room, an "urban lounge."

Design and Transportation Stops

Transportation stops provide public space with an urban, progressive touch. They signal departure and arrival and are therefore always linked with emotions. Design gives visual expression to their function and quality and shapes their presentational aspect. This category of transportation stops can be seen as encompassing smaller scale examples such as stops for trams, buses, cars and bicycles, as well as larger scale constructions such as parking lots, harbors, railway stations and airports.

Transportation stops. Figures 42 and 43: Römerhof, Zurich. These transportation stops have been designed exclusively on the basis of functional and cost-saving criteria. They are completely devoid of emotionality or an image concept.

Figures 44 and 45: Glattalbahn light-rail system stop, Zurich. The design of this tram stop is ambitious, modern and exclusive, and thus promises a great deal.

Design and Green Spaces

Green spaces have a particularly significant role in mega-city regions. They fulfill important functions and are decisive for the quality of life within an urban region as well as for the way it is perceived. Green spaces are synonymous with relaxation and recreation, and these aspects, together with their transboundary character, mean that they can be a potent tool for the shaping of mega-city regions. In the form of parks, for example, green spaces therefore represent a further important facet of design in the context of mega-city regions. A well-known type of park design, which accords with my own preferences, involves the combination of trees, shrubs and flowerbeds with sand, gravel and lawn surfaces in a particular compositional rhythm. It may also include pools, ponds or fountains. A feeling of being close to nature is important for park visitors: the rustling of leaves and the fascinating way in which sunbeams penetrate the treetops, the play of light and shadow, the scent of earth and the places that offer shelter to all kinds of small animals. This need for recreation and relaxation within the urban space is not met by the new parks being constructed in Zurich. The current development of facilities for recreation and relaxation in fact seems to be moving in the opposite conceptual direction. We are seeing a predominance of zones that are oriented more toward architectural and design vernaculars than to the users of hitherto existing parks. The new facilities tend to radiate the feeling of an "event," offer "lifestyle" rather than relaxation and are more form than content. The designs are aesthetically structured to a high degree and offer a range of visually appealing aspects. However, they do not satisfy users' basic need for recreation and relaxation. What is required here is design that also embraces the imperative of adding value for the consumer.

Parks.
Figure 46 (left):
Paris, aerial view of a classically laid out park.

Figure 47 (right):
Park from the user's point of view. A green space can be defined by certain distinctive trees, bushes and the spaces between them.

Figure 48:
City park: Central Park, New York. New Yorkers have an enduring love affair with their city park. Central Park seems to offer the full range of possible uses: walking, games, riding, rowing, daydreaming, seeing and being seen.

Green zones within urban space.
Figure 49: Wahlenpark Oerlikon, Switzerland. Broad, elongated lawn areas with four dominant sculptural elements – the space offers an aesthetically pleasing view but does not invite the observer to take a walk or linger for a while.

Figure 50: MFO Park. Neu Oerlikon, Switzerland. Completed growth: The picture shows the target state of the installation. The vegetation is limited to the contours of the scaffold and thus tends to suggest a further building.

Figure 51: MFO Park. Neu Oerlikon, Switzerland. Current state: Creepers planted around a multilevel metal scaffold that combines wonderfully with its built environment. The interior contains seating and a sandbox with tiny rounded pieces of glass where children and adults can play. A very interesting installation that does not however encompass the added value aspect referred to above.

Identity Formation through Design in a Section of the Mega-City Region – the Example of the Alpine Rhine Valley

Having briefly discussed the different elements relevant to a design-based approach to a mega-city region, I will now explore a number of design ideas that can help crystallize the identity of a mega-city region with reference to the concrete case of the Alpine Rhine Valley.

Studies of the Alpine Rhine Valley from 2005 to 2006 led the Image and Region (Bild der Region) working group – made up of Ernst Basler + Partner, Freicom, the Sotomo research group at the University of Zurich, Hosoya Schaefer Architects and Bencseky-ID – to identify this area as a potential region that fulfilled many of the preconditions required to become part of the larger mega-city region of northern Switzerland. The group's work involved a close examination of the region's particularities and an analysis of its geographical potential. A mega-city-regional dimension is evident in the fact that the area in question has either no or several urban centers. The geographical particularities of the Alpine Rhine Valley are based on the convergence of Switzerland, Austria, Germany and Liechtenstein with the Rhine as a dividing element.

The Alpine Rhine Valley has enormous economic potential due to the presence of a large number of innovative and internationally active companies. In addition, it offers a wonderful, picturesque landscape. Nevertheless, many opportunities are being missed due to the region's lack of identity. The absence of a regional profile is contributing not only to a loss of potential investors but also employees, who are unable to convince their families to relocate to such a bland rural environment. Skilled employees who are in demand internationally will of course, together with their families, be inclined to compare living conditions on an international scale as well. As yet, senior employees still prefer to commute from larger urban centers such as Zurich and St. Gallen. The Alpine Rhine Valley has been unable to focus its energies economically, culturally or politically. The relevant actors tend to focus on the short term and their own needs. Activities and measures dedicated to identity formation are thus urgently required if this unsatisfactory situation in the Alpine Rhine Valley metropolitan region is to be improved.

Figures 52 and 53:
Alpine Rhine Valley.
Atmospheric impressions –
images of the Rhine Valley.

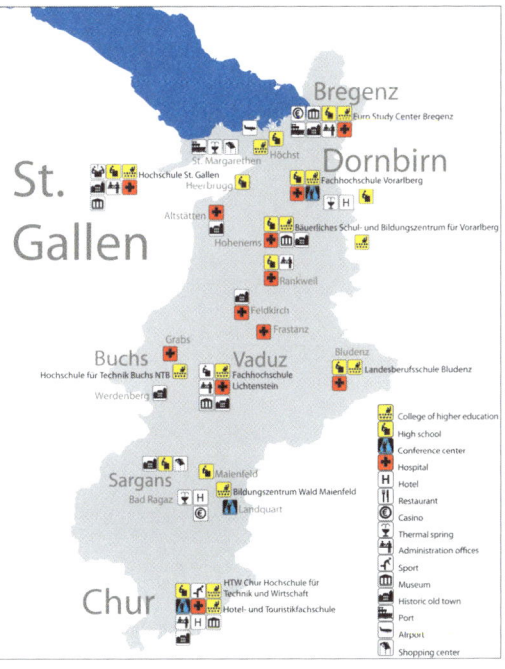

Figure 54:
The diagram shows the economic potential of the Alpine Rhine Valley: the size of the lettering indicates the degree to which the respective firm is an established name and internationally active.

Figure 55:
The diagram provides an indication of the way a lack of political will is leading to a dissipation of energies. As a result, too many institutions, schools, universities and hospitals are being maintained.

Lines of Identity Traced by Pyramids

The analysis of the Alpine Rhine Valley gave rise to two design models geared to the promotion of a lived, active and contemporary identity for this section of a mega-city region. A central aim was to develop an identity that was rooted in the Alpine Rhine Valley area and was linked to the particular geographic character of the area and the existing economic situation.

The point of departure and a core element of the design proposals is an understanding of the Rhine as a connecting rather than a dividing line.

The first model proposes placing a series of terraced pyramids along the Rhine within visible distance of one another. The simple form and the repetition of individual elements oriented toward one another provide an allegory for the interconnectedness of the Alpine Rhine Valley region.

The archaic, simple form of the pyramid symbolizes constancy and longevity. As a form, the terraced pyramid makes an immediate impression. The increasing height of the steps symbolizes the eternal and constant development. The fact that one pyramid is visible from the next emphasizes interconnectedness while also making for an entertaining, playful aspect. Observing the next pyramid, with or without field glasses, enables one to see what sorts of activities are being initiated there. The pyramids are also invested with emotional associations, for example, when a family member or friend is living in the region. The very form of the pyramids imbues them with presence. Their visual effect fits well into the fluvial topography while at the same time causing them to stand out.

Whether the pyramids projecting from the landscape are regarded as landmarks or observation towers will depend on local interpretations. Moreover, their scale will determine whether they are seen as recreational sites, excursion destinations or buildings that provide a new center of identification and a space for regional and cultural activities such as markets and music and theater performances. The model has been designed to provide orientation even in the case of flooding.

Figure 58:
Terraced pyramids of different sizes and with different functions shape the landscape and signal interconnectedness through their visual proximity.

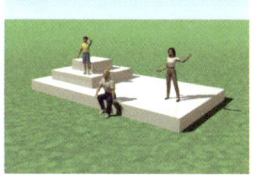

Figure 57:
The pyramid as outside furnishing: The model illustrates the variable function of the pyramids as seating.

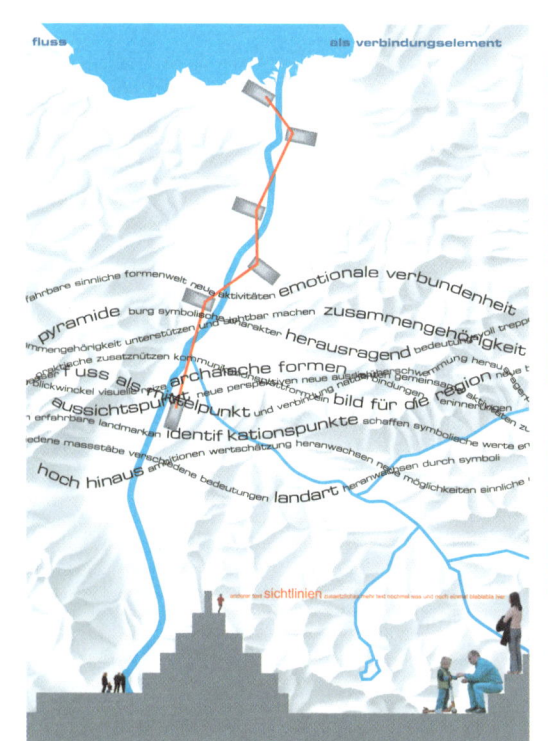

Figure 56:
The river (Rhine) is defined as a connective line and provides the foundation of the design concept for the Alpine Rhine Valley region.

Lines of Identity Traced by Lighting

The second model refers to a particular economic characteristic of the Alpine Rhine Valley. The region is commonly associated with the production of cutting-edge technology. Indeed, those living and working there like to refer to it as "Precision Valley."

The model envisions circular observation platforms mounted with a reflective sphere. A dividing wall reflects natural light and as a result produces different effects depending on the time of day and weather conditions. These observation platforms are similarly positioned to the pyramids in the previous model; they are within visible distance of one another and thus allow for visual contact. A central motif is their dual aspect, i.e., the difference between the platforms by day and by night.

During the day, the reflective spheres mounted on the observation platforms provide an accent within the landscape. The platforms can serve as meeting points and as recreation locations.

At night, the sphere provides an additional visual and sensory experience. Laser beams connect the different regional centers of competence, thus enabling them to "communicate" with one another. The lasers create visible connections and generate an emotional atmosphere while at the same time symbolizing the highly specialized technology of "Precision Valley."

Figure 59:
By night, the light units project laser beams into the landscape, creating a visual network connecting different locations.

Figure 60:
Light is shown here, on the one hand, as a connective, communicative element that sends and receives signals, and on the other as symbolizing economic progress through technology.

Figure 61:
The circular platforms provide a focus for excursions and panoramic views.

Creating Identity

Design as an Important Component of Spatial Development

The Alpine Rhine Valley project illustrates the importance of interdisciplinary work when identifying the strengths and weaknesses of a region. The project also shows that design can communicate the character of what is in this case a section of a mega-city region in a way that makes it comprehensible, tangible and visible. Design covers a range extending from everyday objects to buildings, but it can also be related conceptually to far broader spatial contexts such as that of mega-city regions. Conversely, this conceptually elaborated spatial scale can be related to design, which can be used to forge an identity for mega-city regions. The more individual spheres become specialized and develop in a specific way, the more indispensable design becomes the putty that holds them together at their core. The design applied to mega-city regions as a tool of identity formation distinguishes between the planning scale and the implementation scale. The planning scale can vary according to the intended effect and can encompass an entire mega-city region; the implementation scale is always 1:1. As indicated above, I define this 1:1 scale as the scale that allows the human observer to comprehend a design in its totality. Giving a mega-city region a recognizable character requires both a spatial and temporal process that encompasses a number of coordinated plans with varying planning scales. Design can be compared to acupuncture: on the one hand, it can be applied in a very specific and localized way, while, on the other, the multiplication of these applications can achieve an effect that is sustained, spatially comprehensive and visually generative and can thus contribute to communication.

The two models of identity lines traced by pyramids and lighting provide an indication of the potential qualities that design can generate and show how design can actively support the evolution of a defined sector of a mega-city region and generate identity. Design creates images for the region.

Scale Design

The complex and multifaceted nature of spatial development and the rapidly increasing formation of mega-city regions have enormous implications for our understanding and definition of design. The conventional view no longer suffices. In my opinion, the elaboration of my two theses, "A mega-city region must, like an individual, develop

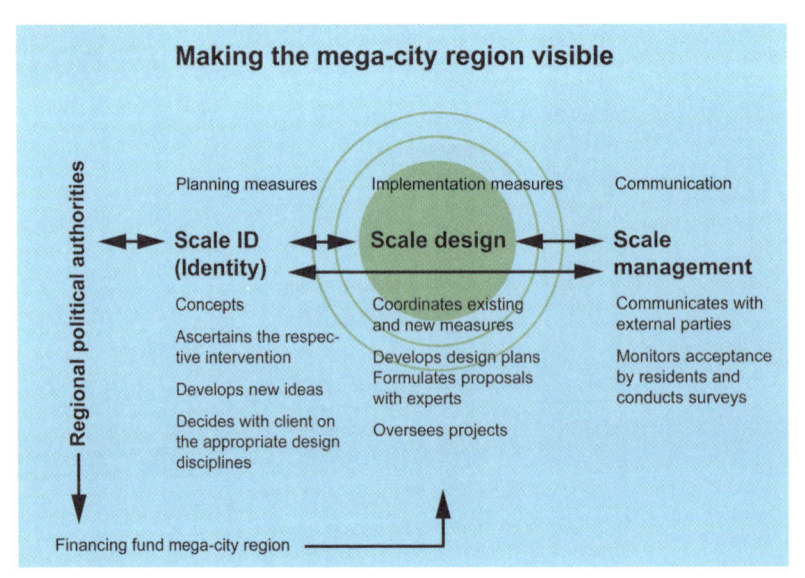

Figure 62:
Organizational chart of scale design. Scale identity, scale design and scale management interlock with regional and political entities in the process of generating the identity of a mega-city region.

Figure 63:
Advertisement for scale designer. Qualified professionals sought for new occupational field: scale design.

an identity and a personality" and "Giving mega-city regions an identity requires design," suggests the need to delineate an area of professional specialization that I would term "scale design."

Thesis III: Scale design: The generation of images for mega-city regions requires a new type of design professional.

A scale designer's work involves contributing to identity formation in public space on different scales and for different areas of application. Scale design requires design professionals with a developed two-dimensional and three-dimensional spatial sense. They work in conjunction with specialists from other disciplines such as urban planning, traffic planning, architecture, landscape architecture, visual design, sociology, etc. Scale design specifically involves the planning scale, while scale identity concerns the implementation scale and scale management involves communicating with affected parties. Scale design involves interventions, invention and research around the theme of identity in public space.

Scale design locates gaps and neuralgic points in the intermeshing of urban and rural spaces. The degree of scale differentiation is of course also dependent on the available resources.

Concluding Thoughts

If we are to deal with the challenges being presented by current spatial development, we need to develop mega-city regions with their own personality profiles. This task requires a widening of perceptual boundaries and a new category of design. Interdisciplinary team-based design is required that can create different scales for extensive social and economic spheres and generate "images" that provide value for the user and cultivate identity. The formation of identity in mega-city regions urgently requires networks forged through design.

addi

Agnes Förster
Alain Thierstein

Adding Value to Spatial Development

Towards a Value Chain Approach to Large-Scale Spatial Development

The different articles can be viewed as either single spotlights or layers that are accentuated by distinct colors of the program laid out by "Making Mega-City Regions Visible!" The overall picture remains in the dark though. The layers' superposition and interplay will provide a tentative collage rather than a continuous smooth pattern. The program of "Making Mega-City Regions Visible!" does not bring about one all-embracing picture. It rather points to multiple coexistent and complementary visualization strategies.

This concluding article does not aim to present a final synthesis of the approaches presented so far. Rather it hopes to explore some preliminary results that both offer a debate and lead the way toward further research and practice.

The composition of this book draws on the hypothesis that the program of the title, the idea of "making mega-city regions visible," requires a multilayered approach. This is reflected in the decision to join the articles on the level of content and the way this was carried out, as well as in the design of the book. In this concluding article this hypothesis will be examined and particularized. If we consider the idea that the immense task posed by the invisibility of mega-city regions cannot be managed by a single strategy of "making visible" but demands multifaceted strategies, the way these different approaches complement each other has to be laid out in detail. To accept the suggestion of complementary visualization as proposed by Burkhard and Wandeler, the meaning of "complementary" has to be explored in our context of mega-city regions. Therefore we propose breaking down the hypothesis into individual aspects (see Burkhard and Wandeler in the present book).

From Single Spotlights to an Integrated Approach

The program of "Making Mega-City Regions Visible!" is intended to stimulate governance processes in these new large-scale contexts. Thus when distilling from the collected articles the lessons learned, it might be helpful to proceed with a concept that offers interfaces between the visualizing work, on the one hand, and the conditions of collective action on the other. We'll adapt then the St. Gall management concept, which integrates the level of contents with the level of processes, to the task of "making visible" (Rüegg-Stürm 2002). This kind of management teaching is based upon the systems approach; it aims at integral thinking and acting when dealing with the complexity of a business company. We can thus identify three basic interacting components that help steer corporate processes, viz., strategy, structures and culture.

Strategy	Function	Why? What for?
	Content	What?
Structures	Technique	How?
	Process, context	When? Where?
Culture	Producer	Who?
	Recipient	For whom?

Figure 1:
An integrated approach for "Making Mega-City Regions Visible!"

When applying these interconnected areas to the program of "Making Mega-City Regions Visible!" the different layers of the perceptional work – presented in separate articles so far – will be part of an integrated approach.

- First the *visualization strategy* describes the tasks that occur when awareness of the relevant stakeholders inside and outside the region is raised. *Why* and *for what* will mega-city regions be visualized? These functions have to be conceived in succession vis-à-vis the evolutive process of the emergence of mega-city regions. Second the strategy implies a choice of relevant and promising contents to be visualized. *What* shall be made visible?
- The *visualization structures* refer, on the one hand, to the different techniques of "making visible." *How* shall mega-city regions be made visible? These visualization types may include the proposed differentiation between real, media and mental images. On the other hand, structures relate to the contexts and processes within the perceptional work that has to be done. Modes of integration in planning processes have to be conceived and tested. *When* and *where* shall mega-city regions be made visible?
- The *visualization culture* points to behavior patterns, capacity, and expectations of the producers as well as the recipients of the images and visualizations. Who makes mega-city regions visible? *Whom* does the visualization work address? Different disciplinary backgrounds and the fact that people belong to dif-

ferent "worlds" inducing different spatial realms of activity and individual logics of action have to be considered.

These questions will guide the summary and evaluation of the collected articles and approaches. The lessons learned will be drawn at two levels, i.e., for each area of strategy, structures and culture, fundamental theses will be presented that give reason to corresponding exemplary questions. In their totality the resulting questions can be understood as a raw version of an agenda of further research and practice. The concluding thesis of this article sketches out the potential of a value-chain approach to spatial development when purposefully integrating the program of "Making Mega-City Regions Visible!" into efforts of analysis and communication.

I Strategy

When designing a strategy for the program of "Making Mega-City Regions Visible!" the perceptional work's driving power has to face the challenges imposed by the awareness issue. When having specified the relevant functions of "making visible," adequate subject matters have to be chosen: What are the important contents for pursuing the chosen challenges? What contents are qualified for making mega-city regions visible?

Thesis I: The program of "Making Mega-City Regions Visible!" serves multidimensional purposes. It fulfils numerous functions as a tool as well as a communication instrument within governance processes.

Dealing with the connection of "image" and "region," one might jump to the conclusion that this work mainly focuses on questions of place marketing or branding. In our opinion the program is not restricted to such a narrow function. Basically two main interrelated layers of function can be distinguished. First the program of "Making Mega-City Regions Visible!" relates to a working process that secondly provides output to communication. Looking to the domain of relevant players and stakeholders to bear large-scale metropolitan governance, the working instrument of "making visible" stimulates, enriches and conducts these processes of cooperation. Awareness among the responsible bodies will gradually rise when they succeed in making mega-city regions more and more visible. This process includes self-knowledge, common objectives as well as common concepts and visions for the future. When turning to the results of these kinds of processes, the acquired visibility serves communication purposes inside and outside the mega-city region. The added value of the cooperation can be demonstrated and felt inside the region; simultaneously the mega-city region's distinct role in its wider spatial and functional context becomes apparent. A successful internal and external communication strategy potentially reinforces the process of cooperation when self-perception is reflected and strengthened and additional supporters join. Consequently these two functions are interrelated and complementary.

Questions to research and put into practice:
When putting the two basic functions – the working and the communication instruments – together, what is their interdependence and temporal succession? How do they intertwine?
The working instrument points to a process character found in the program of "Making Mega-City Regions Visible!"; it needs to be based upon a tentative and explorative approach. Communication, on the other hand, demands ready and coordinated products. How can the different and simultaneous requirements be reconciled?

Thesis II: Visualizations potentially add cognitive, social and emotional benefit. The program of "Making Mega-City Regions Visible!" unfolds its full strength when taking into consideration all three levels.

Burkhard gives three sorts of benefits provided by visual representation for processing information, viz., cognitive, social and emotional benefits (see Burkhard in the present book). When being applied to the program of "Making Mega-City Regions Visible!" some of its possible benefits are:

- Cognitive benefits are generated when highlighting the complex functional interrelations within and between mega-city regions. This gives rise to new insights among the relevant players. The identification and classification of mega-city regions as an analytical, normative and strategic construct can be considerably promoted by their visual representation in corresponding maps.
- Social benefits occur when "making visible" helps the relevant players to raise their motivation, coordinate a shared perception or formulate a shared vision and strategy.
- Emotional benefits might include the creation of attention potentially induced by powerful or seductive visual representations such as maps, illustrations or images. Furthermore emotional points of reference for citizens and players of a mega-city region might be provided by suitable real images.

When conceiving complementary strategies of visualizing mega-city regions, these different benefits can be made use of. This applies to the working as well as the communication instrument of "Making Mega-City Regions Visible!"
Questions to research and put into practice:
What kind of social, cognitive and emotional benefits can be expected from the program of "Making Mega-City Regions Visible!"?
How can these different benefits be purposefully combined and balanced within the program of "Making Mega-City Regions Visible!"?

Thesis III: The program of "Making Mega-City Regions Visible!" needs mediating between two poles: Illustrating complexity, on the one hand, and pushing concreteness on the other hand.

The challenge that lies in the program of "Making Mega-City Regions Visible!" is to mediate between two different, complementary functions. First the enormous size of the new spatial scale, with its complex functional, polycentric interrelations, has to be illustrated to foster understanding and insight. Secondly the large-scale abstract concept of mega-city regions has to be translated into concrete and tangible places, objects, events, etc. This book's articles reflect this duality. Kruse, Leuthold and Zonneveld pursue overarching analytical or designing approaches of the perceptional work. Wandeler, Bencseky and Stein Schultz, on the other hand, realize "making visible" as the transfer of the abstract concept of mega-city regions to the reality of its citizens' everyday life.

Different degrees of complexity and concreteness of mega-city regions		
Strategic, conceptual	←→	Concrete, tangible
Metropolitan scale	←→	Local scale
Functional characteristics	←→	Morphological characteristics
Comprehensive planning	←→	Sectorial issues

Figure 2:
Mega-city-regions
between complexity and
concreteness.

Conceiving the program of "Making Mega-City Regions Visible!" in this duality refers to a combination of two distinct planning approaches, viz., planning by strategy and planning by project. The assumption is that visualizing the superordinate strategy alone has limited impact. Motivation, attention, emotions are very much bound to individual and collective experience and learning processes. First of all mega-city regions are a concept, they are the object of strategic spatial planning; this concept has to be enriched by concrete and tangible aspects. On the one hand mega-city regions' complexity has to be illustrated; on the other, comprehension needs to be fostered by reducing its complexity and providing concreteness. However, beacon projects without a visible strategic framework are likely to fail their purpose. "Making visible" needs the reciprocal translation between general view and integrated details.

Questions to research and put into practice:
When visualizing mega-city regions, what understanding can really be provoked by "making visible" the overarching structures and strategy, and – simultaneously – what degree of concreteness can effectively be attained?
How should one combine and complement the different focal lengths stretching between general view and detail? Can strengths and weaknesses of the respective approaches be purposefully countervailed?

Thesis IV: Mega-city regions are characterized by diversity, discontinuity and shifting perspectives. When their image is more than the sum of its parts, the combination of different levels of content is crucial.

> The multifaceted character of mega-city regions relates to different aspects; the horizontal and vertical superposition of different spatial scales with the related authorities; different dimensions of space that are of relevance, such as functional and morphological; the diversity of the different parts relating to different categories of space, such as highly urban centers, hybrid urban landscapes or semi-rural areas. So "making visible" means interpreting these single components in a broader context and searching for potential syntheses. This work has to be done primarily on the level of contents, before further questions of realization are addressed. On what subject matters may the synthesis work be based upon? Three dimensions seem to be of special relevance, viz., questions of scale, of dimensions of space, and of time and topicality. The following hypothesizes will highlight these aspects.
>
> When assuming that the perceptional work needs to be based upon suitable contents first, it might turn out that existing expectations of the relevant players will not be met. The program of "Making Mega-City Regions Visible!" is no off-the-shelf product that can be completely delegated to external experts. It demands commitment and work on self-perception, something that professionals from different disciplines may help with.
>
> Questions to research and put into practice:
> When questions of content precede questions of visual realization, how can this working process be organized? How can one discuss unborn images?
> Can rough and sketchy images stimulate the collective work on the adequate contents? Might their imprecision, exaggeration or even wrongness be thought-provoking and move forward the working process?

Thesis V: "Making Mega-City Regions Visible!" needs to be based upon a combination of sets of images on different spatial scales.

> When regarding the potential "image" of a metropolitan area – here the term image refers to the mental maps of the inhabitants – Lynch (1960) supposes an arrangement by levels as a necessity of the large and complex environment. "Rather than a single comprehensive image, there seemed to be sets of images, which more or less overlapped and interrelated. They were typically arranged in a series of levels, roughly by the scale of area involved, so that the observer moved as necessary from an image at street level to levels of a neighborhood, a city, or a metropolitan area" (Lynch 1960: 85-86). When the image of the metropolitan area can only be conceived as changing and shifting between different spatial scales, the question of pinning together these different levels of organization is crucial. Instead of one fixed all-embracing picture, "Making Mega-City Regions Visible!" means permanently zooming in and out. This interplay of different spatial scales and changing perspectives brings about different contents that appear on the screen. These contents are interdependent. According to Ipsen (2000), the meaning of places and the related potentials for the inhabitants to

identify with them can be transferred from one spatial level to another. Significance of a place exists only in relation to another one; the space of reference determines the intensity – high or low – and the orientation – positive or negative – of the rating. The transfer of meaning can take place in two directions, i.e., inductive transfer operates from small regions to the larger ones they are part of; deductive transfer acts from higher to lower-ranking spatial scales (Ipsen 2000). Within mega-city regions the spaces of reference that provide the mental context for the evaluation of its different parts are always shifting. Places, objects and skills that are of importance on a regional or metropolitan scale are not necessarily of equal significance on a national, transnational or global level. The program of "Making Mega-City Regions Visible!" aims at a set of different and coordinated images that are nested like a matryoshka doll.

Questions to research and put into practice:
When referring to the image of matryoshka dolls, what contents are they concealing and flaunting in each case? What is the spatial realm of the corresponding images? Might "making visible" be associated with different functions and potentials on the different spatial levels of mega-city regions? What is the resulting relative importance of the different spatial levels within the program of "Making Mega-City Regions Visible!"?

Thesis VI: Intermediate scales potentially play a crucial role in perceptional work; they help to proceed from available images at existent spatial scales to new images at the unfamiliar spatial scale of mega-city regions.

The transition from present conceptions of space to the new conception of mega-city regions rests upon adequate intermediate scales; like a stepping stone, their visibility might further the visibility of the whole mega-city region. Consequently the preoccupation with the relevant parts of mega-city regions seems to be important and promising. When investigating large-scale social topography, Leuthold proposes to scale up the idea of quarters, originating from the city scale, to mega-city regions (see Leuthold in the present book). The criteria for the creation and differentiation of these quarters have to be identified with regard to their size, relative functional importance and complementary role within the mega-city region. When being conceived as a mediator between old and new, present and future, these quarters or part-regions – this is our assumption – already have to be of a cross-border nature. Taking cross-border literally they will comprise several municipalities or subregions; figuratively existent mental barriers will be cut across. Consequently major characteristics and challenges of mega-city regions are also reflected within its parts. Making up mega-city regions out of these kinds of quarters is comparable to Ungers' concept of the city as parts. The design of the city can be thought of as the design of its constituent parts (Ungers et al. 1977). Therefore Frei reflects on the mental images provided by smaller regions and Stein and Schultz are preoccupied with the visibility of urban landscapes being a typical part of mega-city regions (see Frei; see Stein and Schultz in the present book).

Apart from all the remaining questions with regard to the parts, what relevant quarters can be identified? Will they feature homogeneity or heterogeneity? What is their identifiable profile? There remain major questions concerning the composition of the whole. Facing this kind of polymorphism, can mega-city regions ever be pictured as a totality? As to the matter of metropolitan form, Lynch states that "the environment is still not treated as a whole but rather as a collection of parts (the sequences) arranged so as not to interfere with each other. Intuitively, one could imagine that there might be a way of creating a whole pattern ... Perhaps this pattern of a whole cannot exist. In that case, the previously mentioned techniques remain possibilities in the organization of large regions: the hierarchy, the dominant element, or the network of sequences" (Lynch 1960: 114-115).

When images of mega-city regions are made up of parts, it does not mean these parts are area-wide. "Total imageability of an extensive area such as a metropolitan region would not mean en equal intensity of image at every point. There would be dominant figures and more extensive backgrounds, focal points, and connective tissue" (Lynch 1960: 112). In several German mega-city regions one major challenge to the program of "Making Mega-City Regions Visible!" seems to be the visual dominance of the core city in contrast to the rather invisibility of the region (Thierstein, Goebel and Förster 2006).

Questions to research and put into practice:
What kind of portions of mega-city regions might serve as strategic stepping stones towards making the whole visible?
How does one cope with the latent discontinuity of mega-city region's images and their unequal intensity within its perimeter?

Thesis VII: Understanding the interaction of functional and morphological space is decisive for the program of "Making Mega-City Regions Visible!" These different dimensions of space have to be linked within an image of the region.

Mega-city regions are essentially characterized by material and immaterial functional interrelations; inside, between their constituent parts and outside, between different mega-city regions. Substantially determined by the driving forces of the knowledge economy, these characteristics point to a relational understanding of space. Despite their immateriality, these economic, cultural and social relations are bound to material space like physical infrastructure, significant concentration of the built environment producing the necessary proximity of the economic players, or high-quality green spaces. The program of "Making Mega-City Regions Visible!" cannot solely be based upon "making visible" the immaterial structures of relational space in the form of maps, diagrams or sketches. Furthermore, physical space seems to be an important resource for "making visible." It can be directly perceived in everyday life; it provides emotional points of reference; its visible qualities influence the media and mental images of the region. Therefore those physical elements and places within mega-city regions are of special importance for the perceptional work that provide spatial fixes within the network of the knowledge economy. What are the space of flow's physical points of reference? Schaafsma gives the example of the international gateway infrastructure of hub-airports that also emerge as urban generators (see Schaafsma in the present book). Translating functional space into morphological space and vice versa helps to reveal those contents that might be turned into significant and powerful images.

Questions to research and put into practice:
What physical locations, objects and places of mega-city regions are of functional importance for the performance of the knowledge economy?
What spatial elements within mega-city regions join functional significance and potential physical visibility and legibility?

Thesis VIII: The program of "Making Mega-City Regions Visible!" has to balance different temporal orientations; while history matters to properly understand the present constitution of a mega-city region, innovations are needed to face major tasks and challenges related to the future.

The concept of mega-city regions not only invalidates in part familiar spatial scales and existing administrative borders, or shifts the functional importance of the region's morphological characteristics, it also changes the role of historical references within mega-city regions. There are different aspects to the question of the temporality. On the one hand the specific history of mega-city regions decisively determines their present character; the process of their emergence is path-dependent. The POLYNET project with its studies of eight European mega-city regions revealed that polycentrism at the metropolitan level comes in many different forms; their spatial arrangements vary greatly (Lambregts 2006). Here understanding the specific historical development might be a valuable resource for realizing and formulating their distinctness and profile. On the other hand adhering to traditional conceptions of space or specific local or regional history rather hinders the comprehension of the new spatial scale of mega-city regions with its related present and future challenges. When looking for new images for mega-city regions, how is one to deal with the old ones that belong to their different parts? Breaking with them or linking them up? Placing historical landmarks in the new map of a mega-city region – even if they are strong images – doesn't necessarily add value to the whole. Meeting the players, stakeholders and citizens at their current perception is an important task though. The program of "Making Mega-City Regions Visible!" implies a work of synthesis regarding the temporal dimension. It has to provide links to existent historical images – helping to conceive its distinctiveness and giving motivation to the relevant players – as well as orient one toward future challenges.

Questions to research and put into practice:
How can different temporal orientations be integrated into the program of "Making Mega-City Regions Visible!"?
How can existent conceptions of space be overcome? When trying to establish new mental images of the large-scale functional contexts of mega-city regions, would it be helpful to deliberately destroy old ones?

II Structures

Having discussed different strategies that the program of "Making Mega-City Regions Visible!" will pursue, questions of implementation arise. First the visualization *structures* point to the different techniques of "making visible." The book started with the hypothesis that "making visible" needs to be based upon a simultaneous and coordinated work of real, media and mental images. The respective techniques have to be discussed for all three dimensions. What is their relative importance and specific role? What are the potentials for interventions? Secondly "making visible" always takes place in a certain context, within planning processes. What might these interfaces look like, what might modes of integration be?

Thesis IX: Real images can hardly reach out physically to the mega-city region's spatial scale. They unfold their strength when they succeed in visualizing in everyday life the added value of the large-scale cross-border cooperation.

How can real, physical space that is of persistent visibility and potentially guides perception tell something about the mega-city region's spatial scale? When thinking about modes of intervention in real space to foster the visibility and image quality of the whole, the enormous size of mega-city regions, their heterogeneity in terms of internal polycentric functional hierarchy and discontinuity turn out to be major obstacles. How can one purposefully fit single components of the built environment into the big picture of mega-city regions? When the whole cannot be accomplished at once, one has to think about individual approaches. Large-scale components of the mega-city region's morphology such as vast empty spaces, ample network infrastructures such as rail-bound public transport or significant points within the metropolitan tissue like urban nodes might provide promising locations for interventions. It seems to be crucial then to attach further value to these real images by feeding the locally experienced quality of life within the cross-border region. Real images have to be put piecewise into the context of the mega-city region; their everyday functional relation to the whole might help in doing so. Consequently, the resulting real images of mega-city regions have the potential to provide focal points for the identification of the players, stakeholders and inhabitants.

Significant real images of mega-city regions can either be new creations or – and this seems to be even more likely – based upon processes of reinterpretation of existent images within the new functional context. When providing noticeable benefit in everyday life, even very economical interventions may enhance the visibility of the new spatial scale. Scale design offers ways to enhance the legibility and distinctiveness of mega-city regions by choosing an "acupuncture" strategy that is based upon repetitive, minimal interventions with a maximum of effect. It can also be applied to existent structures of mega-city regions (see Bencseky in the present book).

Questions to research and put into practice:
How can large-scale strategic orientations meet the locally experienced quality of life, which is potentially added to by cross-border cooperation within mega-city regions?
What kind of real images are suitable for visualizing in everyday life the added value of the kinds of cooperation processes that are demanded?

Thesis X: When applying the question of real images not to the whole but to the constituent parts of mega-city regions, large-scale urbanistic challenges have to be addressed.

What real, material spaces form the image of mega-city regions? When turning to the idea of its quarters, these large-scale identifiable parts might be conveying the image quality of mega-city regions. On that scale the perceptional work of changing, strengthening or creating real images points to urbanistic questions. Where to locate these urbanistic challenges? Schaafsma gives one example when specifying the importance to mega-city regions of international airports as major network infrastructure. They serve as a kind of gateway to the whole region and their function can be compared to the role played by central train stations in the city in the railway age, i.e., they are generators of urban development within mega-city regions. Concepts such as Airport City, Airport Corridor or Aerotropolis potentially link the main city and the region (see Schaafsma in the present book). Looking into the possible urbanistic qualities of airports is at the same time a way of reworking the image of the mega-city region. With regard to Munich International Airport, the Airport Region of Munich identifies a new spatial context – extending far beyond existing regional borders – that faces mutual challenges concerning land use as well as structure and quality of built infrastructure, housing or large green spaces. Collective action is called for when trying to leave behind uncoordinated spatial development dominated by municipal perspectives in order to take advantage of the enormous urbanistic potentials of the respective spatial context (Droß and Thierstein 2006). It is only when realizing the importance of the mega-city region that its constituent parts can tackle their specific challenges and potentials.

The program of "Making Mega-City Regions Visible!" aims at detecting those places and subregions that are both of strategic functional importance and conveyors of meaning to the whole mega-city region. Their functions and potentials for the image quality of the whole have to be discussed.

Questions to research and put into practice:
What might large-scale urbanistic conceptions look like? What kind of qualities and structures can be proposed and at what level of detail or abstraction?
What are the necessary features of the constituent parts of mega-city regions in order to contribute to the whole artifact?

Thesis XI: The strategic role of media images bears on "making visible" mega-city regions' initially invisible spatial characteristics. The choice of appropriate modes of representation and visual languages is crucial when discussing the performance of different techniques of visualization.

When visualizing unfamiliar, novel contents, what is the preferred way of addressing the recipients? New contents, new style, or new contents, old style? The question of visual language or style points to the expectations, experience and knowledge of the recipients – for whom the visualizations need to be legible – and the desired effects of the visualizations. Lange expounds this problem when raising the question of "how real is real," reflecting on highly realistic renderings and their possible application in scenario studies (see Lange in the present book). Leuthold analyzes the social differentiation within mega-city regions; the unfamiliar contents are visualized by means of topographical relief, already common to every schoolchild (see Leuthold in the present book). The preoccupation with questions of composition and style is also highly present in the photographic work of Wandeler (see Wandeler in the present book). A visual language is never neutral. As a kind of subtext, a certain style of mapping already tells something about the mental disposition on the basis of the contents that are visualized. In the context of mega-city regions major challenges are the opposition of functional and territorial thinking and the aptness of looking for clearcut spatial categories. What mode of visualization corresponds to the understanding of mega-city regions as functional spaces with flexible, changing boundaries?

Questions to research and put into practice:
How to represent dynamic relational space with its nonphysical flows? What visual techniques and languages are suitable and powerful enough to capture the ambiguous and shifting positions within the resulting maps?
What visual means are of help to the recipient in order to orientate himself within the relational space?

Thesis XII: Maps are "hybrid tools" that constantly switch between different functions such as analysis, design and communication. Their inherent constituent power has to be explored for the process of emergence of mega-city regions.

Maps are very powerful instruments for "making visible" because they serve various functions at the same time. Rarely are they purely analytical, but contain the momentum of design and therefore wield enormous power in communication. Maps provide a basis, a resource for design. Maps as "hybrid tools" are of special interest when the program of "Making Mega-City Regions Visible!" is carried out over time (see Primas in the present book). Their different functions can be related to the different steps of "making visible"; in one and the same medium these stages are synthesized. It thus seems crucial to conceive the interfaces between the different functions of mapping. When proceeding from analysis to design, to communication, many questions have to be addressed. Design is not the linear extension of analysis and the finding of the appropriate communication strategy needs to take into account more than the layer of content, the sender's and recipient's perspective and the question of the communication medium.

Questions to research and put into practice:
How does one apply maps as rough, sketchy, and thought-provoking instruments within planning processes despite their enormous power, which is difficult to control? When maps are means of analysis as well as of design and communication, who elaborates these maps and who is involved in the process? How does one conceive the interfaces between the different functions of mapping?

Thesis XIII: Stories might be important tools to manage mental images of mega-city regions. Being made up of single identifiable components they can be deliberately created, manipulated and controlled.

When a mental image is thought of as an integrated whole, its immaterial nature is difficult to control. Breaking it down into the single components of a story it becomes manageable. As stories are immaterial – their image quality only exists in the mind – they can be attached to the category of mental images. Paasi (2003) identifies narratives as important building blocks of regional identity (Paasi 2003). In stories the totality of the image results from linearly joined identifiable parts. The whole image can be purposefully created out of these components. The potential of narratives for the program of "Making Mega-City Regions Visible!" relies on their capacity to join varied, diverse parts within one story. They turn out to be strategic instruments that help to combine different kind of contents such as functional and morphological characteristics, different subregions, varying spatial scales as well as different kind of images – real, media and mental ones. By potentially providing an associational context, stories add value to heretofore separate images of mega-city regions.

Questions to research and put into practice:
What is the actual strength of stories in joining the diverse parts of mega-city regions' images? What are the stories' adequate structure, form and character?
How are stories about mega-city regions received? What is the experience with the stories' role and impact in communication?

Thesis XIV: The program of "Making Mega-City Regions Visible!" needs an active communication between the different kinds of images, real, media and mental, given that spatial perception is steered by a synthesis of all three dimensions.

The three layers of images are interdependent; they comprehend and influence one another. Real images can act upon mental and media images; media images affect mental images. Knowing about and understanding this interplay is crucial for the program of "Making Mega-City Regions Visible!"

Moreover the relative weight of the single components within this triad of images has to be considered. In the case of the Øresund Region, Hospers (2006) reflects on the reciprocal importance of branding and place marketing, basically focusing on the region's mental images, on the one hand, and the internal real lived and experienced spatial qualities of the region on the other. "Thus, place marketing must find a balance between identity, image and the desired reputation, i.e., its brand. If these elements fit, the brand really is the greatest common denominator between the different pillars (e.g., economy, infrastructure, education and culture) and arenas (citizens, entrepreneurs, authorities) making up an area. This requires that the area should be marketed in a realistic way; in other words, the selected brand must suit the identity of the locality in question" (Hospers 2006: 1017). In addition to external marketing, Hospers demands an internal marketing – a kind of bottom-up process – that fosters the cross-border identity of the inhabitants. Otherwise, when externally communicated mental images and internally lived real images diverge, the region risks becoming only an "imagined space" (Hospers 2006). Hence, the program of "Making Mega-City Regions Visible!" requires coordinated and simultaneous work on all three levels of images.

Beyond that, an active communication between real, media and mental images potentially strengthens the individual components. Real images will be taken up by mental and media ones and vice versa. The quality and usefulness of real images – created or modified by interventions in real space – also has to be measured according to their potential of adding to communication by media images. Looking for and elaborating such kind of interfaces and points of contact have to be part of an integral approach to the program of "Making Mega-City Regions Visible!"

Questions to research and put into practice:
In practice, can the reciprocal added value of real, mental and media images actually be put into effect?
When real, mental and media images are issues of different preferential disciplines, who has to be involved when trying to translate different dimension of images into one another?

Thesis XV: The program of "Making Mega-City Regions Visible!" points to continuous learning processes of perception that have to be purposefully integrated in planning processes.

When mega-city regions are of a latent invisibility that hinders the attention, comprehension, and motivation of the players, learning to perceive and adapting the present perception to the new challenges of spatial development have to be an integrative part of governance and planning processes. Thinking of modes and techniques of this integration is crucial. Individual building blocks of this integrative approach of "making visible" have been proposed within this book.

Interactive visualizations aim at integrating the players that will foster their perception in the visualizing process. Stein and Schultz propose to visualize urban landscapes on the basis of collective experience of the relevant players (see Stein and Schultz in the present book). Held and Kruse create the relational landscape of the creative industry of Zurich with the help of insider-knowledge; representatives of the creative industry contribute to these kinds of visualizations in focus group workshops and think-tanks (see Kruse in the present book).

Long-term monitoring through photography, proposed by Wandeler, systematically accompanies the implementation of the planning strategy of a municipality within the mega-city region of northern Switzerland. Photography as a perceptional instrument links the strategic and abstract level of spatial development to the reality of the built environment that can be directly perceived (see Wandeler in the present book).

Spatial visioning is a method of leaving behind – reframing – familiar mental maps within transnational planning processes. According to Zonneveld, the process of "visioning," mainly based on drawing new maps collectively, helps to develop a shared identity that stimulates and provides a basis for the cooperation (see Zonneveld in the present book).

Questions to research and put into practice:
What further modes and techniques of integrating perceptional work in the planning processes can be thought of?
Within the sequence of planning processes, what design steps can be supported by what instruments of "making visible"?

Thesis XVI: The program "Making Mega-City Regions Visible!" potentially adds to planning processes in all their steps, from A to Z. Thus the manifold facets and functions of the perceptional work loosely and situationally intertwine, accumulate and complement one another.

Fostering perception and visibility of mega-city regions is a constant challenge within governance and planning processes with their different design steps. How can the whole process of "making visible" be conceived and organized? Can the program of "Making Mega-City Regions Visible!" be thought of as an all-embracing approach that adds value, through awareness, to products and processes? Although the idea of a master plan or blueprint to this process is enticing, it is not likely something that can be found; it even seems to be an inappropriate attempt. A causal and linear connection of the different ways of visualizing mega-city regions with their related functions can hardly be established. The transition between different functions of visualizations such as from analysis to design and communication is ambiguous; there are always multiple solutions.

In this spirit we would interpret the proposition by Stein and Schultz only as one out of many different ways of proceeding, as a situational approach to a particular project. They try to conceptualize the process of "making visible" from the very beginning of the planning process to its formalized result at the end. The perceptional work is thought to be a value chain that includes in a first step the work on the individual and collective experience of the region in an interactive and communicative process that breaks open familiar perceptions. The documentation of this experience and the experiment with interventions that modify perception are further important steps. Finally the newly gained insights result in a map – a vision – that complements the legal instrument of the regional plan with qualitative statements (see Stein and Schultz in the present book).

Can one really go to such lengths? Zonneveld is more restrained when assigning spatial visioning the capacity of formulating strategic propositions (see Zonneveld in the present book). Petrin even conceives the perceptional work as mere stimulation to planning processes. "Stimulating the second space" is thought to be an independent layer of design that is not directly linked to planning in the sense of town or regional planning. The interdependency between real, mental and media images – Petrin speaks of a spiral of perception – will be exploited to change attitude and behavior of players and citizens towards large-scale urban regions. The purposeful intervention in the present perception of the region – that is the idea – may ultimately stimulate planning processes (see Petrin in the present book).

Questions to research and put into practice:
How much and in what way, directly or indirectly, may visualizations contribute to the performance of planning processes on the spatial scale of mega-city regions?

Consequently, how close or loose will the perceptional work be linked to these planning or governance processes?

When conceiving the process of "making visible," with its different design steps, for a specific mega-city region, how situationally or universally should one proceed?

III Culture

The program of "Making Mega-City Regions Visible" needs to be reflected against the background of the culture of those who produce and those who receive the gathered and designed images. This points to an important aspect of communication. Here we shall discuss the implications of different disciplinary backgrounds and the fact of belonging to different spatial scales and different "worlds."

Thesis XVII: Mega-city regions are multiscalar spatial systems of functional interrelations where internal and external perspectives are interlinked and nested on different spatial scales. Given that, changing perspectives turns out to be a fundamental method in the "Making Mega-City Regions Visible!" program.

The perceptional work has to be broken down to different spatial scales, and on each relevant scale internal and external points of view matter. There are always two directions of questioning: What is our self-image? What makes us identify with our community, city or region that is part of a mega-city region? And, how are we looked at from the outside? What can we contribute within the larger functional, spatial context? These questions are of importance to every policy-maker that has to act and decide as a specific component within the mega-city region's network and at the same time has to justify his or her decisions to those who vote, pay for services and use the infrastructure. The added value of this endeavor then also has to become apparent internally. Hence the program of "Making Mega-City Regions Visible!" demands a process of communication that embraces a series of different spatial scales, at any one time simultaneously providing internal as well as external images.

Questions to research and put into practice:

What are the strategic and decisive combinations of perspectives out of the many possible ones within mega-city regions?

When simultaneously working on images on different spatial scales, how does one cope with the practical problems that may occur? So far images are not managed centrally; on the contrary, the predominance of different legal competences might turn out to be long lasting.

Thesis XVIII: Changing perspectives as a method also applies to the different "worlds" that mix and confront one another within mega-city regions. "Making visible" has to empathize with, address and meet these "worlds" with their corresponding realm of activity and individual logic of action.

In a first step mega-city regions are recognized as functionally interlinked economic spaces. The economic dynamic also extends to other domains; beyond the corporate perspective people show up who also belong to cultural, social, political spheres. Their self-conception differs greatly; for the different social groups the concept of the six "worlds" of Boltanski and Thevenot (1991) is to be applied on a trial basis (Boltanski and Thévenot 1991). According to this concept mega-city regions can be understood as intersection points of different worlds that have different spatial orientations, from local to global, with corresponding differing logics of action. The merchant world is based upon free flows of information, communication, trade relations, merchandise and finances; it is alone globally organized and oriented. Boundaries are almost nonexistent. The domestic world, however, is primarily locally bound. On the basis of that kind of foundation global orientation can be ventured. A dialectic between proximity and distance is established based upon immaterial borders. The world of the civil society features a multilevel spatial organization according to political and administrative spatial units. Boundaries matter in nested and hierarchically connected spatial scales. In one and the same place – in mega-city regions – these kinds of orientations coexist and overlap. At first glance such logics or worlds are quite invisible; even those who are involved are not always aware of them. When producing different claims of interpretation, conventions and land use, these worlds may even compete and come into conflict.

The program of "Making Mega-City Regions Visible!" will purposefully switch between these worlds and provide links between local, national and global thinking. When picking up on these different perspectives, the program responds to its different recipients.

Questions to research and put into practice:
How does one introduce shared perceptions and perspectives into the different "worlds"?
What kind of images may be legible for the greatest range of recipients within mega-city regions?

Thesis XIX: As the program of "Making Mega-City Regions Visible!" features multiple functions, techniques and applications, "making visible" has to be based upon various disciplinary approaches. The connectivity of the different disciplines thus turns out to be a decisive factor of success.

The program of "Making Mega-City Regions Visible!" cannot be attached to one single discipline. When one considers the three interdependent layers of strategy, structures and culture, the complexity of the program becomes apparent. It is not only different visualizing techniques that are relevant, but when conceiving an integrative strategy of "Making Mega-City Regions Visible!" analytical and communicative competencies are of equal importance. Within this kind of value chain of qualifications and methods it is not only the single quality but also the connectivity of each contribution that is very important. What does the capacity to connect one design step to another depend upon? Breaking free of one's professional domain requires an awareness of the core as well as the limitations of the respective competencies and functions and needs that may be served. The interfaces with required suppliers as well as with possible further processing have to be recognized.

It is necessary to conceptualize the single disciplinary position within the superior framework of the program of "Making Mega-City Regions Visible!"
Questions to research and put into practice:
Who feels addressed and activated by the program of "Making Mega-City Regions Visible!"? What will the resulting team look like?
How should one manage such a broad multifaceted team in practice?

**Analysis, Visualization, Communication –
a Value Chain Approach to Large-Scale Spatial Development**
Visualizing mega-city regions is no end in itself. The introductory article identified the crucial role of perception as an essential building block to stimulating large-scale metropolitan governance processes. With the concept of strategy, structures and culture – the chosen framework for this concluding article – the program of "Making Mega-City Regions Visible!" can be embedded in this overarching challenge in different respects: Visualization strategy, for example, discusses the different functions that the program may serve; visualization structures implies the dimensions of process and context where the possible integration of "making visible" into planning processes is discussed; finally visualization culture conceptualizes the hoped-for embeddedness of the perceptional work from a disciplinary and methodological point of view. In this final section the so-called transdisciplinary approach shall be specified and structured. "Making visible" does not add value to mega-city regions on its own but – according to our hypothesis – has to be integrated into a value chain approach with analyzing and communicating. Analysis, visualization and communication are indispensable tools of spatial planning that have been around a long time, each of them featuring specific functions and potentials and applying specific techniques and specialized knowledge. The concept of the value-added chain gives new meaning to these three planning tools when putting them together and redesigning them within this new context. As strategic methodological components of planning processes, they release a penetrating power to transform the analytical and normative concept of mega-city regions into spaces of collective action. Thus analysis, visualization and communication have to work together in a coordinated and complementary way.

The value chain approach provides the "Making Mega-City Regions Visible!" program with a framework. It describes a comprehensive procedure that the visualizing work has to be embedded in. What does added value mean and how does it come about? The value-added chain from the corporate context is a metaphor; specialized individual production steps add to one another in a process of upgrading that results in a market-ready product. When applying this procedure to the interplay of analysis, visualization and communication, the specific capacities of each tool and its possible interfaces have to be developed. It is the task of further theoretical and empirical research to explore the potential and the impact of this productive interplay. So far the proposed value-chain approach to large-scale spatial development is a hypothesis. In the following, some aspects of the assumed reciprocal action will be specified. Analysis, visualization, communication add to one another in different relationships. The value-added process does not work in a linear way only, but simultaneously in multiple directions. Analysis adds value to both visualizations, by providing the contents to be visualized, and communication, by detecting the different "worlds" and backgrounds of the players involved. Visualizations facilitate understanding of analytical results as well as communication with the actors. Communication provides the knowledge for the goal-oriented transfer of contents and examines the effectiveness of visualizations for different types of recipients.

Figure 3:
The concept of the value-added chain: exemplary interplay of analysis, visualization and communication.

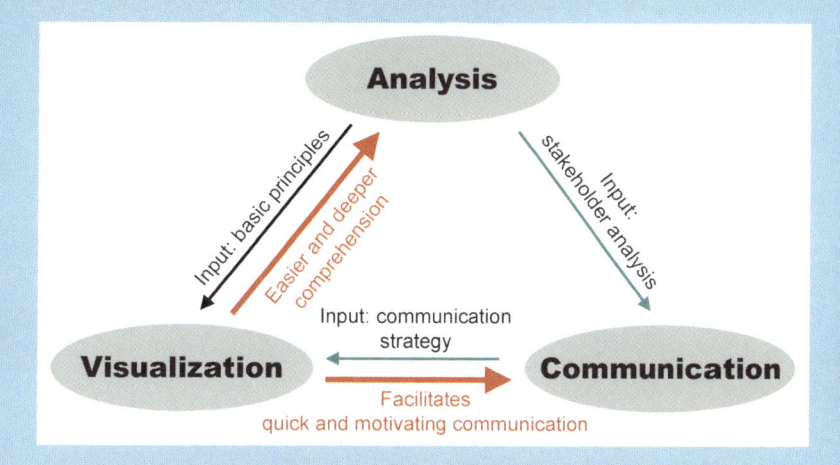

When applying the value-chain approach to the challenge of emerging governance processes in mega-city regions, analysis, visualization and communication face some basic questions.

Analysis:
- What are the spatio-functional characteristics of the mega-city region? How does "spatial development on the quiet" come about? What new division of labor and what spatial hierarchies can be detected between the various functional spaces that together make up the mega-city region?
- What are the current and future challenges to spatial development in the mega-city region? And in light of that question, what functions and objectives arise for visualizations and communication?
- What are the relevant players and stakeholders that are involved and have to be addressed? What are their interests and "worlds"?

Visualization:
- What is the internal self-image of the mega-city region? What is the shared vision of the different players? How does one create one single map out of the different parts?
- How can the mega-city region be perceived in everyday life? What are potential focal points for the identification of the citizens?
- What is the external image of the mega-city region? What messages does "mindware" bear on? What is the spatial realm of the mega-city region's different landmarks?

Communication:
- How can insight and comprehension be fostered among the relevant players? How can their motivation be intensified?
- How can the different spatial scales that the players belong to be integrated and coordinated within a communication strategy?
- What potential intersection points between the different "worlds" can be identified? Where do the stakeholders' different logics of action and distinct spatial realms of activity meet?

The proposed questions form a source that has to be developed further depending on the specific case where they are applied. As a practical tool the three dimensions of analysis, visualization and communication facilitate the conception of "making visible" as an integrative part of governance strategy, structures and culture in a particular mega-city region. First taking into account the right questions in the right dimensions assures the integration of the perceptional work in a broader context of spatial development and planning. Secondly the interfaces of the different disciplines involved in this work can be detected and the individual production steps can be fitted together.

References

Boltanski, L. and L. Thévenot. 1991. *De la justification. Les économies de la grandeur.* Paris: Gallimard.

Droß, M. and A. Thierstein. 2006. *Airport Region Munich. Von der Genese eines Handlungsraumes. Ergebnisse des Seminars "Airport Region Munich" im Wintersemester 2005/2006.* Lehrstuhl für Raumentwicklung, TU München. http://www.raumentwicklung-tum.de/publikationen.php.

Hospers, G.-J. 2006. "Borders, Bridges and Branding: The Transformation of the Øresund Region into an Imagined Space." *European Planning Studies* 14 (8): 1015-1033.

Ipsen, D. 2000. "Poetische Orte und regionale Entwicklung." *Informationen zur Raumentwicklung* (9/10): 567-574.

Lambregts, B. 2006. "Polycentrism: Boon or Barrier to Metropolitan Competitiveness? The Case of the Randstad Holland." *Built Environment* 32 (2): 114-123.

Lynch, K. 1960. *The Image of the City.* Cambridge, Massachusetts, and London, England: The M.I.T. Press.

Paasi, A. 2003. "Region and Place: Regional Identity in Question." *Progress in Human Geography* 27 (4): 475-485.

Rüegg-Stürm, J. 2002. *Das neue St. Galler Management-Modell.* 2. ed. Bern: Haupt.

Thierstein, A., V. Goebel and A. Förster. 2006. *Das Feuer in der Europäischen Metropolregion München entfachen. Expertise zum Aufbau eines Initiativkreises Europäische Metropolregion München.* München: Landeshauptstadt München. http://www.raumentwicklung-tum.de/publikationen.php.

Ungers, O.M., R. Koolhaas, P. Riemann, H. Kollhoff and A. Ovaska. 1977. *Die Stadt in der Stadt. Berlin, das grüne Stadtarchipel. Ein stadträumliches Planungskonzept für die zukünftige Entwicklung Berlins.* Köln: Studioverlag für Architektur, Liselotte Ungers.

Appendix

The Authors

Beatrix Bencseky (1961), architect and designer. From 1989 to 1993, studies in architecture, interior and product design at Kingston University (London, UK) and University of Applied Sciences, School for product- and interior design (Zurich, Switzerland), Diploma. Experience in several architecture and design offices. She teaches various classes in fashion and interior design. In 2003 she founded her own design studio, Design Identity Bencseky. In 2006 she became a partner at By ABBT, design concepts and spatial development. Main working fields are identity for public and private spaces, remodeling, lighting and color concepts, exhibition design and concepts.

Remo Burkhard (1976), PhD, architect, is senior researcher at ETH Zurich. He both studied architecture and obtained his doctorate on Knowledge Visualization at ETH Zurich. He is a co-author of the Science City Project and is involved in the Strategic Planning Process 2008 – 2011 of ETH Zurich. Since 2003 he has been a Project Manager at the University of St. Gallen, where he has founded and built the Competence Center Knowledge Visualization at the Institute for Media and Communications Management. Remo Burkhard is a founding partner of vasp datatecture GmbH, a company that focuses on visualizing business contents.

Simin Davoudi (1957) holds the Chair of Environmental Policy and Planning in Global Urban Research Unit (GURU) and is Director of Social Systems at the Institute for Research on Environment and Sustainability (IRES) at Newcastle University. Her research has focused on UK and European spatial planning, institutional relationships and governance, and sustainability and strategic waste planning. The list of her responsibilities includes Past President of the Association of the European Schools of Planning (AESOP), former coordinator of the Planning Research Network for the UK government department, and a member of the expert panel for the Irish and Austrian EU Presidency Seminars on territorial development.

Agnes Förster (1976), architect, research associate at the Chair of Spatial and Territorial Development at Munich University of Technology, and partner at the architectural firm 4architekten, Munich. Her main fields of research and practice are "analysis, visualization, communication" as basic tools of spatial development and planning, the interface of spatial development and urban planning and design, viz., the interplay of functional and morphological spatial strategies, and perception and identity of urban landscapes.

Reinhard Frei (1956) studied economics at the St. Gallen University of Applied Sciences after completing an internship and training program in public administration. He initially worked in marketing, export and association management before turning to the field of communications. In 1993 he founded a PR agency and went on to supervise a range of locational marketing projects. He was a co-initiator of the

Chancental Rheintal (Rhine Valley – Valley of Opportunity) project. In 1994 he completed an MBA in Business Engineering at the University of St. Gallen. He is particularly interested in the interface between politics and business and has been a member of the cantonal parliament.

Christian Kruse (1970), PhD, economic geographer and cultural anthropologist, is currently working at Morgan Stanley Global Wealth Management in Zurich. He has been senior researcher at the Swiss Banking Institute of the University of Zurich, focusing on financial centers, European metropolitan regions and the creative industry. Prior to this he spent seven years working at the Chair of Territorial Development at ETH Zurich. In recent years his research has specifically examined the efficiency of networks of both financial intermediaries in asset management and investment banking and entrepreneurs of the creative industry.

Eckart Lange (1961), landscape planner, is Professor of Landscape at the University of Sheffield (UK). He holds a Dipl.-Ing. degree from TU Berlin, a Master's in Design Studies from Harvard University and a PhD and PD from the Department of Civil, Environmental and Geomatic Engineering from ETH Zurich. His research focuses on how landscape and environmental planning can influence anthropogenic landscape change, and how landscape visualization and modeling can be used to explore human reaction to these changes.

Heiri Leuthold (1967), PhD, geographer, graduated in geography and economics 1999 and completed his doctorate in 2006 at the Department of Geography at the University of Zurich. Together with Michael Hermann he manages the independent research unit sotomo, specialized on spatial analysis of politics and society. His main research interests are the impact of contemporary globalization on social structure and political values at the urban and regional level. He teaches political geography and methodology of empirical research for students in geography at the University of Zurich.

Wilhelm Natrup (1959), city and regional planner, is a partner at Ernst Basler + Partner Ltd with offices in Zurich (CH) and Potsdam (D). He manages the firm's urban planning-related activities and projects in Switzerland and abroad. As a consultant he has worked on several concepts, programs and strategies for the metropolitan regions of Berlin-Brandenburg and Zurich, among others.

Julian Petrin (1968), city planner and economic and social geographer, is a partner at urbanista, Hamburg, working on the interface of urban development and communication. Since 2005 he is a research associate at the Institute of Regional and Urban Planning at HafenCity University Hamburg, and since 2007 a postgraduate member of the International PhD Program "Research Lab Space." His recent work focuses on the relationship between theoretical concepts of space and planning practice, e.g., the question of how the perception of space affects the production of space.

Urs Primas (1965), architect, graduated from ETH Zurich in 1991. From 1995 to 2002 he lived in Amsterdam, working for several architecture offices and as a Dutch correspondent for the Swiss architectural magazine "werk, bauen + wohnen." In 2002 he opened an architecture firm in Zurich, engaging in a number of realized projects and competitions in the fields of innovative housing and urban planning. He is lecturer at the Chair for Urban Landscape at the Zurich University of Applied Sciences in Winterthur, Switzerland. His research interests include scenario planning and urban morphology.

Maurits Schaafsma (1958), urban planner, is a senior planner at Schiphol Real Estate, the real estate development company of the Schiphol Group. His responsibilities cover architecture, urban design, urban and landscape planning and the development of AirportCity concepts. His area of interest is the interaction of traffic nodes with urban development and he has lectured on this subject (and on airport development in general) at several universities in the Netherlands and abroad. He is a former regional planner at the Province of North-Holland and the Randstadovreleg Ruimtelijke Ordening.

Henrik Schultz (1976), landscape architect, is a partner at Stein+Schultz, Frankfurt am Main. Since 2004 he has been teaching and conducting research at the Studio Urbane Landschaften of the Leibniz University of Hannover. He was the 1999/2000 project manager for neighborhood improvement initiatives and the Massachusetts Organization of Conservation Commissions, Boston (USA). His areas of interest include regional landscape design, perception and development of urban landscapes, development of open space and landscape architecture.

Ursula Stein (1957), Dr.-Ing., planner and organizational development consultant, is a partner at Stein+Schultz, Frankfurt am Main, and honorary professor at the University of Kassel (Faculty of Architecture, Urban Planning and Landscape Planning). "Communication in Planning" is the main idea running through her research, teaching and consulting on topics that include neighborhood and urban development, regional cooperation and new urban landscapes.

Alain Thierstein (1957), PhD, economist and planner, is a full professor for territorial and spatial development at the Munich University of Technology and head of urban and regional economic development at the consultancy of Ernst Basler + Partners Ltd, Zurich. His areas of interest include regional and territorial development, urban development, sustainable regional development, regional and innovation policy, airport city research, cross-border cooperation and policy evaluation.

Meret Wandeler (1967), photographer and artist, is Project Director of Research & Development at the Institute for Contemporary Arts Research and teaches in the photography study program at the Zurich University of the Arts. She has designed and carried out research projects on photography and spatial and territorial development with Prof. Ulrich Görlich. She is also pursuing her own artistic projects in photography as well as the fields of actionism, happenings and performance.

Wil Zonneveld (1955), PhD, spatial planner, is a senior lecturer and head of the Urban and Regional Development research program at the OTB Research Institute of Delft University of Technology. His main field of research is strategic planning at the national, transnational and European levels, including cross-border and transnational co-operation. A main area of interest is the use of both spatial planning concepts at various policy levels and visualization in policy.

Illustration Credits

Numbers below refer to the figures in each chapter.

Calling for Pictures
1 BBR Bonn 2004.

2–10 Chair of Spatial and Territorial Development, Munich University of Technology.

11 Chair of Spatial and Territorial Development, Munich University of Technology. Source: Weichart, P. 1999. "Raumbezogene Identitäten 4, Intensivkurs." Paper read at Alexander von Humboldt Lectures in Human Geography, 16.–17.09.1999, at Nijmegen, The Netherlands.

12 Chair of Spatial and Territorial Development, Munich University of Technology.

Mapping Hybrid Value-Added Landscapes
1–9 Thomas Held and Christian Kruse.

Governing Polycentric Urban Regions
1–2 BBR Bonn 2000.

3 Chair of Spatial and Territorial Development, Munich University of Technology. Source: Meijers, E.J., A. Romein, E.C. Hoppenbrouwer (eds.) 2003. *Planning Polycentric Urban Regions in North West Europe; Value, Feasibility and Design, Eurbanet Report 2*. Housing and Urban Policy Studies 25. Delft: Delft University Press.

Accessing Global City Regions
1 United Airlines advertisement, 2005.

2 Schiphol Real Estate.

3 Province of North Holland.

4 Chair of Spatial and Territorial Development, Munich University of Technology.

Cooperating and Competing

1 Chair of Spatial and Territorial Development, Munich University of Technology.

2 BFS VZ2000, Statistisches Amt Kanton Zürich.

3 BFS, ThemaKart, Neuenburg 2003 / K00.16.

4 Greater Zurich Area AG.

5 Verein Metropole Schweiz.

6 ETH Studio Basel / Contemporary City Institut.

7 Ernst Basler + Partner AG, Zurich.

8–9 Kommunale Nachbarschaftsforen und Senatsverwaltung für Stadtentwicklung (eds.) 2001. *Stadt und Nachbarn, Kommunale Zusammenarbeit im Spree-Havel-Raum*. Berlin.

Managing Reputation

1–4 Reinhard Frei.

Visioning and Visualization

1–2 MVB, Ministerie van Volkshuisvesting en Bouwnijverheid. 1960. *Nota inzake de ruimtelijke ordening in Nederland* [Report on spatial planning in the Netherlands]. Den Haag: Staatsuitgeverij.

3 RNP, Rijksdienst voor het National Plan. 1962. *Jaarverslag 1961* [Annual report 1961]. Den Haag: Staatsuitgeverij.

4 Ley, N. 1967 "Die Zukunft der Raumordnung in Nordwesteuropa." *Wegwijzers naar een goed bewoonbaar Nederland* [Signposts to a more livable Holland], Beschouwingen aangeboden aan Mr. J. Vink bij zijn afscheid als directeur-generaal van de Rijksplanologische Dienst. Alphen aan den Rijn: N. Samsom nv.

5 Brunet, R. 1989. *Les Villes "europeennes"*; Rapport pour la DATAR: Délégation à l'aménagement du territoire et à l'action régionale. Paris: La Documentation Française.

6 Kunzmann, K.R. and M. Wegener. 1991. "The Pattern of Urbanization in Europe." *Ekistics* 350 (September/October).

7 CPMR, Conference of Peripheral Maritime Regions of Europe; Peripheries Forward Studies Unit. 2002. *Study on the Construction of a Polycentric and Balanced Development Model for the European Territory*. Rennes: CPMR.

8 CEC, Commission of the European Communities; Directorate General XVI. 1996. *The Prospective Development of the Central and Capital Cities and Regions, Regional Development Studies* No. 22. Luxembourg: Office for Official Publications of the European Communities.

| 9 | NWMA Spatial Vision Group. 2000. *A Spatial Vision for North-West Europe: Building Cooperation*. The Hague: Ministry of Housing, Spatial Planning and the Environment of the Netherlands. |
| 10–11 | Wiersma, A. 2004. *Het ruimtelijk concept in transnationale planning* [The spatial concept in transnational planning]. Master thesis, Nijmegen School of Management, University of Nijmegen. |

Revealing the Social Topography of Mega-City Regions

1	Blöchliger, H. 2005. *Baustelle Förderalismus*, edited by Avenir Suisse. Zürich: Verlag NZZ.
2	sotomo – Gesellschaft, Politik und Raum, Department of Geography, University of Zurich. Source: Flückiger, H. and M. Koll-Schretzenmayr. 2000. "Das vernetzte Städtesystem der Schweiz. Eine schweizerische Strategie, ein europäisches Modell?" *DISP* 142/2000: 4–9.
3–7	sotomo – Gesellschaft, Politik und Raum, Department of Geography, University of Zurich.

Experiencing Urban Regions

| 1–6 | Stein+Schultz, Frankfurt am Main. |

Stimulating the Second Space

| 1 | Photo: Rudolf Sterflinger. |
| 2 | Julian Petrin. |

Visualizing Desires, not Cities

1	Macrofocus GmbH, www.macrofocus.com.
2	Remo Burkhard.
3–4	vasp datatecture GmbH, www.vasp.ch.

Perceiving and Visualizing Changing Environments

| 1 | Lenné3D / Lange, Wissen & Schroth. |
| 2–4 | Lange, Thoma und Weber. |

Going Beyond Identity

1	EFL Stichting. Source: Physical Planning Department, City of Amsterdam. 2003. *Planning Amsterdam. Scenarios for urban development 1928 – 2003*. Rotterdam: NAI Publishers.
2	Federal Office of Topography swisstopo.
3	Reproduced by permission of Federal Office of Topography swisstopo (BA071643).

4	Th. K. van Lohuizen, De bevolkingsgroei in de Randstad, 1869–1920. Source: Rossem, V. van. 1993. *Het Algemeen Uitbreidingsplan van Amsterdam. Geschiedenis en ontwerp.* Rotterdam: NAI Publishers.
5	Bosma, K., H. Hellinga.1997. *De regie van de stad II. Noord-Europese Stedebouw 1900–2000.* Rotterdam: NAI Publishers.
6	Office for Metropolitan Architecture.
7	Stichting CASE, Amsterdam.
8–9	London School of Economics and Political Science.
10	The National Archives and Records Administration. Source: University of Pennsylvania, Cartographic Modeling Laboratory, Amy Hillier.
11	gta Archive / ETH Zurich.

Setting up a Perception Instrument

1–10 Ulrich Görlich / Meret Wandeler / Zurich University of the Arts.

Creating Identity

1	Photo: Katrin Ritz.
2–3	Photo: Beatrix Bencseky.
4–5	Architect: Stücheli Architekten, Zurich. Color and lighting concept, furnishings and design: Beatrix Bencseky. Photo: Beatrix Bencseky.
6–7	Komitee "Weltoffenes Zürich," poster campaign 2006.
8–11	Design concept and name design: Beatrix Bencseky for Marie-Luise Hilbert, KO AG 1994.
12	Dr. Renate Kostrzewa.
13	SkyscraperCity.
14	U.S. Geological Survey.
15	Photo: Matthew Wharmby.
16	Verein Aktion Pro Sächsitram.
17	Ricardo Media Office.
18	Photo: David Tenser.
19	Photo: Fabio Consani.
20	Photo: Michael Reeve.
21	Photo: Nina Aldin Thune.
22	Schaffhausen Tourismus.
23–24	Photo: Michael Reeve.

25	Photo: Guido Allieri.
26	Photo: Markus A. Jegerlehner/www.fotojeger.ch.
27	Photo: Beatrix Bencseky.
28	Photo: Nizar Krayem.
29	Sun Star Models Development Ltd.
30	Photo: George Fremin III - K5TR.
31	Photo: Laszlo.
32	Photo: Beatrix Bencseky.
33	Naciketa Datta, Photo: David Blaine.
34	Photo: Beatrix Bencseky.
35	www.bigfoto.com.
36	© Land Berlin/Thie.
37	Photo: Alain Thierstein.
38–39	Photo: Beatrix Bencseky.
40	Photo: Lisi Gradnitzer & MQ Errichtungs- und BetriebsgesmbH.
41	RAIFFEISEN SCHWEIZ.
42–45	Photo: Beatrix Bencseky.
46	Fotosearch.de.
47	Batey, M. and D. Lambert. 1991. *The English Garden Tour: A View into the Past*. London: John Murray.
48	Photo: Family Ambühler-Hauenstein, Schwitzerland.
49	Photo: Natalie Madani, BA Photographic & Digital Arts.
50	Photo: Beatrix Bencseky.
51	Grün Stadt Zürich.
52–53	The Image and the Region working group.
54–55	Hosoya Schaefer Architects, Zurich.
56–63	Beatrix Bencseky.

Adding Value to Spatial Development

1–3	Chair of Spatial and Territorial Development, Munich University of Technology.

Acknowledgments

The editors would like to thank the authors for their stimulating contributions to the still very emerging challenge of "Making Mega-City Regions Visible!" Their commitment inspired a fruitful discussion that proved to be an indispensable source for both the introductory and the concluding articles.

We also wish to express our gratitude to Lars Müller and Katharina Kulke of Lars Müller Publishers for their belief in the need for and urgency of "Making Mega-City Regions Visible!" They facilitated the realization of this book by their long experience and by being invaluable partners in a useful dialog throughout the process.

And we would like to extend a mega-city region's worth of warm thanks to Valerie Kiock, whose expertise was essential in "making visible" the present book, including all the subtle facets of its wide-ranging contents. Her design and realization of the graphics encouraged us in turn to specify with ever-greater precision the overall concept of the program laid out in "Making Mega-City Regions Visible!"

The printing of the book was generously supported by
- BURRI public elements AG, Zurich
- Department of Labor & Economic Development, City of Munich
- Ernst Basler + Partner AG, Zurich
- Hamasil Foundation, Zurich

Finally, we would like to thank Christina Smoravek for her active support in requesting sources and copyrights for the many illustrations.

Imprint

Editors
Alain Thierstein, Agnes Förster

Translation
Joe O'Donnell

Copyediting / Proofreading
John O'Toole

Litho
Reproline Genceller, München

Printing and Binding
Kösel, Altusried-Krugzell

Design
Valerie Kiock, München

Publisher
Lars Müller Publishers
5400 Baden / Switzerland
www.lars-muller-publishers.com

©Lars Müller Publishers 2008

ISBN 978-3-03778-131-9

We have taken great pains to locate all copyright holders. Should we have been unsuccessful in individual cases, copyright claims should be addressed to the editors. All rights reserved.